THE
Cancer-Fighting
Kitchen

THE
Cancer-Fighting Kitchen

Nourishing, Big-Flavor Recipes for Cancer Treatment and Recovery

SECOND EDITION

Rebecca Katz with Mat Edelson

PHOTOGRAPHY LEO GONG

TEN SPEED PRESS
Berkeley

For Waz Thomas, who showed me the way

Contents

Foreword

When I first sit down with someone to consult on how to integrate complementary therapies into their cancer care, I remark that cancer is like a weed in the body's garden. I say that their conventional oncologist is focused on ridding them of the weed through conventional means (such as surgery/chemo/radiation), while my job, as their integrative oncologist, is to work with their garden to make its soil as inhospitable as possible to the growth and spread of the weed. The first step is to discuss how they are fertilizing their garden—that is, what do they eat? And that launches into a lengthy conversation about an organic, plant-based, antioxidant-rich, anti-inflammatory whole foods diet—what I consider to be the optimal anticancer fertilizer. At the end of the consultation, to help them start following my recommendations, I bring out a stack of books, including a number of cookbooks. The first one I show I refer to as the bible of anticancer cuisine—*The Cancer-Fighting Kitchen*. It is hard to believe that this amazing guide to healthful eating for the whole family could be made any more wonderful, but Rebecca has gifted us with an exciting second edition, chock-full of the power of yum!

Oncologists are frequently asked whether what one eats has any real impact after a diagnosis of cancer. So many of my colleagues advise their patients to "eat whatever you want; it doesn't really matter." Oncologists are very evidence-based because of the very nature of the disease we treat and the treatments we use. We want to have clear data to support that what we recommend is safe and effective. Trying to do large-scale trials demonstrating that what one eats impacts one's cancer outcome is difficult; historically, this has limited such nutritional research. It is much easier to study a new drug compared to an old one or a placebo. But now, more and more evidence is accumulating that diet after cancer occurs *does* make a difference. This is based on dietary information collected as part of conventional cancer treatment trials and the large (approximately 185,000 men and women) American Cancer Society Cancer Prevention Study II Nutrition Cohort. Not surprisingly, participants consistently fared less well on the standard American diet, high in saturated fats and refined carbohydrates, than on the plant-based diet with fish and poultry as the main animal foodstuffs.

It is becoming harder to ignore the importance of nutrition in the health of all of us. A report on "The State of US Health, 1990–2010," published in the *Journal of the American Medical Association*, ranked "dietary risks" as the leading cause of morbidity and mortality in the United States, surpassing tobacco smoking. The fourteen components of dietary risk include diets low in fruits, vegetables, whole grains, nuts and seeds, milk, fiber, calcium, seafood-sourced omega-3 fatty acids and polyunsaturated fatty acids, and diets high in red meat, processed meat, sugar-sweetened beverages, trans-fatty acids, and sodium.

What I love about the easy-to-make recipes in this incredible book is that they're bursting with health-promoting nutrition and they are also scrumptious. Rebecca has done all the work regarding what foods work best on the plate to both fight and prevent cancer, and, in the process, made them delicious and accessible. I speak from firsthand knowledge. Over the past decade, I have had ample opportunity to enjoy Rebecca's cuisine on numerous occasions. We have done a number of lecture/cooking demonstrations for doctors, wellness professionals, and patients, where she cooks up a meal and I describe the science behind her ingredients. These fun sessions always end with a tasting of the delightful final products. I've also enjoyed group dinners at her home where we all get to pick up even more tips on how to do things right in the kitchen. This second edition is like receiving an invitation to enter into Rebecca's kitchen, with recipes that will allow you to begin to explore and appreciate firsthand the benefits of healthful eating. I frequently see people, three months after my initial consultation with them, who have successfully modified their diets, usually with a little help from Rebecca. They report that they feel great and have much more energy. In addition, their spouses may have been able to lower or discontinue their cholesterol or blood pressure medications (yes, studies are increasingly showing that the foods you'll find in these pages are great not just for fighting cancer, but also for limiting the development and/or ameliorating the systemic effects of many chronic diseases).

Enjoy Rebecca's wonderful guide to wellness for all! Bon appétit!

—**DONALD I. ABRAMS**, MD, Chief, Hematology-Oncology, San Francisco General Hospital; Professor, Department of Medicine, University of California, San Francisco (UCSF); Integrative Oncology, UCSF Osher Center for Integrative Medicine; Editor, *Integrative Oncology* (2014, Oxford University Press, second edition)

Preface to the Second Edition

In the eight years since *The Cancer-Fighting Kitchen* was first published, the research linking what you eat to how it affects the occurrence, treatment, and recurrence of cancer has exploded; hence this second edition. The great news is that no matter where you are on the journey—a concerned mother looking to safeguard her family's health, a patient currently in treatment (or a caregiver looking to help), or a cancer survivor looking to stay cancer free—science has shown, with increasing certainty, that nourishing foods have a healthful impact on all sorts of cancer-related pathways.

By "nourishing," we're not talking hippie gruel. Incredibly delicious meals have cancer-fighting ingredients. Blueberries, almonds, carrots, salmon, olives, cabbage—all bring something to the table.

What have really caught my eye are recent studies emphasizing the fantastic role herbs and spices play in combating cancer. Gram for gram, they pack in more cancer-fighting phytochemicals than just about any other food. I'm so impressed with both the taste and nutritional power of herbs and spices that I've increased their content in many of the recipes.

Here's an emerging theory of cancer on which many integrative oncologists and I agree, and which Dr. Donald Abrams touched upon in this book's new foreword: The best way to beat back the disease is by creating a healthy biological environment that makes it difficult (or impossible, in the best-case scenario) for cancer cells to flourish. The right foods can help accomplish this task.

Here's how—there are four cellular processes, always busy doing their thing, that have been linked to either controlling or promoting the growth of cancer: inflammation, oxidative stress, blood sugar regulation/insulin production, and normal cell death (aka apoptosis). When any of these processes go out of balance for a long period of time, the body's cellular defenses fail and cancer can proliferate. The typical Western diet, which is low in plant foods (produce) and high in sugars, saturated fats, and processed foods, is known to weaken the control of all of these mechanisms.

Fortunately, the flavorful recipes in this book have been shown to greatly lessen inflammation, provide an antioxidant boost, keep blood sugar levels from spiking (which decreases insulin production), and inhibit molecular pathways such as nuclear factor kappa B (NF-KB) that cancer cells use to stave off their own demise. Perhaps equally important, many of the recipes included here help keep the ratio of good bacteria high in the gastrointestinal tract (this environment is also known as the "gut microbiome"). Chemotherapy often impacts good bacteria, breaking down the lining of the gut in nearly half of all patients. This promotes serious short- and long-term issues including inflammation and poor food absorption. But using the right foods before, during, and after treatment can help keep the gut microbiome robust and healthy.

If all this sounds complex, well, cancer *is* complex (at any rate, its causes are). Researchers increasingly agree that it takes multiple genetic mutations and systemic malfunctions for cancer to take hold. That's why, if you're bringing nutrition to bear on your cancer concerns, it makes sense to go after multiple cancer-causing targets. That's always been the approach of this book, and we're heartened to see that many of the world's leading cancer organizations have jumped on board. The American Cancer Society, the American Institute for Cancer Research, the American Association for Cancer Research, and the Physician's Committee for Responsible Medicine all have published recently updated diet and nutrition guidelines for limiting cancer risk. They generally support the idea that getting the nutrition you need from your diet (as opposed to supplements) is the best way to go, and that nutrition should ideally come from a diverse, plant-based diet.

Why diverse? Because just like personalized medicine, the evolving field of nutrigenomics suggests that a one-size diet doesn't fit all. Put another way, two people eating the same exact food don't absorb the same amount of nutrients. Eventually, science will figure out which individual foods are best assimilated by your particular genetic makeup, but until then it's best to play the odds and set your palate up to range far and wide. Besides—as you'll find inside these pages—it's a lot more fun!

Another reason all this science has me excited is that it doesn't operate in a vacuum. When we first wrote *The Cancer-Fighting Kitchen*, many readers felt they had been left to fend for themselves when it came to nutritional concerns. Outside of integrative oncologists, most physicians had little knowledge of the interplay of food and fighting cancer. That's not a knock on doctors; most oncologists at the time saw their role as being diagnosticians and medical managers. But that's changed. The National Cancer Institute now has more than four hundred clinical trials looking at associations between diet and cancer. Some, including the Women's Health Initiative and the Women's Healthy Eating and Living Study, are long-term longitudinal cohorts involving thousands of participants.

All told, these trials and studies have built on thousands of other published, peer-reviewed works. Over time, the consciousness-raising effect of this science has been impossible to ignore. From the top down, the knowledge has been incorporated into school curricula (finally!) and disseminated outward to community physicians.

We're glad to be back, and overjoyed to show you how great-tasting food and outstanding cancer-fighting nutrition can joyfully coexist on the plate. Thanks for welcoming us into your kitchen.

Introduction

For the last fifteen years, I've felt like one of those wild-eyed Hawaiian surfers riding a wave that, instead of cresting, just keeps gathering momentum and strength. That wave is the food-as-medicine movement, the idea that what we eat can keep diseases at bay, including cancer. When I wrote my first two books—*One Bite at a Time* and the first edition of *The Cancer-Fighting Kitchen*—the initial goals were modest, yet vital. What we knew at the time (2003–2008) was that 80 percent of cancer patients were malnourished. Indeed, most of the people who picked up those books, either as caregivers or recently diagnosed patients, had but two questions regarding food that burned in their minds: *Am I going to enjoy eating during treatment?* and *Heck, am I going to be able to eat at all?*

These were—and still are—crucial concerns. This book is *all* about enhancing your appetite during treatment. The key concept is what I call "the power of yum," the mind-blowing notion that great nutrition and fabulous taste can joyfully coexist on the plate. As one of my colleagues noted years ago, "If food doesn't taste great, people won't eat it, no matter how good it is for them." Essentially, I work as a culinary translator, teaming up with oncologists, nutritionists, and cancer wellness professionals to help their patients stay well fed during treatment by translating nutritional recommendations into delicious, nourishing meals. The positive results I've seen in thousands of patients have been heartening. People who had completely disconnected from food have been brought back to the table and nourished by engaging three easy-to-follow ideas:

1. Make the food appealing to all the senses.

2. Offer lots of choices to fit often changing tastes and appetites (think small, easily stored, and reheated nutrient-dense portions).

3. Create ways that patients or caregivers can comfortably shop for, prep, and cook said meals.

But now, nearly a generation into the food-as-medicine journey, it turns out that there's far more to "the power of yum" than taste. I've watched as research into food and how it can restore and maintain health (aka sustainable nourishment) has matured in numerous mainstream peer-reviewed journals including the *Journal of the American Medical Association* and the *New England Journal of Medicine*. I've chronicled this explosion of knowledge in three more recent cookbooks: *The Longevity Kitchen*, *The Healthy Mind Cookbook*, and *Clean Soups*. What I've learned researching those books—such as the wonderful roles herbs and spices play in improving health—also applies to those fighting cancer. Many people, not surprisingly, become motivated to eat well when taking on a disease. I try to capitalize on that motivation to help folks realize that the very foods that weed the body's garden of cancer can create long-term downstream benefits that help ward off recurrence.

As a chef, I've been awed by this data, and I went and got a master's in nutrition to better converse with the rapidly growing number of doctors and scientists researching foods that impact cancer. I then took their input to create more outrageously scrumptious cancer-fighting dishes. This updated melding of science and taste is the cookbook and resource you hold in your hands, and I'm proud and humbled that many doctors—including conventional and integrative physicians—refer their patients to the book as part of their care.

But there's more. Being diagnosed with cancer is very scary. I've seen that firsthand, with my father, who battled throat cancer. My coauthor, Mat, has had his own up-close-and-personal encounters, with both his mom (colon cancer), and long-time partner, Deb (ovarian cancer). Dealing with cancer is enough to scramble anybody's mental GPS. At a time when everything seems out of one's control, cooking and eating well offers more than nourishment; it's downright empowering. The knowledge that you can influence both short- and long-term outcomes, and help alleviate some of the side effects associated with cancer treatment, is a tremendous psychological boost for many patients and caregivers. What's on the end of your fork *really* matters, for both body and soul.

The delightful aspect of this work is that so many common foods—everything from broccoli to tomatoes—have multiple cancer-fighting phytochemicals and nutrients. In the preface to this new edition (page xi) we covered how cancer pathways can be affected by food. This includes controlling blood sugar and insulin spikes as well as lowering systemic inflammation. Everyday herbs and spices such as ginger, cinnamon, and turmeric are both taste and anticancer powerhouses. If you'd like to learn more, see the Culinary Pharmacy, page 28, which details the beneficial properties of the foods used in the recipes in this book. I've included the science because many people I work with get interested in the particulars once they realize how much better they often feel as they become well nourished.

It's my belief that we all have the ability to nourish ourselves, even in the direst of circumstances. This book was designed to meet you wherever you are in your journey. Whether your appetite is robust or waning, everything from the teas and smoothies to the entrées presented in these pages contain maximum nutrition and taste. *The Cancer-Fighting Kitchen* emphasizes a whole foods approach: these are foods coming straight from farm to table with their nutrients intact, unlike refined and processed foods, such as white flour and sugar, which are stripped of their nutritional value (aka "empty" calories).

In addition to offering the broadest range of nutrients, the whole foods approach serves another purpose. People often ask me, "If science knows specific foods that fight cancer, why don't I just eat those?" Ah, if only a single food had such abilities. But that's not the way it works—at least not yet. Eating a wide variety of foods allows you to hedge your bets, as each of us absorbs nutrients differently (this is being uncovered by the emerging field of nutrigenomics). Since we can't yet identify which specific foods work best for each individual, a wide-ranging diet is the best guarantee you'll get the nourishment you need.

Now, I know I've just put a lot on your plate. And I understand that stepping into the kitchen to cook for someone dealing with cancer (whether that's you or someone else) takes a lot of courage. You *so* want them to like the food so they'll eat. But take comfort in this: I'll be holding your hand all the way. Life is serious enough for you and your loved ones right now. Although this book deals with a difficult topic, it comes at eating from a stance of joy and fun. Believe me, when you see the results—and the healing effect they have on all who partake—your motivation to get into the kitchen will take a quantum leap.

How to Use This Book

First and foremost, have fun with this book, and celebrate every act of eating, be it large or small. There are probably going to be days when swallowing a few sips of broth is an accomplishment. By all means, celebrate that accomplishment. Don't beat yourself up for the meals you miss. When you accentuate the positive, your connection to food remains intact during treatment and even builds upon itself.

Think of this book as a toolbox, full of great ideas that can entice you to eat with a minimum of kitchen stress. The tools give you ways to address issues that commonly crop up during treatment and throughout recovery.

Chapter 1: Cancer-Fighting Tool Kit is a guide to scrumptious foods, recipes, meal planning, and kitchen techniques. These foods can lessen the impact of side effects, improve appetite and immunity, and overcome taste changes stemming from impaired taste buds that are a common consequence of treatment (you'll want to pay special attention to the tool I call FASS on page 18; it uses four basic pantry staples to course-correct and vastly improve the taste of any dish).

The tool kit includes specific suggestions on what to eat before, during, and after chemotherapy, along with showing you ways to get maximum nutrition even on those days when your appetite wanes. There's also an easy questionnaire that uncovers people's food preferences. Treatments can throw people's tastes for such a loop that old favorites may not be appetizing. When that's the case, knowing more about a person's inherent preferences is valuable information. Chapter 1 also includes what I call *global flavorprints*—lists of herbs and spices that characterize different cuisines (it's amazing how easily you can change a dish from, say, an Asian to an Indian feel, just by swapping a few spices and herbs). Another popular feature in the chapter is the Culinary Pharmacy mentioned earlier; it's an introduction to the powerhouse foods used in the recipes, including their amazing cancer-fighting properties and other nutritional attributes. Many people find the Culinary Pharmacy incredibly enlightening and motivating; there's nothing like discovering that a favorite food can also help you battle cancer.

Chapter 1 ends where many people choose to begin: with strategies for showing how friends and family can help. The idea is that cooking, shopping, and cleanup shouldn't add stress to a caregiver's day. I'll show you how to organize friends, family, neighbors, and others into a culinary support team to cover shopping and cooking tasks, and how to clearly define roles so people don't step on each other's toes (including the patient's). The suggestions allow everyone to contribute in a desired and appreciated way. On a practical level, these concepts show people how to make sure a wide variety of healthy, yummy meals and snacks are available for the person in treatment whenever hunger strikes, even in work, hospital, and treatment settings. Eating small portions at frequent intervals is often the best route for delivering nourishment to the body during treatment. You'll also find detailed instructions on various food preparation techniques, and advice on storage and reheating. Being able to prepare meals in quantity and store single-portion containers in the fridge and freezer greatly cuts down on cooking and prep time.

Chapters 2 through 8 are the recipes and variations that are the heart and soul of the book. They've been tried and tested by a battery of tasters who refused to be satisfied until they were moaning with delight. You've paid for a cookbook expecting that every recipe will deliver in terms of both taste and nutrition; my team and I have done the utmost to meet, and hopefully exceed, those expectations.

Throughout the recipes, you'll find suggestions on substitutions for common food sensitivities. For those who want to avoid dairy, you can generally use soy or rice milk—just be sure to use an unsweetened variety. Folks with gluten intolerance will find substitutions for wheat, as well.

Whenever possible, I suggest that people in treatment eat organically. That's especially true for those who eat meat and dairy. I realize organic food can cost a bit more across the board, but consider that undergoing treatment means you're already dealing with plenty of toxins in your body; you don't want to introduce more, in the form of pesticides, hormones, antibiotics, and other drugs, in your food. Plus, organically grown food often offers more nutrients and phytochemicals than its commercially grown counterparts. As for taste, organic, fresh-picked produce, pasture-raised chicken, and fish caught in the wild are absolutely delicious, offering the finest flavors that can land on your plate. Speaking as a chef and the little pixie in your ear, why would you settle for anything less?

One other important note about the recipes: Some people are intimidated when they see a recipe list with more than three ingredients. I get that. But if you look closely at my recipes, you'll find they often include lots of easily stored herbs and spices, the unsung heroes of cancer-fighting cuisine. You'll see variations on these herbs and spices come up time and again in the book, meaning you won't have to shop for them each time you want to make a dish. That's comforting to know, and should put you in a good space as you embrace these delicious recipes.

Finally, for those without easy access to a farmers' market or well-stocked grocery stores, the Resources section in the back of the book provides online sources for many of the ingredients in the recipes. It also includes information on cancer support groups and medical information. The extensive bibliography documents sources for the information used in this book.

CHAPTER 1

Cancer-Fighting Tool Kit

The first thing you need to know about this chapter is that there won't be a test at the end. The point of all of the tools herein is to use them as you like, take from them what you will, and know that they're all country roads leading to the same joyous place: a dish, a meal, a snack, or a liquid refreshment that will help you or your loved one feel a little better and live a little easier.

These tools all come from firsthand experience working with thousands of people in treatment and their families. They've often told me that eating well gives them a chance to forget what they're dealing with during the rest of the day. Over the years, I've also been delighted to rub elbows with hundreds of cancer wellness doctors, nurses, nutritionists, dieticians, and researchers, many of whom have generously imparted their own nutritional tips and explained the science behind them.

These tools are powerful, capitalizing on the power of yum and food to tackle many difficult aspects of treatment, including:

- Lessening the impact of common side effects, including nausea, fatigue, and muscle loss

- Improving appetite, which enhances the immune system and keeps people stronger, allowing them to get the maximum benefit from cancer treatments

- Warding off the impact of impaired taste buds by using simple ingredients to boost flavor

- Utilizing strategies to ensure that people can eat delicious nourishing foods whenever they want, no matter how quickly or often their tastes and appetite changes

- Offering outstanding anticancer properties—not to mention unparalleled flavor—by harnessing the power of generous amounts of herbs and spices

Side Effects

Ah, the things we're supposed to endure to retain or regain our health. Most people I've worked with have dealt with one or more side effects due to chemotherapy, radiation, surgery, and immunotherapy. The good news is that, between medication and sound nutrition, many side effects can be greatly reduced. But—and this is a huge but—you have to speak up and let your doctor and/or caregivers know you're not feeling well. I know this can be hard to do. You may want to be a good patient with the "grin and bear it" attitude. At the same time, some doctors are so tightly focused on treatments that they may not take the time to prompt conversations about side effects, while caregivers may be afraid to ask.

Not addressing side effects, however, can have larger consequences. Cancer treatments can negatively impact immunity, inflammation, blood sugar regulation, digestion, and a whole host of other bodily systems; as you'll learn, eating well may lessen these issues, but if your side effects make you want to avoid food, the net result could impact your treatment schedule.

Think of it this way: The clinical goal of treatment is to give you the maximum therapeutic dose possible to wipe out your cancer while still keeping your body intact. Any side effect that isn't addressed can leave your body less than 100-percent prepared for the next treatment. At times, this may force your doctor to lessen your chemo dose or skip a treatment altogether to give your body more time to recover. The odds suggest you don't want to be missing treatments too often.

There are dozens of healing foods that appear in this book's recipes—foods that can help you deal with fatigue, nausea, anemia, constipation, dehydration, diarrhea, mouth sores, swallowing issues, weight loss, and low immune function or low white blood cell counts. There are also foods that deal with lowering inflammation and restoring blood sugar regulation, systemic functions that need to be in balance to best fight cancer. It's also worth noting that many, if not all of the recipes contain foods that take on suspected cancer pathways, including oxidative stress.

You'll find a listing of these foods and their anticancer properties in the Culinary Pharmacy (page 28), but let me suggest that you first take a look at the listing of side effects and recommended recipes that follows. I'm steering you toward these sections because consulting them is quick, easy, and provides solutions. A glance, a flip of the page, and you're right where you need to be. Feeling a little queasy? There you are, Ginger Peppermint Green Tea, on page 158. *Flip-flip, sip-sip,* and in no time at all, you'll most likely be feeling better.

There's another reason I'm nudging you toward recipes versus individual foods. Science shows it's generally best to get nutrients from multiple foods at once, which is the very definition of a recipe. The reason is rooted in our individual unique DNA, which determines the enzymes we produce to break down and assimilate food. Put another way, two people eating grapes off the same bunch may get vastly different health benefits. Science doesn't yet have a way of figuring out each individual's digestive "blueprint," but it's getting there; it's the emerging field called nutrigenomics, which eventually will allow us to determine which enzymes each individual is capable of producing, and what foods they can best digest to make nutrients bioavailable. In the meantime, experts suggest that you hedge your bets during treatment by eating a wide variety of healthy foods—just what a cook like me *loves* to hear.

Recipes for Specific Side Effects

ANEMIA

Nourishing Soups and Broths	Pasture Beef Bone Broth (page 51), Minestrone (page 57), Velvety Red Lentil Dal (page 70)
Vital Vegetables	Kale with Sweet Potatoes and Pecans (page 84), Kale with Carrots (page 86)
Anytime Foods	Mediterranean Lentil Salad (page 144)

ANTI-INFLAMMATORY

Vital Vegetables	Baby Bok Choy with Yam and Ginger (page 76), Emerald Greens with Orange (page 78), Broccoli with Ginger and Garlic (page 87), Stir-Fried Baby Bok Choy with Shiitake Mushrooms (page 93), Shredded Carrot and Beet Salad (page 95)
Protein-Building Foods	Lemon Mustard Salmon Salad (page 115), Poached Salmon with Moroccan Pesto (page 116), Triple-Citrus Ginger Black Cod (page 119)
Tonics and Elixirs	Commonweal's Most Nourishing and Healing Tea (page 157), Green Tea Ginger Lemonade (page 158), Triple Berry Smoothie (page 168)

BLOOD SUGAR REGULATION

Nourishing Soups and Broths	Italian White Bean Soup (page 52), Minestrone (page 57), Rockin' Black Bean Soup (page 63)
Vital Vegetables	Green Beans with Brazil Nuts and Basil (page 77), Arugula with Edamame, Radish, and Avocado (page 89)
Protein-Building Foods	All of the recipes in Chapter 4
Anytime Foods	Edamame Avocado Dip with Wasabi (page 131), Cannellini Bean Dip with Kalamata Olives (page 131), Navy Bean and Sun-Dried Tomato Dip (page 132), Black Bean Hummus (page 132), Curried Hummus (page 133), Spiced Toasted Almonds (page 138), Mediterranean Lentil Salad (page 144)

Recipes for Specific Side Effects, *continued*

CONSTIPATION

General recommendations	Drink warm fluids throughout the day and eat fruit.
Nourishing Soups and Broths	Magic Mineral Broth (page 49), Chicken Magic Mineral Broth (page 50), Pasture Beef Bone Broth (page 51), Italian White Bean Soup (page 52), Velvety Red Lentil Dal (page 70)
Vital Vegetables	Basil Broccoli (page 75), Baby Bok Choy with Yam and Ginger (page 76), Emerald Greens with Orange (page 78), Kale with Sweet Potatoes and Pecans (page 84), Kale with Carrots (page 86), Stir-Fried Baby Bok Choy with Shiitake Mushrooms (page 93), Shredded Carrot and Beet Salad (page 95)
Anytime Foods	Anytime Bars (page 125), Mediterranean Lentil Salad (page 144)
Tonics and Elixirs	Commonweal's Most Nourishing and Healing Tea (page 157), Ginger Peppermint Green Tea (page 158), Green Tea Ginger Lemonade (page 158), Cinnamon Ginger Tea (page 159)
Dollops of Yum!	Dried Fruit Compote (page 183), Seasonal Stewed Fruit (page 184)
Sweet Bites	Baked Apples Filled with Dates and Pecans (page 195), Poached Pears with Saffron Broth (page 205)

DEHYDRATION

Nourishing Soups and Broths	All of the recipes in Chapter 2
Tonics and Elixirs	All of the recipes in Chapter 6

DIARRHEA

Anytime Foods	Best Oatmeal Ever (page 128), Creamy Polenta (page 134), Simple Tuscan Farro (page 147)
Tonics and Elixirs	Annemarie's Calming Kudzu Elixir (page 156)
Sweet Bites	Chocolate Tapioca Pudding (without the chocolate) (page 196), Coconut Rice Pudding (page 201)

FATIGUE

Nourishing Soups and Broths	Magic Mineral Broth (page 49), Chicken Magic Mineral Broth (page 50), Pasture Beef Bone Broth (page 51), Italian White Bean Soup (page 52), Lemony Greek Chicken Soup (page 53), Chicken Vegetable Soup with Ginger Meatballs (page 55), Ma's Mushroom Barley Soup (page 56), Thai It Up Chicken Soup (page 58), Velvety Red Lentil Dal (page 70)
Vital Vegetables	Gregg's Stuffed Acorn Squash with Quinoa, Cranberries, and Swiss Chard (page 81)
Protein-Building Foods	All of the recipes in Chapter 4
Anytime Foods	Anytime Bars (page 125), Edamame Avocado Dip with Wasabi (page 131), Cannellini Bean Dip with Kalamata Olives (page 131), Navy Bean and Sun-Dried Tomato Dip (page 132), Black Bean Hummus (page 132), Curried Hummus (page 133), Orange Pistachio Quinoa (page 141), Rice Paper Moo-Shu Rolls (page 148), Curried Hummus and Vegetable Pinwheels (page 151)
Tonics and Elixirs	Commonweal's Most Nourishing and Healing Tea (page 157), Ginger Peppermint Green Tea (page 158), Green Tea Ginger Lemonade (page 158), Cinnamon Ginger Tea (page 159), Peach Ginger Smoothie (page 166), Triple Berry Smoothie (page 168), Chocolate Banana Smoothie (page 169)

LOW WHITE BLOOD CELL COUNT (LEUKOPENIA)

Nourishing Soups and Broths	Magic Mineral Broth (page 49), Chicken Magic Mineral Broth (page 50), Pasture Beef Bone Broth (page 51), Chicken Vegetable Soup with Ginger Meatballs (page 55)
Vital Vegetables	Basil Broccoli (page 75), Kale with Sweet Potatoes and Pecans (page 84), Stir-Fried Baby Bok Choy with Shiitake Mushrooms (page 93)
Protein-Building Foods	Chicken and Broccoli Stir-Fry with Cashews (page 106), My Family's Favorite Chicken (page 110)

NAUSEA AND VOMITING

Nourishing Soups and Broths	Magic Mineral Broth (page 49), Chicken Magic Mineral Broth (page 50), Pasture Beef Bone Broth (page 51)
Tonics and Elixirs	Ginger Peppermint Green Tea (page 158), Cinnamon Ginger Tea (page 159), Ginger Tea Spritzer (page 159), Ginger Ale with Frozen Grapes (page 165)

Recipes for Specific Side Effects, continued

SORE MOUTH AND DIFFICULTY SWALLOWING

General recommendations	Omit spicy ingredients and ginger from all recipes.
Nourishing Soups and Broths	Magic Mineral Broth (page 49), Chicken Magic Mineral Broth (page 50), Pasture Beef Bone Broth (page 51), Bella's Carrot, Orange, and Fennel Soup (page 61), Cooling Cucumber Avocado Soup (page 62), Rockin' Black Bean Soup (page 63), Spiced Sweet Potato Soup (page 66), Summer's Best Zucchini Soup (page 67), Creamy Broccoli and Potato Soup (page 71)
Anytime Foods	Best Oatmeal Ever (page 128)
Tonics and Elixirs	Annemarie's Calming Kudzu Elixir (page 156), Commonweal's Most Nourishing and Healing Tea (page 157), Ginger Peppermint Green Tea (page 158), Green Tea Ginger Lemonade (page 158), Cinnamon Ginger Tea (page 159), Mouthwatering Watermelon Granita (page 161), Cantaloupe Granita with Mint (page 162), Peach Ginger Smoothie (page 166), Triple Berry Smoothie (page 168), Chocolate Banana Smoothie (page 169)

WEIGHT LOSS

Nourishing Soups and Broths	Italian White Bean Soup (page 52), Lemony Greek Chicken Soup (page 53), Chicken Vegetable Soup with Ginger Meatballs (page 55), Ma's Mushroom Barley Soup (page 56), Minestrone (page 57), Thai It Up Chicken Soup (page 58), Bella's Carrot, Orange, and Fennel Soup (page 61), Curry Cauliflower Soup (page 64), Velvety Red Lentil Dal (page 70)
Vital Vegetables	Gregg's Stuffed Acorn Squash with Quinoa, Cranberries, and Swiss Chard (page 81), Baked Sweet Potatoes with Assorted Toppings (page 90), Roasted Root Vegetables with Rosemary and Thyme (page 92)
Protein-Building Foods	Easy Eggs in a Cup (page 100), Nana's Egg Salad (page 102), Poached Eggs with Basil Lemon Drizzle (page 103), Curried Chicken Salad (page 104), Chicken and Broccoli Stir-Fry with Cashews (page 106), Cozy Comfy Chicken and Rice (page 107), Orange Ginger Roasted Chicken (page 109), My Family's Favorite Chicken (page 110), Middle Eastern Chickpea Burgers (page 112)
Anytime Foods	All of the recipes in Chapter 5
Tonics and Elixirs	Peach Ginger Smoothie (page 166), Triple Berry Smoothie (page 168), Chocolate Banana Smoothie (page 169)
Sweet Bites	Almond Muffin Mania (page 193), Chocolate Tapioca Pudding (page 196), Great Pumpkin Custard (page 197), Cardamom Maple Mini Macaroons (page 198), Chocolate Apricot Date Nut Truffles (page 202), Triple Ginger Snap Cookies with Pecans (page 209)

Menu Planning

If you're undergoing cancer treatment, it's a good idea to schedule your eating in a way that maximizes the benefits of treatment and minimizes side effects. Part of this involves a conversation with your doctor or nutritionist about what you can and can't eat—and, just as important, *when* you can eat—before, during, and after treatment.

That said, here are some recommendations based on science and my personal experience working with others.

Surgery often dehydrates the body due to stress and the required food and water fasting (often up to eight to twelve hours) that usually precedes anesthesia. I suggest that you concentrate on staying well hydrated for two weeks prior to a procedure, with an eye toward eating broths and smoothies with protein. The protein helps with wound healing, while the extra fluids help you stay hydrated. Research is showing that getting your body ready for medical procedures before they take place often sets you up for a quicker recovery.

Similarly, fluids can limit the nausea commonly associated with chemotherapy and immunotherapy. Also, avoiding fried foods, ice cream, or anything with a high fat content can help you limit gastrointestinal issues around treatment days. Believe me, your stomach will thank you.

Radiation treatments often prompt fatigue. To help alleviate this, I focus on high-energy foods you can find in the side-effect chart section (no, they're not laced with sugar, but your body will love them nonetheless).

Now, some ideas about what to eat and when, all with the goal of making treatment as easy as possible. I've focused on people undergoing chemotherapy and immunotherapy, since they often have the same eating issues. Those getting radiation treatment, especially those with head and neck issues, may find the following suggestions helpful. I also recommend taking a look at the "Sore Mouth and Difficulty Swallowing" recipe list on the facing page.

Two Days Before Chemotherapy or Immunotherapy

In the days leading up to your chemotherapy or immunotherapy session, remember that eating right will give your body the extra boost it needs to stay strong and make the most of the treatments you receive—and hopefully minimize side effects as well. Here are three points to remember:

1. Avoid your favorite foods, so you don't develop an aversion to them in the event that you get sick from chemotherapy. (For the same reason, avoid your favorite foods for three days after chemotherapy as well.)

2. Chemotherapy and immunotherapy can cause inflammation; fat-filled, fried, and/or greasy foods have their own inflammatory properties, so it's best to avoid them in the days prior to treatment.

3. Eat lightly. Some research looking mostly at animal models suggests that cutting back on calories prior to treatment may be beneficial.

Treatment Days and the Week That Follows

During treatment, you should try to eat a small nibble every hour or so, even if you aren't especially hungry. Small meals throughout the day will keep your strength up. Set an alarm, if necessary, to make sure you eat something nutritious. You're more likely to feel nauseous if your stomach is empty, so keep it supplied with good food.

If you're at a loss as to what, specifically, to eat during chemotherapy or immuno-therapy, fear not. Here you'll find recommendations for three different appetite levels: bare minimum, regular, and hearty appetite. If you fall into the minimum appetite category, the healing foods and delicious recipes in this book can help you work your way up to a regular appetite, and eventually a hearty appetite. It's true: I've seen it happen over and over in my practice, much to my delight.

One other note. Some people take a week (or more) to get hungry again after treatment, but for others it happens in just a few days. Everyone is different; let your body tell you what it's ready for, and when.

BARE MINIMUM MENU

No matter how awful you're feeling, you need nourishment. At a bare minimum, this is what you should eat during your treatment and the week following your treatment. You may find it helpful, for the day of treatment, to bring at least one of these delicious liquids to your session in a thermos.

4 cups of either Magic Mineral Broth (page 49), Chicken Magic Mineral Broth (page 50), or Pasture Beef Bone Broth (page 51)

2 servings of smoothies with protein powder

2 cups of Commonweal's Most Nourishing and Healing Tea (page 157)

2 cups of green tea or any variation on green tea in this book

Here's a list of recipes that might work well during the week following treatment. All are easy to digest, comforting, nourishing, and full of the vitamins and minerals your body needs to heal. This is a perfect reference list to give to friends and family who offer to cook for you during this time.

Nourishing Soups and Broths	Magic Mineral Broth (page 49), Chicken Magic Mineral Broth (page 50), Pasture Beef Bone Broth (page 51), Chicken Vegetable Soup with Ginger Meatballs (page 55), Thai It Up Chicken Soup (page 58), Bella's Carrot, Orange, and Fennel Soup (page 61), Spiced Sweet Potato Soup (page 66), Summer's Best Zucchini Soup (page 67), Creamy Broccoli and Potato Soup (page 71)
Vital Vegetables	Mashed Cinnamon Butternut Squash (page 83), Baked Sweet Potatoes with Assorted Toppings (page 90), Roasted Root Vegetables with Rosemary and Thyme (page 92)
Protein-Building Foods	Easy Eggs in a Cup (page 100), Nana's Egg Salad (page 102), Poached Eggs with Basil Lemon Drizzle (page 103), Cozy Comfy Chicken and Rice (page 107)
Anytime Foods	Best Oatmeal Ever (page 128), Edamame Avocado Dip with Wasabi (page 131), Cannellini Bean Dip with Kalamata Olives (page 131), Navy Bean and Sun-Dried Tomato Dip (page 132), Black Bean Hummus (page 132), Curried Hummus (page 133), Maple-Glazed Walnuts (page 137), Spiced Toasted Almonds (page 138), Orange Pistachio Quinoa (page 141), Quinoa Porridge with Walnut Cream (page 142), Rice Paper Moo-Shu Rolls (page 148), Curried Hummus and Vegetable Pinwheels (page 151)
Tonics and Elixirs	Annemarie's Calming Kudzu Elixir (page 156), Commonweal's Most Nourishing and Healing Tea (page 157), Ginger Peppermint Green Tea (page 158), Green Tea Ginger Lemonade (page 158), Cinnamon Ginger Tea (page 159), Mouthwatering Watermelon Granita (page 161), Cantaloupe Granita with Mint (page 162), Peach Ginger Smoothie (page 166), Triple Berry Smoothie (page 168), Chocolate Banana Smoothie (page 169)
Sweet Bites	Chocolate Tapioca Pudding (page 196), Great Pumpkin Custard (page 197), Coconut Rice Pudding (page 201), Strawberries with Mango Coconut "Sabayon" Sauce (page 206)

If you're lucky to have a voracious appetite, eat up! Here's a list of additional foods that are beneficial during treatment.

Nourishing Soups and Broths	Italian White Bean Soup (page 52), Minestrone (page 57), Velvety Red Lentil Dal (page 70)
Vital Vegetables	Basil Broccoli (page 75), Warm and Toasty Cumin Carrots (page 96)
Protein-Building Foods	Chicken and Broccoli Stir-Fry with Cashews (page 106), Orange Ginger Roasted Chicken (page 109), My Family's Favorite Chicken (page 110), Middle Eastern Chickpea Burgers (page 112)
Anytime Foods	Orange Pistachio Quinoa (page 141)
Dollops of Yum!	Tomato Mint Chutney (page 173)
Sweet Bites	Almond Muffin Mania (page 193), Triple Ginger Snap Cookies with Pecans (page 209)

ONE WEEK AFTER CHEMOTHERAPY OR IMMUNOTHERAPY

At some point during the week after treatment, your mouth is going to wake up and want to taste food again. Pay attention to this list of recipes that can jump-start your taste buds and get your appetite up and running.

Nourishing Soups and Broths	Lemony Greek Chicken Soup (page 53), Thai It Up Chicken Soup (page 58), Bella's Carrot, Orange, and Fennel Soup (page 61), Rockin' Black Bean Soup (page 63), Curry Cauliflower Soup (page 64), Spiced Sweet Potato Soup (page 66), Velvety Red Lentil Dal (page 70)
Vital Vegetables	Baby Bok Choy with Yam and Ginger (page 76), Emerald Greens with Orange (page 78), Gregg's Stuffed Acorn Squash with Quinoa, Cranberries, and Swiss Chard (page 81), Mashed Cinnamon Butternut Squash (page 83), Kale with Sweet Potatoes and Pecans (page 84), Kale with Carrots (page 86), Stir-Fried Baby Bok Choy with Shiitake Mushrooms (page 93), Shredded Carrot and Beet Salad (page 95), Warm Napa Cabbage Slaw (page 97)
Protein-Building Foods	Middle Eastern Chickpea Burgers (page 112), Poached Salmon with Moroccan Pesto (page 116), Triple-Citrus Ginger Black Cod (page 119), Baked Citrus Halibut with Signora's Tomato Sauce (page 120)

Anytime Foods	Edamame Avocado Dip with Wasabi (page 131), Cannellini Bean Dip with Kalamata Olives (page 131), Navy Bean and Sun-Dried Tomato Dip (page 132), Black Bean Hummus (page 132), Curried Hummus (page 133), Mediterranean Lentil Salad (page 144)
Tonics and Elixirs	Commonweal's Most Nourishing and Healing Tea (page 157), Green Tea Ginger Lemonade (page 158), Mouthwatering Watermelon Granita (page 161), Cantaloupe Granita with Mint (page 162)
Dollops of Yum!	Apricot Pear Chutney (page 172), Tomato Mint Chutney (page 173), Basil Lemon Drizzle (page 175), Avocado Dressing (page 176), Cashew Cream (page 178), Pistachio Cream (page 179), Cilantro Lime Vinaigrette (page 180), Zesty Lemon Fennel Vinaigrette (page 181), Seasonal Stewed Fruit (page 184), Parsley Basil Drizzle (page 187), Signora's Tomato Sauce (page 189)
Sweet Bites	Baked Apples Filled with Dates and Pecans (page 195), Cardamom Maple Mini Macaroons (page 198), Poached Pears with Saffron Broth (page 205)

Between Treatments

Once your appetite returns to what feels like normal, continue to eat in a healthy and nourishing manner. One colorful way to stay well-nourished is to eat a rainbow of deeply hued organic fruits and vegetables, as they generally contain the highest level of cancer-fighting nutrients. Any of the recipes in this book will deliver high-quality nourishment as well. In addition, I recommend the following immune-system boosters on a daily basis.

Smoothie or protein shake

Magic Mineral Broth (page 49), Chicken Magic Mineral Broth (page 50), or Pasture Beef Bone Broth (page 51)

Commonweal's Most Nourishing and Healing Tea (page 157) Ginger Peppermint Green Tea (page 158), Green Tea Ginger Lemonade (page 158), Cinnamon Ginger Tea (page 159), or any other green tea

Enhancing Flavor and Dealing with Taste Changes

There's one side effect I haven't yet discussed, because it deserves a whole section unto itself. The technical term is "transient taste change," but I just say it's what happens when your taste buds go kaflooey during treatment. Many people I've worked with complain of either an altered or a metallic taste in their mouth as they go through their cancer therapies, most notably chemotherapy. They're not imagining things. Cancer therapies can damage or unbalance taste buds and also cause sudden sensitivities to hot and cold. Fortunately, many of these changes wax and wane even between treatments, and often disappear post-treatment. The reason is that taste buds and taste nerves regenerate rapidly, often within weeks. In fact, the average turnover rate of taste bud cells is just ten days!

Normally, the brain combines sensory output from the taste buds and the sense of smell, and the resulting neuronal input is taste. But treatment can distort or impair this output, so the brain picks up just a whisper of the flavor, producing a taste in conflict with what the eater expects. As a result, your all-time favorite treat—say, warm banana bread fresh from the oven—may *look* delicious, and it may even *smell* delicious, but when you taste it, it's anything but. So you push back from the table, disappointed and disengaging from one of the most important things you must do during treatment: eat. Similarly, those metallic tastes, which researchers suggest could be caused by everything from taste bud damage to chemo agents finding their way into the salivary glands, can frustrate patients into avoiding food and drink—and who can blame them? It can be psychologically devastating when our food expectations, built upon a lifetime of experience, suddenly let us down.

Fortunately, there is a simple answer that can revitalize impaired taste buds. It's a tool I call FASS, which stands for Fat, Acid, Salt, and Sweet. In my kitchen, olive oil represents the fat, lemons are the acid, sea salt is the only salt I'll touch, and organic maple syrup is my preferred sweet. You'll find this Fantastic Four of seasonings right next to my stove, as ever-present and important to me as a spreadsheet is to an accountant.

FASS started as a culinary tool to help any dish whose flavor strayed off course during the cooking process, and to bring food to the table bursting with flavor. That's an absolute *must* for someone dealing with subpar taste buds (it's not just people in treatment that encounter this; our taste buds often become desensitized as we age).

Think of cooking as a game of darts, with the bull's-eye being that absolute moment of yum. Each element of FASS represents a culinary quadrant of the dartboard. When they're balanced and work in harmony, you'll hit the bull's-eye. Acid and salt add high notes to taste, each in its own way; fat and sweet tend to bring roundness and fullness to a dish. FASS is really just an acronym to remind you of these fundamentals, which chefs and many cooks do by intuition much of the time.

Here's FASS in action: When I make a soup, I taste it throughout the cooking process. It's a good habit to adopt, a fun way to fix in your memory what each new ingredient brings to the table. Also, constant tasting is the only way to ensure that a dish has optimum flavor without running the risk of having to resort to drastic measures after it's completed. If you've ever tried to put wiring into a house *after* the walls are up, you'll know what I'm talking about. By adding a spritz of lemon here or a pinch of salt there, you can better alchemize the ingredients so that what hits the tongue in the end is pure bliss.

I conduct workshops throughout the country that introduce both patients and cancer wellness professionals to how to use FASS. I usually cook up a batch of carrot-ginger soup, which unbeknownst to the participants has been watered down just enough to throw off the taste. Still, the bright orange color looks just about right, and a hint of the smell is also there. They line up to taste the soup, anticipation in their eyes, but upon taking a sip they look disappointed, to say the least. For people who haven't personally had transient taste changes, this gives them a glimpse into what it's like to live with that reality.

Now that I have their attention, I explain the role that FASS plays for the taste impaired. I start with sea salt, as it has more than eighty minerals and a much fuller flavor than normal table salt. Sea salt stimulates nerve endings and ignites taste. It's kind of like cranking up the volume on your stereo. By contrast, lemons, citrus in general, and other acidic ingredients are like turning up the treble and brighten up whatever tastes you've brought out with the salt.

Sweet—in this case organic maple syrup—adds a depth or roundness to flavor that's the equivalent of hearing an orchestra in a concert hall, rather than on your stereo. Just a bit of sweetness can transform a two-dimensional taste encounter into a memorable 3-D culinary experience.

As for fat, it serves as a chauffeur supreme, transporting the salt, sweet, and acidic tastes to the different islands of taste buds throughout the mouth, guaranteeing that all the buds—impaired *and* healthy—have an opportunity to at least listen to the concert.

Once people understand the FASS components, and the role they play, the application of FASS is a pure delight to watch. That *meh* carrot-ginger soup turns into something that tastes *fantastic* in just a few minutes. One by one, I bring people out of the audience, have them taste the soup, and ask them "What's missing?" Even people with no cooking experience have an innate sense of how something should taste, and can usually point to the right FASS ingredient and say, "How about we add a little of *this?*" The soup quickly comes back into balance with each touch of FASS, getting closer to that culinary bull's-eye. What really gets people is when the soup has gone from so-so to pretty darn good. They're tempted to stop, but I nudge them forward, suggesting just a few more FASS hits. What I'm looking for is that culinary bull's-eye, that involuntary spasm of vocal delight. And when it happens (and it does!), it's pure nirvana.

I've yet to meet anyone in treatment who wasn't helped by an application of the FASS principle. For those with little or no change in the sense of taste, FASS makes a good meal great. For those with more challenging taste issues, it can spell the difference between finding meals palatable, which keeps the appetite engaged, and losing interest in eating. FASS works wonders. Use it, and enjoy!

FASS Fixes for Taste Bud Troubles

IF YOUR TASTE BUDS ARE SAYING	USE THIS FASS FIX
Things have a metallic taste.	Add a little sweetener such as maple syrup, and a squeeze of lemon. You could also try adding fat, such as a nut cream or butter.
Things taste too sweet.	Start by adding 6 drops of lemon or lime juice. Keep adding it in small increments until the sweet taste becomes muted.
Things taste too salty.	Add ¼ teaspoon of lemon juice. It erases the taste of salt.
Things taste too bitter.	Add a little sweetener, such as maple syrup.
Everything tastes like cardboard.	Add more sea salt until the flavor of the dish moves toward the front of the mouth. A spritz of fresh lemon juice also helps.

If you are having trouble swallowing or dealing with mouth sores, add fat, such as a nut cream, to your food. Eat blended or pureed foods, such as blended soups, smoothies, and granitas. Stay away from ginger, curry, red pepper flakes, and other strong spices.

Learning Your Food Preferences

If you're the cook in the house, you know it can be awfully difficult to get some people to answer the simple question, "What do you feel like eating?" That inquiry can become even more confounding for people whose appetite may be constantly waxing and waning due to treatment. Still, it's vital to give those folks the necessary vocabulary so that they can more easily express what they'd like to eat, no matter their mood. That's what this tool—learning your food preferences—is all about.

Uncovering favorite tastes is just one part of the puzzle. An often-ignored part of appetite allure is texture. Let's use mushrooms as an example. People tend to love them or hate them (in my experience there's rarely a middle ground). And the reason, pro or con, usually has nothing to do with taste; it's the slippery texture mushrooms often have once they're cooked.

Figuring out taste and texture preferences—whether yours or someone else's—serves two purposes: If those foods are healthy and nutritious, great. If not, zeroing in on desired taste and texture is the only sustainable way to begin to move people to delicious substitutes that benefit health. Feeding someone something for which they have no natural affinity is guaranteed to be a turnoff, one that can't be remedied by saying "Eat this, it's good for you." There's a vast difference between getting nutrition and feeling nourished; the former is often joyless, mechanical, and not sustainable, while the latter creates an uplifting state of well-being, an empowering sense that one is truly feeding one's body and soul. That's both desirable and sustainable.

I've learned that long-term change occurs only if you meet people where they are, rather than insisting that they start where you'd like them to be. You can't take a meat-and-potatoes guy and expect to perform a culinary coup d'état that lands him in a strict vegan diet. That's counterproductive and will never last. But if you understand someone's preferences, incremental change is not only possible, but also likely—*so long as they consider the new food scrumptious* (which I guarantee will be the case if you apply what you find in this book).

The tool I use that gets to the heart of people's connection or disconnection with food is a questionnaire. I employ it during what I call my "culinary confessional." It's a fun process where I sit down with patients and caregivers to better get to know their situation. I'll ask people what their favorite food is, and because they think of me as the "healthy" chef in the room, they'll say something like "Oh, I really like kale."

And I'll say, "Really? Kale? That's funny, because I love cinnamon jelly beans. Used to eat them by the handful."

The only way to get an honest answer is to drop any judgments. The point is to find the person's comfort level and work within those parameters. If someone is straight with me and admits to being a pretzel addict, that's fine—great, in fact. Why? Because it tells me they love crunchy things. How can I make that work in the person's favor? By making sure to include a crunchy topping on every healthy soup or salad. That helps guarantee that they'll enjoy eating those dishes.

But there's more. By giving them that hit of a taste or texture they like, I help them experience the delicious, nutritious nature of the other outstanding foods in the meal. So a woman who wouldn't go near a broccoli stalk suddenly finds herself enjoying creamy broccoli potato soup. Why? Because potatoes, which she likes, are in the foreground, and the broccoli, instead of being presented in chunks—a texture she eschews—is creamy and colorful, a background canvas for the rest of the meal. Put a small shaving of Cheddar on top—another food she craves—and there's no way she'll turn her nose up at the soup.

Many of the questions that follow are pretty straightforward, but I recommend that you really give them some thought, and even write down your answers. I also suggest paying special attention to one question that may seem a bit unusual: if your taste buds could travel around the world, where would they go? After the questionnaire you'll find a tool I call global flavorprints, which can help you make the most of the insights you gain here.

One last thought: A consultation with a nutritionist who specializes in eating well during cancer is a great idea. Bringing them your answers to the Culinary Preferences questionnaire can be an excellent starting point for a conversation.

Discovering Your Culinary Preferences

Do you have any food allergies? (Examples may include nuts, dairy, or shellfish.)

What are your favorite foods? (Don't hold back; chocolate and potato chips count!)

Why do you like them? (This means what, *specifically*, you like about them.)

What are your comfort foods, or what foods that make you happy?

If you were banished to a desert island, what's the one food you would take with you, and why?

What kinds of food do you crave, and why?

What are your favorite tastes? If your taste buds could travel around the world, where would they go? Multiple landings are allowed!

What are your favorite and least favorite textures? Do you enjoy crispy, crunchy, or smooth textures? For example, do you like chunky, hearty soups, or smooth and creamy soups, or both?

What foods do you not like or not want included in your meals? For example, do you love or hate cilantro?

How many meals do you eat a day—small meals more often, or one big meal?

How do you feel when you're eating? Do you feel nourished and satiated?

Do you cook or does someone else in your family cook?

The Power of Herbs and Spices

Whether we're discussing flavor or nutrition, nothing packs more power, gram for gram, than herbs and spices. That's why I make such extensive use of them in nearly every recipe in this book. What's gratifying, from a cancer-fighting perspective, is seeing the growing body of research showing that everything from turmeric to cinnamon to mint can play a role in controlling many of the systemic disruptions that contribute to cancer. We're talking controlling inflammation, limiting the damage of oxidative stress, and keeping blood sugar from spiking. Sure, lots of vegetables and fruits and other plant foods do this as well, but not as potently as herbs and spices (and for those of you keeping score at home, herbs and spices also count as plant foods). And from a cook's perspective, nothing increases the yum factor of food better than herbs and spices.

Here's a tip about how to use herbs and spices to release maximum flavor and phytochemicals. When using dried herbs and spices, add them near the beginning of the process, especially if the dish is cooked. The reason? Heat, especially in combination with a bit of fat such as olive oil, breaks down the oils in the herbs and spices and releases them into the food. These oils carry much of the taste, and with it the healing benefits of the phytochemicals. As far as fresh herbs like cilantro, mint, and parsley are concerned, it's best to add them at the end, to retain maximum flavor and color.

A lot of people I teach are initially hesitant about adding herbs and spices, worried that they'll overdo it. Don't sweat it. Use the recipes as a guide for how much of each herb or spice to add and when. After a while, you'll get a feel for the amounts that work for you. You'll also find that certain groups of spices like to hang out together, as indicated in the following chart of global flavorprints. It lists many of the herbs and spices associated with a variety of popular cuisines. To capture the essence of a cuisine, I generally recommend using three spices from its list. This will allow you to bring the flavors of your favorite restaurants home to recreate in your own kitchen. The other nice thing is that once you've stocked your pantry with dried herbs and spices, they're there for a long time, always ready and handy.

Global Flavorprints: Herbs and Spices

Mediterranean	Garlic, basil, oregano, mint, nutmeg, parsley, rosemary, bay leaves, fennel seeds, red pepper flakes, sage, saffron, thyme, oregano
Middle Eastern	Allspice, oregano, marjoram, mint, sesame seeds, garlic, cinnamon, cumin seeds, coriander seeds, cilantro
North African (Moroccan)	Red pepper flakes, cumin seeds, coriander seeds, cilantro, mint, saffron, garlic, cinnamon, ginger, turmeric
Thai	Lemongrass, ginger, mint, makrut lime leaves, lime, curry powder, turmeric, coriander seeds, chiles, garlic, cilantro, red pepper flakes
Indian	Red pepper flakes, chiles, saffron, mint, cumin seeds, coriander seeds, cilantro, garlic, turmeric, nutmeg, cinnamon, ginger, cardamom, mustard seeds, curry powder
Mexican	Chiles, oregano, cumin seeds, cinnamon, cilantro

Optimizing Nutrition

Eating well during cancer treatment can be tricky. The brain's appetite center can become finicky, disrupting or even turning off the signals that normally go from the brain to the rest of the body that tell you you're hungry. It has also been noted that chemotherapy, immunotherapy, radiation, and surgery can all impair the normal sensitivity of taste buds, and/or leave a metallic taste in the mouth. Fortunately, there are strategies that patients and caregivers can employ to get the nutritious food they need in a way they can embrace, even on difficult days. Check out these suggestions:

- **Move from three large meals to six "mini" meals.** This is advice you'll hear from just about every nutritionist who works with people in treatment. I take it one step further. *Any* food you can get into your system—even a sip of a nutrient-dense broth (I often serve my soups up in little cups), or a shot glass full of a smoothie—counts as a mini meal in my book. (And *please* don't judge yourself harshly if one nibble is all you can get down. That's fine. Really!) I also suggest using an alarm on your smartphone or some other device to remind you, every hour, that you need a small nosh. Don't depend on your body to tell you when it's hungry, because, as already noted, your appetite signaling may not be reliable during treatment.

- **Have a wide variety of foods available.** It is wonderfully satisfying to open up the fridge or freezer and realize that, on any given day, you have lots of nourishing food and drink choices. If you're not up to doing the prep and cooking yourself, this is where friends and family can help. Give them a list of your food preferences (see the earlier section) and a few recipes from the book; most are designed to yield four to six servings, meaning they're perfect for freezing and storing (see "Food Storage Tips," page 43). Even smoothies in a pitcher will last for several days in the fridge.

- **Make your food portable.** It's a great idea to make food available wherever you go, be it at work, during a long treatment session, or even at the hospital. A thermos full of soup, mineral broth, tea, or smoothie is one way to accomplish this. So are small bags or single-serving containers filled with nuts or Anytime Foods (see Chapter 5). Believe me, if you have foods and drinks that are easily accessible, you'll avail yourself of them, time and again.

- **Get more herbs and spices into what you eat and drink.** We've noted that herbs and spices contain fantastic anticancer phytochemicals that lower inflammation, regulate blood sugar, and bolster cancer-fighting pathways. There are lots of ways to get more herbs and spices into your diet. Sprinkling mint, basil, or parsley on any salad or dish is one idea. A small hit of turmeric on eggs also works. A dash of cinnamon goes well over oatmeal, yogurt, grains, or sweet potatoes.

- **Fiber—a great way to keep blood sugar regulated.** Blood sugar regulation is a key to fighting cancer and other diseases such as Type 2 diabetes. Getting fiber into your diet slows the speed with which sugar enters your system. Combining fiber with just a touch of healthy fat slows this process even further. Fortunately, certain high-fiber foods make a great canvas for adding fat. Apples with a little bit of almond butter is one example. So is celery with hummus. Sprinkling flaxseeds on oatmeal, salad dressing, or smoothies also does the trick. Sweet potatoes with a little olive or coconut oil is another winner.

- **Tea, tea, tea.** Pick your pleasure. Green tea has a huge number of phytonutrients. Some people find it bitter, but making sure the water is hot—but not boiling—can take away much of that bitter taste, as can adding a spritz of lemon. Cinnamon and ginger teas are also excellent for hydration (which is vital during treatment) and can calm the digestive system.

- **Speaking of hydration.** I've often dealt with avid water drinkers who are dismayed to find that a side effect of their treatment is that water suddenly tastes metallic. An excellent way to get rid of that metallic taste is to put a bunch of sliced lemons into a pitcher of water that you keep in the fridge. Mint and berries also work, infusing their wonderful taste and phytochemicals into the water. I'm a big fan of keeping a thermos filled with your favorite water, tea, or other nutrient-dense liquid (aka smoothies) with you whenever you can.

- **Create your own cancer-fighting trail mix.** Walnuts, almonds, seeds, dried blueberries—they're portable, nutrient-dense (meaning you need only a few nibbles to fill you up), and full of great phytochemicals. Again, check out the Anytime Food in Chapter 5 for ideas.

Culinary Pharmacy

If you're interested in how, exactly, certain foods can benefit people dealing with cancer, you've come to the right place. Research into this field has exploded: type "cancer prevention and food" into the National Library of Medicine's PubMed data base, and hits for more than ten thousand peer-reviewed studies appear, with more than half having taken place in the last ten years. This culinary pharmacy looks at the healing properties of the foods in this cookbook: everything from cinnamon's ability to keep blood sugar levels stable (which is important because people on chemotherapy and immunotherapy can be more prone to insulin swings and diabetes) to curcumin's role in regulating nuclear factor kappa B (NF-kB), a protein complex involved in immune and inflammatory processes. Incorrect regulation of NF-kB and inflammation is thought to play a role in many diseases, including cancer. Similarly, cancer treatments often tax the immune system, making people more vulnerable to infection and illness from viruses, bacteria, and the like. I've noted the foods that have antiviral and antimicrobial properties, such as rosemary, cloves, and mustard seed, which may offer protective benefits.

One final point about my benchmark for all these citations, namely peer-reviewed scientific studies. You'll see a lot of qualifiers in how I describe the medicinal activity of foods—lots of "mays" and "coulds," as in "this may help reduce the risk of colon cancer." There's a reason for this. While the number of studies looking at the food/ cancer-fighting connection includes far more human data than ever before, the majority of research still involves animals or basic laboratory work. Promising? Extremely. But what works in mice doesn't always apply to humans. Even in studies analyzing the diets of human populations less prone to cancer, it takes time to tease out which foods—and which compounds in those foods—offer protection. The emerging field of nutrigenomics is really fascinating, as it explores how our genes interact with foods, slowly revealing which nutrients and phytochemicals turn on (or turn off) the metabolic pathways that dictate our health.

All this research is, in my opinion, great news. But the fact that the jury is still out in many areas suggests it's wise to play the odds when it comes to eating by consuming a wide-ranging diet. That way, you'll consume more potentially beneficial nutrients, which is really the name of the game.

I like to think of the culinary pharmacy as a shop that's open 24/7, with something in every aisle that can help people thrive during treatment. It's one of my favorite tools in the tool kit. To find recipes that include each ingredient, consult the index.

Cancer-Fighting Ingredients

EXPLANATION OF SOME TERMS

Antiangiogenesis	Angiogenesis is the process whereby cancer cells grow new blood vessels to stay alive; antiagiogenesis is stopping that process.
NF-kB regulator	NF-kB is a pathway that helps control the body's immune response. When NF-kB is improperly regulated, chronic inflammation that may lead to cancer can occur.
Promotes apoptosis	Apoptosis is the medical term for the death of a cell. Cancer cells are often resistant to normal cell death.
Aids DNA repair	Cells employ DNA repair to ensure limiting damage that could lead to genetic mutations that may be the precursors of cancer development.
Anticarcinogenic	Having an action effective against carcinogens, cancer-causing agents that can enter the body through environmental and dietary exposure.

ALLSPICE/ALLSPICE BERRIES: *Digestion aid, antimicrobial.* Allspice is great if you're feeling bloated or gassy, as it relieves indigestion and soothes discomfort, especially in the upper (small) intestine.

ALMONDS: *Anti-inflammatory.* Almonds are a fantastic source of fiber, which may help prevent colon cancer. They have twice the antioxidant power with their skins on. They're also good blood sugar regulators.

APPLES: *Anti-inflammatory.* Apples have been shown in the lab to keep liver, breast, and colon cancer cells at bay.

APRICOTS: *Anti-inflammatory.* Potassium-rich apricots rebalance the body chemistry, especially for people whose electrolytes have been depleted due to dehydration from treatments. Their iron content benefits oxygen transport, keeping hemoglobin and energy levels steady.

ARUGULA: *Promotes detoxification; cancer pathway inhibitor.* In addition to the general cancer risk–reducing effect of eating cruciferous vegetables, arugula contains sulforaphane, which may slow down the effects of an enzyme known to cause cancer cell progression, notably in prostate cancer cells. Also, arugula's chlorophyll may limit the damage from carcinogens created by high-temperature grilling of meat, fish, and chicken.

ASPARAGUS: *Anti-inflammatory.* The phytochemicals in asparagus mimic an anti-inflammatory called a COX-2 inhibitor. Asparagus is also rich in vitamin A (which in lab and animal models takes on skin, breast, liver, colon, and prostate cancers), vitamin K (prostate and lung cancers), and folic acid (colorectal, esophageal, stomach, and breast cancers).

AVOCADOS: *Anti-inflammatory.* Avocado's monounsaturated fats (notably oleic acid) may protect against breast cancer, while other phytochemicals and vitamin E are believed to combat prostate cancer growth. Glutathione, a combination of amino acids abundant in avocados, removes cancer-promoting carcinogens such as cigarette smoke from the healthy cells they can damage.

BANANAS: *Digestion aid, balances electrolytes.* Bananas' high potassium levels replace the electrolytes sometimes lost during treatments. As with apples, they're full of stomach-soothing pectin, and their fiber sweeps toxins from the intestinal tract, improving bowel function and lowering colon cancer risk.

BARLEY: *Anti-inflammatory.* Lignan, a barley phytochemical, binds with estrogen receptors in the body, which may help women who are sensitive to estrogen-related breast cancer. Barley's high fiber benefits digestion and bowel function, lowering the risk of colon cancer.

BASIL: *Digestion aid, anti-inflammatory, antimicrobial, antibacterial, NF-kB regulator.* Two flavonoids (chemicals that are part of a plant's metabolism) in basil, orientin and vicenin, protect human cells from both radiation and free-radical damage. If your taste buds are off, or a sore throat or irritated mouth is affecting taste, basil can have a corrective effect.

BAY LEAF: *Digestion aid.* Bay leaves relieve abdominal cramps and gas. They soothe and relax the digestive tract.

BEANS AND LENTILS: *Anti-inflammatory.* Studies show that diets high in beans or lentils lowered breast cancer recurrence in women. Their high fiber also lowers colon cancer risk. They help control blood sugar and flush toxins from the body, vital for those in treatment. They are fantastic sources of protein and minerals, notably molybdenum. Molybdenum deficiency is linked to stomach and esophageal cancers.

BEETS: *Anti-inflammatory.* Beets' rich red color comes from the phytochemical betacyanin; it combines with beets' fiber to fight colon cancer. Beet fiber also increases glutathione levels, which cleanses toxins from cells.

BELL PEPPERS: *Anti-inflammatory.* Lycopene—also found in tomatoes—along with vitamin C and lots of fiber in bell peppers may offer protection against colon, cervical, bladder, prostate, and pancreatic cancers. The vitamin A–promoting carotenoid beta-cryptoxanthin lowers lung cancer risk. Antioxidants, including vitamins A, C, K, folic acid, and B_6, also absorb cancer-causing free radicals.

BLACK PEPPER: *Digestion aid, antibacterial, NF-kB regulator.* Black pepper stimulates the taste buds to signal the stomach to produce hydrochloric acid, which aids digestion. Peppercorns also contain piperine, an alkaloid that increases the body's ability to assimilate cancer-fighting nutrients including beta-carotene, curcumin, and selenium.

BLUEBERRIES: *Anti-inflammatory.* The ellagic acid in blueberries interferes with metabolic pathways that feed certain cancers. Another component, the flavonol kaempferol, can reduce pancreatic cancer risk. Also, acids called phenols cause colon cancer cells to self-destruct.

BRAZIL NUTS: *Anti-inflammatory.* Brazil nuts are selenium-rich, which helps fight colon and prostate cancers. The American Cancer Society notes that the Brazil nut antioxidant quercetin may trigger cell death in some cancers.

BROCCOLI: *Anti-inflammatory, antibacterial.* Sulforaphane, a well-studied broccoli phytochemical, appears to slow leukemia and melanoma growth. Another metabolite, glucosinolate, can inhibit breast cancer growth.

BUCKWHEAT: *Anti-inflammatory.* Buckwheat's high fiber content regulates bowel function and speeds toxins out of the body, which may decrease colon cancer risk.

CABBAGE: *Anti-inflammatory, antibacterial.* Cabbage, along with cruciferous kin such as cauliflower, kale, brussels sprouts, broccoli, bok choy, and turnips, is extremely high in anticancer phytochemicals. Indole-3-carbinol (I3C for short) nearly doubles how quickly the liver can break down estrogen so it doesn't remain in the body. Cooking cabbage for the right amount of time (in other words, not too long) helps retain sinigrin, a compound that aids release of molecules that detoxify carcinogens and inhibit tumor cell growth.

CANTALOUPE: *Anti-inflammatory.* Vitamin A–rich cantaloupes can protect against the possible emphysema and lung inflammation linked to exposure to secondhand smoke. The American Cancer Society also suggests eating melon to protect against colorectal cancer.

CARDAMOM: *Digestion aid, anti-inflammatory, NF-kB regulator.* Cardamom can help relieve numerous digestive issues including constipation, gas, and stomachaches. Just chewing on cardamom seeds can ease indigestion and freshen the breath. Cardamom may reduce inflammation and protect against growth of colon cancer cells.

CARROTS: *Anti-inflammatory.* Studies show that eating just one carrot a day, rich in the vitamin A that promotes lung health, could cut lung cancer risk in half. They're also rich in the beta-carotene that accounts for their beautiful orange color; beta-carotene is associated with preventing lung, mouth, throat, stomach, intestinal, bladder, prostate, and breast cancers.

CASHEWS: *Possible tumor suppressor.* Cashews are copper-rich, which is important because copper deficiency is associated with increased risk of colon cancer. As with avocados (see facing page), they're high in oleic acid, an anticancer component of monounsaturated fat.

CAULIFLOWER: *Anti-inflammatory.* See Cabbage.

CAYENNE AND CHILE FLAKES: *Appetite stimulant, digestion aid, anti-inflammatory, antibacterial.* Capsaicin decreases PSA levels—that's the antigen whose level normally rises as prostate cancer develops. Capsaicin may also prevent stomach cancer and perhaps inhibit the spread of brain and spinal cord tumors known as gliomas.

CELERY: *Anti-inflammatory.* A celery phytochemical called coumarin helps white blood cells prevent free radicals from damaging cells, decreasing mutations that can cause cells to become cancerous. In addition, acetylenic compounds in celery can stop the growth of tumor cells.

CHERRIES: *Anti-inflammatory.* Cherries' tartness comes from perillyl alcohol, which may deprive cancer of the proteins it needs to flourish. It's done well in lab studies against advanced breast, prostate, and ovarian cancers. Two other cherry phytochemicals, isoquercitrin and quercetin, inhibit colon cancer cells.

CHICKEN: *Antioxidant, possible heavy metals detoxifier.* Organic, free-range chickens are nice sources of niacin and selenium, both of which have cancer-preventive qualities. Selenium induces cancer cells, especially colon and prostate cancer cells, to stop functioning and replicating.

CHICKPEAS: *Anti-inflammatory.* Protein-rich chickpeas are also good regulators of blood sugar and cholesterol, which can be affected by treatments. Chickpeas' high fiber helps flush toxins from the body and may reduce colon cancer risk.

CHOCOLATE: *Anti-inflammatory.* Chocolate's flavonoids may have chemoprotective effects. Also, go for dark chocolate: it has four times the antioxidants found in tea.

CILANTRO AND CORIANDER: *Digestion aid, anti-inflammatory, antimicrobial, antibacterial, NF-kB regulator.* Cilantro packs a punch in the lab; its antibacterial and antimicrobial properties have taken out salmonella under the microscope. Cilantro is also good at relieving an upset stomach and nausea. It also helps with general anxiety.

CINNAMON: *Appetite stimulant, digestion aid, anti-inflammatory, antimicrobial, antibacterial, NF-kB regulator.* Cinnamon's cinnamaldehyde lessens inflammation associated with certain cancers. Cinnamon also helps keep blood sugar levels balanced, while its antioxidant and calcium/fiber combination lowers cholesterol and reduces colon cancer risk.

CLOVES: *Digestion aid, anti-inflammatory, antibacterial, NF-kB regulator.* Cloves are kaempferol-rich; human studies show that a higher kaempferol intake lowered ovarian cancer risk. As with cinnamon, cloves aid digestion. Cloves also contain a wonderful oil, eugenol, that may protect against digestive cancers, offering anti-inflammatory benefits while attacking toxicities from environmental pollutants. Another phytochemical, rhamnetin, kicks up cloves' antioxidant factor.

COCONUT MILK AND COCONUT OIL: *Anti-inflammatory, antimicrobial, antibacterial.* Half of coconut's saturated fat content comes from lauric acid, which the body converts into monolaurin, a powerful antibacterial and antiviral compound. Monolaurin may also play a role in attacking cancer.

CRANBERRIES: *Anti-inflammatory.* No fruit is better at inhibiting the growth of liver cancer cells in humans. Many cranberry compounds appear to be toxic to other cancer cells, while leaving healthy cells alone. This includes lung, cervical, prostate, and breast cancers, as well as leukemia. Whole cranberries may also target skin, lung, and brain cancers.

CUMIN: *Appetite stimulant, digestion aid, antimicrobial, NF-kB regulator.* Studies suggest that cumin seeds may slow the growth of stomach and cervical tumors. Other studies found they're good for an upset stomach and to relieve cramping, especially when the seeds are toasted.

DATES: *Blood sugar regulation, immune system booster.* Some sugars found in Libyan dates were shown to have potent antitumor properties. Another sugar, beta-D-glucan, regulates cholesterol and blood sugar levels by slowing down gut absorption of glucose.

EDAMAME: *Anti-inflammatory.* Edamame (or soybeans) jump-start the immune system. Their isoflavones appear to act like roadblocks, starving cancer cells by preventing the formation of new blood vessels in the body (also known as *angiogenesis*).

EGGS: *Anti-inflammatory.* A study of 121,000 women suggested that eating three eggs a week during adolescence dropped the risk of breast cancer by 18 percent. Other components of eggs, such as choline and lecithin, improve brain and gallbladder function.

FENNEL: *Digestion aid, anti-inflammatory, NF-kB regulator.* Fennel soothes the stomach, while anethole—a compound that largely accounts for fennel's licorice aroma—lowers inflammation that may affect cancer cell development.

FLAXSEEDS AND CHIA SEEDS: *Anti-inflammatory.* Flaxseeds are perhaps nature's best source for lignans, a phytoestrogen that may help women who are dealing with estrogen-sensitive breast cancer by blocking estrogen receptor sites in the body. Both flax and chia seeds are high in an omega-3 fatty acid called alpha linolenic acid (ALA); ALA has been shown in the lab to induce cell death in certain breast and cervical cancer cells. ALA-rich diets may also reduce breast cancer risk in women.

GARLIC: *Anti-inflammatory, antimicrobial, antibacterial.* A garlic compound called allicin gives this food its pungent smell and cancer-protective punch. Allicin is a strong antibacterial and antiviral agent that appears to keep carcinogens from affecting healthy colon cells.

GINGER: *Nausea reducer, anti-inflammatory, antibacterial, NF-kB regulator.* Ginger is renowned for easing nausea and an upset stomach; that effect increases when it's consumed with some protein. Ginger's active component, spicy gingerol, controlled the growth of bowel cancer cells in animal models.

GREEN TEA: *Anti-inflammatory.* Green tea's polyphenols appear to help keep carcinogens inactive in the body, notably blocking cancers of the gastrointestinal tract. They may also help prevent breast, prostate, and lung cancers. One potentially negative note: USC researchers found that some green tea compounds, notably EGCG, appeared to block the anticancer action of the drug Velcade (also known as Bortezomib), used for multiple myeloma treatment. They suggested that patients taking this drug might want to avoid green tea.

HALIBUT: *Anti-inflammatory.* Regular consumption of the omega-3 fatty acids found in fish such as halibut could reduce the risk of cancers including non-Hodgkin's lymphoma, multiple myeloma, and childhood leukemia. This protection may extend to kidney, colon, breast, prostate, and lung cancers.

KALE: *Anti-inflammatory.* Brassicas, the family of cruciferous vegetables including kale, are high in indole-3-carbinol. This may affect estrogen-sensitive tissues, perhaps preventing lesions from turning cancerous or keeping cancer cells from proliferating.

KOMBU: *Anti-toxins.* Sea vegetables such as kombu have chlorophyllins, which in animal models bind to carcinogens in the digestive tract, potentially limiting their impact. Kombu also contains lignans (as do edamame and barley) that may modestly reduce breast and endometrial cancer risk in post-menopausal women.

KUDZU: *Digestive aid, NF-kB regulator.* Kudzu, a vine, and its vegetable offshoot contain phytochemicals including daidzin and genistein, which in animal studies slowed prostate cancer development.

LEEKS: *Anti-inflammatory, antibacterial.* Leeks, like their allium kin onions and garlic, are linked to a reduced risk of colon and prostate cancers. Kaempferol (also present in almonds, Brazil nuts, and cloves) may offer some protection against ovarian cancer.

LEMONGRASS: *May promote apoptosis.* Lemongrass' powerful citrus taste comes partly from citral, an oil that fights infections, relaxes muscles, and in the lab interfered with cancer cell growth. It's great if you're dealing with cramps or muscle-related headaches.

LEMONS: *Anti-inflammatory, antimicrobial.* Lemons, like most citrus fruits, have a high vitamin C content that benefits the immune system. Lemons also contain several anti-inflammatory and anticancer compounds, including limonene (in the zest), which promotes cancer cell death. Liminoids are helpful with skin, lung, breast, colon, stomach, and mouth cancers.

LIMES: *Anti-inflammatory, antimicrobial.* Limes boost white blood cell activity, which may help fight off treatment-related infections. Lime sugars known as glycosides may stop division of some cancer cells.

MANGOES: *Antioxidant, anti-inflammatory.* Regular mango eaters reduce their gallbladder cancer risk by up to 60 percent. Mango extract may also keep healthy cells from turning cancerous.

MAPLE SYRUP, GRADE A DARK AMBER: *Antioxidant, aids DNA repair.* Maple syrup is high in zinc that benefits the prostate, as low zinc levels are associated with increased prostate cancer risk.

MILLET: *Anti-inflammatory.* Millet's high fiber cleans out the bowel, potentially decreasing colon cancer risk. Also, a huge (over thirty thousand participants) study of women in the U.K. found that those eating the highest fiber diets cut their risk for breast cancer by more than half.

MINT: *Digestion aid, antimicrobial, NF-kB regulator.* Mint can act as an appetite aid, improving the taste of foods for those affected by treatments. It also relieves indigestion. As with cherries, mint contains perillyl alcohol, which in the lab stalls growth of liver, mammary, and pancreatic tumors. Mint's rich vitamin C and beta-carotene content helps lower colorectal cancer risk.

MUSHROOMS: *Anti-inflammatory.* Shiitake, maitake, and reishi mushrooms all appear to enhance the immune system, potentially making it more cancer resistant. Mushroom's polysaccharides sugars, notably lentinan, are potent; gastric cancer cells exposed to lentinan literally disintegrated. Another compound, lectin, stopped cancer cell division. Some mushrooms also trigger the body's ability to create interferon, which can help the effectiveness of certain chemotherapies.

MUSTARD SEED: *Appetite stimulant, digestion aid.* Mustard seed contains sulfur and nitrogen compounds known as glucosinolates, which break down into isothiocynates that slow down GI tract and colon cancer growth. Mustard seed also contains abundant selenium, which may protect against prostate cancer. On the tongue, mustard prompts salivation, which promotes appetite. It can also help prevent indigestion.

NUTMEG: *Appetite stimulant, digestion aid, nausea reducer, anti-inflammatory, antibacterial, NF-kB regulator.* Nutmeg's myristicin, also found in parsley, may prompt tumor-fighting in the body.

OLIVES/OLIVE OIL: *Anti-inflammatory, antibacterial.* The abundance of vitamin E and monounsaturated fats in olive oil translates into lowered colon cancer rates, while its oleic acid reduces expression of a particular breast-cancer gene by 46 percent.

ONIONS: *Anti-inflammatory, antibacterial.* Onions—shallots, in particular—were effective in attacking leukemia in animal studies. Onion extract also showed antitumor properties, possibly because it helps quickly flush carcinogens from the body.

ORANGES: *Anti-inflammatory, antimicrobial.* Citrus—including oranges—helps against mouth, throat, and stomach cancers. Some of the oils in citrus, called monoterpenes, help remove carcinogens in animals, slowing tumor growth. Oranges' abundant vitamin C is also associated with cutting colon cancer risk.

OREGANO: *Digestion aid, anti-inflammatory, antimicrobial, antibacterial, NF-kB regulator.* Two antioxidants in oregano, thymol and rosmarinic acid (also found in rosemary), scavenge for potentially cancer-causing oxygen molecules. Oregano is also a good source of antibacterial and antimicrobial agents, which help immune systems taxed by treatment.

PAPAYAS: *Digestion aid, antioxidant, anticarcinogenic.* Papayas are rich in the vitamin C that can negate the effect of nitrosamines, potentially carcinogenic agents often found in the soil and processed foods. Other papaya vitamins, such as folic acid and vitamin E, have cancer-fighting properties, and the fruit's high fiber content can reduce colon cancer risk. Papayas are rich in the potent antioxidant lycopene, more commonly associated with tomatoes. Lycopene may protect against pancreas, prostate, breast, and colon cancers.

PARSLEY: *Appetite stimulant, digestion aid, anti-inflammatory, NF-kB regulator.* Parsley's oils, such as myristicin, have strong antitumor properties, especially with regard to lung tumors. Parsley also appears to neutralize carcinogens such as the benzopyrenes present in cigarette smoke, charcoal grill smoke, and fried foods.

PARSNIPS: *Anti-carcinogen, blood sugar regulator.* Parsnips have a high fiber content, which benefits GI function and lowers colon cancer risk.

PEPPERMINT: *Digestion aid, nausea reducer, anti-inflammatory, antibacterial.* Great-tasting mint relaxes abdominal and stomach muscles, making it excellent for relieving cramps, decreasing gas, and aiding overall digestion.

PINEAPPLE: *Anti-inflammatory.* One of pineapple's enzymes, bromelain, contains two molecules that block cancer-related proteins and turn on immune cells that, in animals, attacked lung, ovarian, bowel, and breast cancer cells.

POTATOES: *Antioxidant, possible antiangiogenesis.* Vitamin B_6 in potatoes appears to control activation of a tumor-suppression gene. Also, potatoes may have an overall detoxifying effect, with phytochemicals that seek out cancer-causing free-radicals.

QUINOA: *Anti-inflammatory.* Quinoa contains lignans; the body converts lignans into enterolactone, which may mimic estrogen in a way that may protect against hormone-dependent breast cancer.

RADISHES: *Anti-inflammatory.* The sulfur compounds in radishes go right to the liver and gallbladder, increasing the flow of bile to organs important in detoxifying treatments. Radishes also improve digestion.

RAISINS: *Antioxidant.* Raisins are rich in antioxidants known as phenols; Cornell researchers found that mice fed a phenol-rich diet had a 70-percent reduction in intestinal tumors.

RASPBERRIES: *Anti-inflammatory.* Raspberry pigments called anthocyanidins jump-start a process that blocks tumor growth. Ohio State researchers found that black raspberries prevented the beginning of esophageal cancer in animals and interfered with preexisting precancerous growths.

RICE: *Anti-inflammatory.* Whole grain rice is a fantastic fiber source and may protect premenopausal women against breast cancer, particularly those who are overweight. Whole grain rice fiber can also reduce colon cancer risk.

ROSEMARY: *Digestion aid, anti-inflammatory, NF-kB regulator.* A rosemary antioxidant, carnosol, inhibited skin and breast tumor development in animals. In people, rosemary improves digestion, circulation, immune function, and blood flow to the brain.

SAFFRON: *Digestion aid, anti-inflammatory, NF-kB regulator.* A saffron pigment, crocin, appears to cause human leukemia and liver cancer cells to die. Saffron is also great for digestion.

SAGE: *Antitumor.* Another member of the mint family, sage mimics rosemary in many of its medicinal properties. Sage's essential oils are being investigated by many cancer researchers; in animals, some effectiveness against skin cancer lesions has been observed.

SALMON: *Anti-inflammatory.* Researchers think that fatty fish such as salmon have compounds that help release ceramides, lipids that may tell cancer cells to stop functioning. Salmon's selenium may also offer protection against colon and pancreatic cancers.

SEA SALT: *Appetite stimulant.* Unlike table salt, which is generally stripped of minerals and had iodine added, sea salt contains numerous essential minerals, including calcium, magnesium, and potassium.

SESAME SEEDS: *Anti-inflammatory.* As with flaxseeds, sesame seeds are rich in lignans, which may offer protection against hormone-related cancers. Similarly, sesame seeds are high in gamma-tocopherols (a form of vitamin E), which can help men dealing with prostate cancer.

SPELT: *Antioxidant, blood sugar regulation.* A single serving of spelt has more than 100 percent of the daily recommended intake of manganese, an über-antioxidant and blood sugar regulator. Spelt is also fiber-rich, which may play a role in combating colon cancer.

SPINACH: *Antioxidant, antiangiogenesis.* Spinach carotenoids may offer help in fighting prostate cancer; another by-product, kaempferol, induces the death of ovarian cancer cells and also prevents the growth of tumor-feeding blood vessels.

SQUASH: *Antioxidant, blood sugar regulation.* Reports suggest that the juice from squash may slow mutations that turn healthy cells cancerous. The fiber in squash, particularly winter squash, is thought to offer colon-cleansing benefits.

STRAWBERRIES: *Anti-inflammatory.* As with raspberries, strawberries are loaded with anthocyanidins and ellagitannins that appear to inhibit tumor growth. (In one study, ellagitannins taken from pomegranates limited the growth of prostate cancer in the lab.) Strawberries also slow the growth of liver cancer cells.

SWEET POTATOES AND YAMS: *Antioxidant, blood sugar regulation.* Those beautiful orange-yellows of yams and sweet potatoes indicate they are loaded with cancer-fighting beta-carotene and vitamin C. One note: For a time, some medical professionals considered wild yams as an alternative to hormone replacement therapy because of their alleged ability to affect estrogen levels. More recent studies show no such link between yams and estrogen levels.

SWISS CHARD: *Anti-inflammatory.* Swiss chard is a powerful cancer-fighting food, loaded with beta-carotene, fiber, and vitamins A and C. Betalain, a Swiss chard pigment, has shown lab potential for slowing tumor growth in numerous cancers, possibly by lowering systemic inflammation.

THYME: *Antimicrobial, antibacterial.* Think of thyme as nature's version of a throat lozenge. Soothing to the mouth and oral cavity, it's also helpful with nagging coughs and congestion. It also has antiseptic and antibacterial properties.

TOMATOES: *May inhibit cancer cell growth pathways.* Tomatoes contain the powerful antioxidant lycopene. When lycopene is eaten with a healthy oil (such as olive oil) the combination reduces the risk of pancreatic, prostate, breast, and colon cancer. In other studies, eating tomatoes and broccoli together seems to have a protective effect against prostate cancer.

TURMERIC: *Appetite stimulant, digestion aid, anti-inflammatory, NF-kB regulator.* When turmeric is consumed with a cruciferous vegetable, the curcumin in turmeric lowered the growth and spread of prostate tumors. Curcumin is also an anti-inflammatory. Turmeric is used by Eastern Indian Ayurvedic medicine physicians for treating digestive disorders.

WALNUTS: *Anti-inflammatory.* Walnuts contain ellagic acid (as do many berries), which in the lab has caused cancer cells to die. It also appears to limit estrogen's growth potential regarding breast cancer cells and may help the liver detoxify potential carcinogens.

YOGURT: *Digestion aid.* Plain yogurt, especially when fortified with probiotics such as lactobacillus, can moderate diarrhea and fight GI tract infections. It can also enhance the immune system.

Receiving Support—and How Family and Friends Can Help

Cancer treatment can be a daunting process. Remember, the goal is to emerge with body and soul intact. To that end, there's one piece of advice I want to offer above all others: Please, if you have the choice, don't try to go it alone. I know how hard this is for many people. A cancer diagnosis is so frightening and can threaten your sense of self. In the days following a diagnosis, you may feel you're drowning in confusing torrents of information and emotion. That's normal. The treatment options—and their potential side effects and consequences—can be bewildering. You're trying to make the best choices while coming to grips with this thunderbolt that is reverberating off of everyone and everything you hold dear.

While you may be tempted to pull a blanket over your head and duck for cover (which you're allowed to do—but not for too long), there are strategies you can use to improve your body's ability to physically and emotionally thrive during treatment. Many revolve around building a support team. Please don't think that asking for support is a sign of weakness; it's actually quite courageous—and smart. Your support team helps you accomplish the all-important goal of staying well-nourished during treatment. Equally as important, the team approach keeps family, friends, and, most important, you from feeling overwhelmed or fatigued. It's important to avoid burnout, because treatment and caregiving can go on for quite some time. Stress is also important to avoid; stress actually increases levels of corticosteroids, hormones that can impair immune function.

Here are some tips.

- **Choose a captain for your support team.** This can be a spouse, partner, adult offspring, parent, friend, or neighbor. The captain should have an excellent rapport with the patient or someone close to them, because it's up to the captain to relay the patient's culinary desires to the rest of the team. The person in the captain's role can be changed weekly, or as often as desired. The captain assigns tasks to team members, including shopping, prepping, cooking, dishwashing, etc. If you're the captain:

  - Give people tasks they enjoy.

  - Recognize that caregivers have other responsibilities they need to attend to.

  - Take everyone's emotional temperature every few weeks to make sure no one is getting crunched.

  - Always keep feelers out for other people who want to join the team, as it's normal for some volunteers to drop out over time. (Remember, treatment can last a year or more.)

  - Buy a cooler for the team. It's a great way to transport food, and you can leave food in the cooler at the doorstep if nobody is home.

Shopping for Organics

Why go organic? Where do I begin?! Taste, color, nutrient-density—organic food is superior in all these areas. Why would you opt for food raised with commercial pesticides, additives, and artificial color and flavoring if you have a better choice? Best of all, the groundswell toward eating organic foods in the last few years has made them less expensive and more widely available. Growers who meet the standards of the Federal Organic Foods Production Act and receive state or federal certification can label their foods as organic, but they're not the only entities providing organic foods. Small farmers who sometimes don't want to incur the cost or time involved in meeting the requirements of the federal organic act also grow organic foods, including hormone- and chemical-free poultry and meats. You'll find these purveyors most often at farmers' markets, where they often enjoy chatting about the foods they've raised. If you can't afford to buy all organic produce, I recommend you steer clear of the most compromised items. The Environmental Working Group (www.ewg.org), a nonprofit that conducts research and publishes information on the effects of environmental factors on health, recommends avoiding the following nonorganically raised produce (Dirty Dozen) and notes which produce is least likely to hold pesticide residues (Clean Fifteen):

Dirty Dozen	Clean Fifteen
Peaches	Avocados
Apples	Sweet Corn
Sweet Bell Peppers	Pineapples
Celery	Mangoes
Nectarines	Papayas
Strawberries	Sweet Peas (frozen)
Kale/Collard Greens	Asparagus
Grapes (imported)	Kiwi Fruit
Spinach	Grapefruit
Potatoes	Cantaloupe
Cherry Tomatoes	Cabbage
Cucumbers	Onions
	Eggplant
	Cauliflower
	Sweet Potatoes

For a pocket guide and more comprehensive pesticide food list, visit www.foodnews.org

For the latest science and news about organics, visit the Organic Center: www.organic-center.org

For more information on organic foods, visit the Organic Trade Association: www.ota.com

- **Use Google Calendar.** Google Calendar (or some other online calendar sharing app) is a great resource that allows the captain and all team members to see online what tasks need to be accomplished. It also allows for posting of recipes and necessary ingredients. Everyone has access, so they can update the calendar in real time. You'll need a free Google account to use their calendar. For more information, do an Internet search on the term "Google Calendar."

- **Lower your appetite expectations.** Treatments often throw one's appetite into chaos: one moment you can't stand the idea of food, the next thing you know you're as hungry as a linebacker. Captains and other caregivers need to realize this, so they don't get frustrated when an asked-for meal is barely touched (that's why I always recommend having storage containers standing by so nothing good goes to waste). Similarly, patients should let go of the guilt they may feel if suddenly they're not really hungry; any eating, even a nibble, is an accomplishment. Remember, the traditional concepts of a regular breakfast, lunch, and dinner may no longer apply.

- **For caregivers, hypervigilance can be counterproductive.** There's a fine line between caring and pestering. This is especially true of people who have always been the traditional caregiver in a home. They may feel it's their responsibility to do everything within their power to make sure someone in treatment survives. Unfortunately, from a food perspective, that can lead to a caregiver going off the rails if the patient desires something the caregiver considers unhealthy. If, as a caregiver, you find yourself slipping into this mindset, I suggest you ease up. People in treatment may have cravings for all kinds of foods; in my experience letting them indulge in them once in a while makes it far more likely they'll go along with you when you want them to eat healthy fare.

- **For potential team members, surmount your fears.** Many emotions can keep people from pitching in. Awkwardness, embarrassment, worries about saying the wrong thing—anything that gets in the way of common sense and clear conversation needs to take a hike. Pick up the phone, send an email or text, hire a blimp to do a flyover, walk across the den, do whatever you have to do, but please let that special someone know that you want to bring them a bite to eat. And if you *are* that special someone, please see these gestures of support as a loving opportunity to gently guide your caregivers in making you the foods you truly need.

- **Be flexible with what you cook.** The person you're caring for should have lots of different meals on hand, everything from extremely light fare (soups) to something more hearty (veggies, protein, and the like). Most of the recipes in this book store well in the fridge or freezer in individual containers, ready to

Kitchen Smarts

Food Storage Tips

It's worth taking the time to think of how you're going to store these wonderful meals once you've made them. The first time I made soup for an ill friend, I delivered it in a monstrously huge 8-quart container. It quickly dawned on me—and my friend—that unless she drowned her family in soup for dinner that night, there was no way to fit the container in her freezer. I want to save you from similar pitfalls. These tips for making, storing, and delivering food in the safest and most practical manner guarantee that everything is good to the last drop, even weeks or months later.

- Build a freezer inventory so that you have broths and cooked dishes on hand in easy-to-use portion sizes. Think about the size of your freezer so that you don't end up with more food than storage space.

- Freeze food in sizes you will use at one time. One-, two-, four-, and eight-cup sizes are convenient and freeze well.

- Label all of your containers with the date, contents, and quantity. A permanent marker and blue painter's tape (looks like blue masking tape) works great.

- Do not fill plastic containers with hot liquids. To speed the cooling, put the pot in some ice water in the kitchen sink or a large dish and stir the soup occasionally.

- When freezing liquid, leave ½ to 1 inch of space at the top of the container to allow for expansion, especially in glass containers, which can shatter in the freezer if over filled.

- As a general rule, fruits and vegetables will stay freezer fresh for up to six months; meat, poultry, fish, and shellfish are good for three months.

Cooking and Reheating Tips

- Use cast-iron or stainless steel pots and pans for cooking instead of aluminum and nonstick surfaces.

- To prevent bacterial growth, thaw frozen food in the refrigerator or in cold water, not on the counter. If thawing in cold water, change the water every 30 minutes. Frozen meat should always be thawed in the refrigerator, which can take up to 48 hours.

- When reheating food in a microwave, avoid using plastic containers, as chemicals in plastic can leach into the food. Instead, reheat foods in glass or ceramic containers.

be reheated and served in a flash, with all of their delightful original flavors intact. Though some people go back to the same food again and again (and that's fine), I've found that having a variety of foods at one's fingertips generally enhances the desire to eat.

- **Let the person in treatment participate in the kitchen.** Sometimes the person receiving all this caregiving doesn't want to be a bystander. The kitchen is a great place for them to contribute in ways small or large. I've worked with people who said it meant the world to them to be able to just sit at the kitchen table and chop up fresh basil. Food—and its preparation and cooking—can be extremely life-affirming.

- **Take care of yourself.** There's a reason why flight attendants tell you to put on your own oxygen mask before attending to others. If you're a caregiver, it is absolutely essential that you tend to your own health as well. It's easy to put your needs second. In the short term that can work, but a month of this attitude will leave you exhausted. Eat well, get plenty of sleep, download your emotions to someone who cares about you, and take a nice walk whenever you can. So say I. With these tips and suggestions, it's my hope to make you and your loved ones realize that this sojourn into a new, exciting, *healing* culinary world is one that we all can take together. The experiences of thousands of people who've been exactly where you are now, who've graciously allowed me to work with them and help them deliciously achieve their eating goals, infuses and informs every word and recipe in this book. Don't worry: I've got you, and I'm not letting go. *Mangia*!

CHAPTER 2

Nourishing Soups and Broths

Just as every artist has a favorite medium, every chef has a favorite outlet. For me, that's soup, hands down. I love giving people a culinary hug: a warm, comforting dish I can wrap around them like a cashmere sweater. (In fact, I call some of my favorite soup recipes exactly that: my cashmere sweater collection.)

Soup allows me to throw my entire heart, soul, and cooking ability into one incredibly nourishing pot. Soup completely captures the mind and body by engaging all of the senses. It's practically aromatherapy in a bowl, with the heady smells, the enveloping heat, and the stimulating scaffolding of tastes.

Best of all, especially for people in treatment, is that soup is the perfect vehicle for delivering enticing taste and sumptuous nourishment. That notably includes those all-important phytochemicals and other nutrients that boost immunity and challenge cancer head-on. The combination of broth and heat alchemizes the vegetables, breaking them down and releasing more nourishment.

As you make your way through the soup recipes, you'll develop a sense of my formula for optimizing flavor. I've made sure to put in variations and combinations guaranteed to appeal to people who like everything from hearty stews to smooth and creamy soups to light broths. It all comes down to what I think of as layering the flavors. Each ingredient is added in a way that brings out its maximum taste and nutrition.

The best part is that these nutrient-dense soups will appeal to everyone around the table. Sip for sip and spoon for spoon, soup will always be my go-to dish when I want to show people that I really care for them. Because for me, soup is where the love is.

Magic Mineral Broth

This is my Rosetta stone of soup, a broth that transforms to meet numerous nutritional needs. It serves as everything from a delicious sipping tea to the powerful base for more hearty soups and stews. So no matter what a person's appetite, it can provide a tremendous nutritional boost. Chemotherapy often saps strength due to dehydration, which pulls vital nutrients out of your system. This rejuvenating liquid, chock-full of magnesium, potassium, and sodium, allows the body to refresh and restore itself. I think of it as a tonic, designed to keep you in tip-top shape.

Rinse all of the vegetables well, including the kombu. In a 12-quart or larger stockpot, combine the carrots, onions, leek, celery, potatoes, sweet potatoes, garlic, parsley, kombu, peppercorns, allspice berries, and bay leaves. Fill the pot with the water to 2 inches below the rim, cover, and bring to a boil.

Remove the lid, decrease the heat to low, and simmer, uncovered, for at least 2 hours. As the broth simmers, some of the water will evaporate; add more if the vegetables begin to peek out. Simmer until the full richness of the vegetables can be tasted.

Strain the broth through a large, coarse-mesh sieve (remember to use a heat-resistant container underneath), then add salt to taste. Let cool to room temperature before refrigerating or freezing.

COOK'S NOTE: Like fine wine, this broth gets better with age. The longer the simmer time, the better tasting and more nutrient dense the broth will be. You can also cut the recipe in half and make it in a slow cooker or a pressure cooker. Kombu is dark brown seaweed (kelp) that is dried and folded into sheets. It's used in Japanese cooking to add depth and flavor to soups and stocks. It also adds a tremendous amount of valuable trace minerals to this broth. Look for kombu in the Asian section of many grocery stores, or online (see Resources, page 211).

STORAGE: Store in an airtight container in the refrigerator for 5 to 7 days or in the freezer for 4 months.

PER SERVING: Calories: 45; Total Fat: 0 g; Carbohydrates: 11 g; Protein: 1 g; Fiber: 2 g; Sodium: 140 mg

MAKES: 6 quarts
PREP TIME: 10 minutes
COOK TIME: 2 to 4 hours

---

6 unpeeled carrots, cut into thirds

2 unpeeled yellow onions, cut into chunks

1 leek, white and green parts, cut into thirds

1 bunch celery, including the heart, cut into thirds

4 unpeeled red potatoes, quartered

2 unpeeled Japanese or regular sweet potatoes, quartered

1 unpeeled Garnet sweet potato, quartered

5 unpeeled cloves garlic, halved

½ bunch fresh flat-leaf parsley

1 (8-inch) strip of kombu

12 black peppercorns

4 whole allspice or juniper berries

2 bay leaves

8 quarts cold, filtered water

1 teaspoon sea salt

Chicken Magic Mineral Broth

MAKES: 6 to 7 quarts
PREP TIME: 20 minutes
COOK TIME: 4 hours

6 unpeeled carrots, cut into thirds

2 unpeeled yellow onions, cut into chunks

2 leeks, white and green parts, cut into thirds

1 bunch celery, including the heart, cut into thirds

4 unpeeled red potatoes, quartered

2 unpeeled Japanese or regular sweet potatoes, quartered

1 unpeeled Garnet sweet potato, quartered

8 unpeeled cloves garlic, halved

1 bunch fresh flat-leaf parsley

1 (6-inch) strip of kombu

12 black peppercorns

4 whole allspice or juniper berries

2 bay leaves

1 tablespoon apple cider vinegar or freshly squeezed lemon juice

1 organic chicken carcass or 2 pounds of chicken bones

8 quarts cold, unfiltered water

1 teaspoon sea salt

My neighbor Julie and I are soup sisters. We have one of those friendships where I can barge into her house uninvited and nine times out of ten I'll find Julie in the kitchen making soup. She's so good at it that whenever I return from an out-of-town job, the first place I make dinner reservations is her house. Last winter we were canoodling on a hearty chicken broth recipe. Suddenly we realized that we already had an incredible foundation in the Magic Mineral Broth recipe (page 49), with its rich color, aroma, flavor, and impressive nutritional profile. Here, we've enhanced Magic Mineral Broth by adding chicken bones, infusing the soup with even more bone-building calcium and phosphorus.

Rinse all of the vegetables well, including the kombu. In a 12- to 16-quart stockpot, combine the carrots, onions, leeks, celery, potatoes, sweet potatoes, garlic, parsley, kombu, peppercorns, allspice berries, bay leaves, vinegar, and chicken carcass. Fill the pot with the water to 2 inches below the rim, cover, and bring to a boil.

Remove the lid, decrease the heat to low, and skim off the scum that has risen to the top. Simmer, uncovered, for at least 2 hours. As the broth simmers, some of the water will evaporate; add more if the vegetables begin to peek out. Simmer until the bones begin to soften and fall apart, about 4 hours, or as long as you're willing to let it simmer away.

Strain the broth through a large, coarse-mesh sieve, then stir in salt to taste. Let cool to room temperature, then refrigerate overnight. Skim off as much fat as you can from the top of the broth, then portion into airtight containers and refrigerate or freeze.

COOK'S NOTE: Here's a trick of the trade: Once you've skimmed the fat from the surface of the broth, you can remove even more by dabbing the surface of the broth with paper towels to sop it up.

STORAGE: Store in an airtight container in the refrigerator for 3 to 4 days or in the freezer for 3 months.

PER SERVING: Calories: 50; Total Fat: 0 g; Carbohydrates: 11 g; Protein: 1 g; Fiber: 2 g; Sodium: 145 mg

Pasture Beef Bone Broth

In many cultures, beef broth is a traditional healing beverage. Beef bones are filled with collagen and minerals that build connective tissues, such as calcium, magnesium, and phosphorus. It's a perfect sipping medium for people figuring out how to get five or six hits of nutrition a day. I've had clients with eating difficulties who have literally lived on this broth for days or weeks at a time.

Preheat the oven to 350°F.

Place the bones on a baking sheet or roasting pan and roast until the bones are well browned, about 30 minutes.

Rinse all of the vegetables well, including the kombu. In a 12-quart or larger stockpot, combine the bones, carrots, onions, leek, celery, potatoes, sweet potatoes, garlic, parsley, kombu, peppercorns, allspice berries, bay leaves, and vinegar. Pour in the water, cover, and bring to a boil.

Remove the lid, decrease the heat to low, and skim off the scum that has risen to the top. Simmer gently, uncovered, for 8 to 12 hours. As the broth simmers, some of the water will evaporate; add more if the vegetables begin to peek out.

Remove and discard the bones, then strain the broth through a large, coarse-mesh sieve. Stir in salt to taste. Let cool to room temperature, and then refrigerate overnight. Skim off as much fat as you can from the top of the broth, then portion into airtight containers and refrigerate or freeze.

COOK'S NOTE: To make a shortcut version, roast the marrow bones as directed and place in a 6½-quart slow cooker. Cover with Magic Mineral Broth (page 49) and add the vinegar. Set the slow cooker on low for 8 to 24 hours, and allow the broth to simmer away. Strain the broth and refrigerate it overnight, then skim the fat, and add another 2 quarts of Magic Mineral Broth.

STORAGE: Store in an airtight container in the refrigerator for up to 4 days or in the freezer for up to 4 months.

PER SERVING: Calories: 50; Total Fat: 0 g; Carbohydrates: 11 g; Protein: 1 g; Fiber: 2 g; Sodium: 140 mg

MAKES: 6 quarts
PREP TIME: 25 minutes
COOK TIME: 8 to 12 hours

3 pounds marrow bones from grass-fed organic beef

6 unpeeled carrots, cut into thirds

2 unpeeled yellow onions, cut into chunks

1 leek, white and green parts, cut into thirds

1 bunch celery, including the heart, cut into thirds

4 unpeeled red potatoes, quartered

2 unpeeled Japanese or regular sweet potatoes, quartered

1 unpeeled Garnet sweet potato, quartered

5 unpeeled cloves garlic, halved

½ bunch fresh flat-leaf parsley

1 (8-inch) strip of kombu

12 black peppercorns

4 whole allspice or juniper berries

2 bay leaves

1 tablespoon apple cider vinegar

8 quarts cold, filtered water

1 teaspoon sea salt

Italian White Bean Soup

SERVES: 6

PREP TIME: 20 minutes (after soaking the beans overnight)

COOK TIME: 1 hour 30 minutes (25 minutes with canned beans)

BEANS

1½ cups cooked cannellini beans, or 1 (15-ounce) can drained, rinsed, and mixed with a spritz of fresh lemon juice and a pinch of sea salt

SOUP

2 tablespoons extra-virgin olive oil

1¾ cups finely diced yellow onion

3 cups finely diced fennel

Sea salt

1½ cups peeled and finely diced carrots

1½ cups finely diced celery

1 cup peeled and diced Yukon gold potato

2 cloves garlic, minced

¼ teaspoon dried sage, or 1 tablespoon chopped fresh sage

¼ teaspoon dried thyme, or 1 tablespoon fresh thyme

⅛ teaspoon saffron

8 cups Magic Mineral Broth (page 49), Chicken Magic Mineral Broth (page 50), or store-bought organic stock

1 tablespoon freshly squeezed lemon juice

¼ cup fresh parsley, coarsely chopped

¼ cup fresh basil, coarsely chopped

When it comes to cooking, Italians believe in region first, country second. That makes this recipe my version of culinary heresy. By taking white beans, a notoriously Tuscan legume, and mixing them with saffron, which is more common to northern Italy's Lombardi region, I've committed what might be considered a food felony. My defense for breaking with tradition is justified in this case: saffron is a powerful cancer-fighting spice. It's best to soak the beans overnight before cooking them, so plan ahead.

To make the soup, heat the olive oil in a soup pot over medium heat, then add the onion, fennel, and a pinch of salt, and sauté until golden, about 4 minutes. Stir in the carrots, celery, potato, garlic, and ¼ teaspoon of salt, then add the sage, thyme, and saffron and sauté until the vegetables are soft, about 15 minutes.

Pour in ½ cup of the broth to deglaze the pot and cook until the liquid is reduced by half. Add the remaining 7½ cups broth and the beans, then lower the heat and simmer until the vegetables are tender and the beans are heated through, about 10 minutes. Stir in the lemon juice, parsley, basil, and another ¼ teaspoon of salt and serve right away.

VARIATION: For a more southern Italian flair and some added lycopene, add 1 cup of canned diced tomatoes (drained) after you add the garlic. Since tomatoes are naturally acidic, skip the lemon juice.

COOK'S NOTE: This is a soup that swings well both ways, as a hearty soup or as a blended soup. If you serve it blended, top it with a generous amount of Parsley Basil Drizzle (page 187) for extra yum.

STORAGE: Store in a covered container in the refrigerator for 5 to 7 days or in the freezer for up to 2 months.

PER SERVING: Calories: 275; Total Fat: 4.5 g (0.7 g saturated, 3 g monounsaturated); Carbohydrates: 48 g; Protein: 12 g; Fiber: 11 g; Sodium: 680 mg

Lemony Greek Chicken Soup

I always thought my people had the market cornered when it came to making chicken soup. I mean, there's a reason they call it Jewish penicillin, right? Well, the Greeks know a thing or three about chicken soup as well. Their Mediterranean take is to fold a little lemon and egg into the mixture. And unlike my beloved *yiddishe* version, which can be a little fatty, this riff is light and bright. Because of the egg, which provides protein, and the Chicken Magic Mineral Broth, this a nutrient-dense bowl of yum. You'll need to cook the farro in advance, so plan ahead.

Heat the olive oil in a soup pot over medium heat, then add the onion and a pinch of salt and sauté until translucent, about 4 minutes. Stir in the carrot, celery, oregano, and ¼ teaspoon of salt, and sauté for about 30 seconds. Pour in ½ cup of the broth to deglaze the pot and cook until the liquid is reduced by half. Add the remaining 5½ cups broth and the farro and bring to a boil, then lower the heat to maintain a simmer.

Whisk the lemon juice, lemon zest, and egg yolks together, then stir the mixture into the simmering soup and cook until it clouds and thickens a bit, about 3 minutes. Stir in the mint, parsley, pepper, and ½ teaspoon of salt, then add the chicken and taste. If the soup tastes too sour, add a pinch of salt.

COOK'S NOTE: You can substitute ½ cup of cooked brown rice for the farro. To make a vegetarian version, omit the chicken and use Magic Mineral Broth (page 49).

STORAGE: Store in an airtight container in the refrigerator for up to 5 days or in the freezer for up to 2 months.

PER SERVING: Calories: 170; Total Fat: 7.4 g (1.6 g saturated, 4.45 g mono-unsaturated); Carbohydrates: 22 g; Protein: 5 g; Fiber: 4 g; Sodium: 255 mg

SERVES: 6
PREP TIME: 10 minutes (after cooking the farro)
COOK TIME: 15 minutes

---

2 tablespoons extra-virgin olive oil

1 cup finely diced onion

Sea salt

½ cup peeled and finely diced carrot

½ cup finely diced celery or fennel

½ teaspoon dried oregano

6 cups Chicken Magic Mineral Broth (page 50) or store-bought organic chicken stock

½ cup Simple Tuscan Farro (page 147)

¼ cup freshly squeezed lemon juice

2 teaspoons lemon zest

3 egg yolks

¼ cup fresh mint, finely chopped

¼ cup fresh parsley, finely chopped

Pinch of freshly ground pepper

1 cup thinly sliced cooked organic chicken breast meat

Chicken Vegetable Soup with Ginger Meatballs

Here's an embarrassing admission for a cook who loves making Italian food: For the life of me, I could not figure out how to keep my meatballs from falling apart, even after I studied under an Italian signora on the Isle of Elba. Then I stumbled upon basmati rice. Now my meatballs taste great and don't disintegrate on the fork. These are actually mini meatballs, closer to the Latin American version known as *albóndigas*, with the ginger providing a little zing. If timing is an issue, prepare the meatballs in advance and refrigerate them until you're ready to cook. This recipe makes twice as many meatballs as you'll need for the soup. To save the remainder, place them in the freezer for 1 hour to firm up, then transfer to an airtight container and refrigerate for up to 5 days or freeze for up to 3 months.

To make the meatballs, line a sheet pan with wax paper. Combine the chicken, ginger, garlic, parsley, salt, cayenne, egg, and rice in a bowl and mix with your hands or a spatula until well combined. Don't overwork the mixture or the meatballs will be tough.

Wet the palms of your hands so the mixture doesn't stick, roll it into 1-inch balls, and place them on the prepared pan.

To make the soup, heat the olive oil in a soup pot over medium heat, then add the onion and a pinch of salt and sauté until translucent, about 4 minutes. Add the carrot, celery, garlic, ginger, and ¼ teaspoon of salt and continue sautéing for about 3 minutes.

Pour in ½ cup of the broth to deglaze the pot and cook until the liquid is reduced by half. Add the remaining 7½ cups broth and another ¼ teaspoon of salt and bring to a boil. Lower the heat to maintain a vigorous simmer, then gently transfer half of the meatballs into the simmering broth. (Refrigerate or freeze the remainder to use later.) Cover and allow the meatballs to simmer for 15 minutes.

Add the peas and cook for 3 minutes more, then stir in the parsley and basil. Serve each bowl garnished with a wedge of lime.

VARIATION: Replace the peas with 1 cup of baby spinach or arugula.

STORAGE: Store in an airtight container in the refrigerator for up to 5 days or in the freezer for up to 2 months.

PER SERVING: Calories: 210; Total Fat: 7 g (1.6 g saturated, 3.4 g monounsaturated); Carbohydrates: 23 g; Protein: 15 g; Fiber: 3 g; Sodium: 380 mg

---

SERVES: 4

PREP TIME: 20 minutes

COOK TIME: 35 minutes

MEATBALLS

1 pound ground organic dark-meat chicken or turkey

2 teaspoons grated fresh ginger

1 teaspoon minced garlic

¼ cup fresh parsley, finely chopped

½ teaspoon sea salt

Pinch of cayenne

1 egg, beaten

⅓ cup cooked basmati or jasmine rice

SOUP

2 tablespoons extra-virgin olive oil

1 yellow onion, diced small

Sea salt

1 large carrot, peeled and diced small

1 large celery stalk, diced small

2 cloves garlic, minced

1 teaspoon grated fresh ginger

8 cups Chicken Magic Mineral Broth (page 50) or store-bought organic chicken broth

½ cup fresh or frozen sweet peas

¼ cup fresh parsley, finely chopped

¼ cup fresh basil, finely chopped

1 lime, cut into quarters, for garnish

Ma's Mushroom Barley Soup

SERVES: 6

PREP TIME: 20 minutes (after soaking the barley overnight)

COOK TIME: 45 minutes

½ cup pearl barley

Juice of 1 lemon

2 tablespoons extra-virgin olive oil

1 small onion, diced

½ teaspoon sea salt

1½ cups peeled and finely diced carrots

1½ cups finely diced celery

1 parsnip, peeled and diced small

¼ pound white mushrooms, thinly sliced

¼ pound shiitake mushrooms, thinly sliced

2 cloves garlic, minced

¼ teaspoon dried oregano

¼ teaspoon dried thyme

¼ teaspoon ground caraway

Pinch of freshly ground pepper

9 cups Pasture Beef Bone Broth (page 51) or Magic Mineral Broth (page 49)

¼ cup loosely packed chopped fresh parsley

This soup is for both mushroom maniacs and those on the fungi fence. I guarantee this soup will sway you! There's simply no taste in the culinary world that mimics the umami sensation of mushrooms, and that flavor is backed up by a host of health-supportive properties. Between the shiitakes, the barley, and the rich broth, this is a warming meal in a bowl. One note: the barley needs to soak overnight.

Place the barley in a pan or bowl with the lemon juice and water to cover and soak overnight, or for at least 8 hours.

Drain and rinse the barley.

Heat the olive oil in a soup pot over medium-high heat, then add the onion and ¼ teaspoon of the salt and sauté until golden, about 3 minutes. Add the carrots, celery, and parsnip and sauté for 3 minutes more. Add the white mushrooms, shiitake mushrooms, garlic, oregano, thyme, caraway, pepper, and barley and sauté for 3 to 4 minutes, until the mushrooms release their juices. Pour in 1 cup of the broth to deglaze the pot and cook until the liquid is reduced by three-quarters.

Add the remaining 8 cups broth and bring to a boil, then lower the heat and simmer for 20 minutes.

Stir in the remaining ¼ teaspoon salt and the parsley, then taste. You may want to add just a spritz of fresh lemon juice or another pinch of salt before serving.

COOK'S NOTE: If you have leftover soup, you'll find that it has much less broth, as barley loves to expand in liquid. Keep an extra cup or two of broth on hand to add when you reheat the leftovers.

STORAGE: Store in an airtight container in the refrigerator for up to 4 days or in the freezer for up to 2 months.

PER SERVING: Calories: 230; Total Fat: 5.4 g (0.8 g saturated, 3.4 g mono-unsaturated); Carbohydrates: 42 g; Protein: 6 g; Fiber: 9 g; Sodium: 460 mg

Minestrone

The Italians are beautiful because they've turned essentially peasant fare into an internationally renowned cuisine. Take *pappa al pomodoro*. Fancy, huh? Can you say, "Day-old knot of stale bread in tomatoes and water"? A staple there, a delicacy here. The same goes for minestrone, which I've always claimed is Italian for "Whatever is in the pantry goes in the pot!" Actually, minestrone comes from the array of dishes known as *cucina povera* or "poor kitchen." It's a bit of a misnomer, though, as minestrone is rich in vital nutrients, most notably lycopene, a tomato phytochemical that has anticancer properties, especially with regard to prostate, lung, and stomach cancer.

Heat the olive oil in a soup pot over medium heat, then add the onion and a pinch of salt and sauté until golden, about 5 minutes. Add the carrot, celery, zucchini, garlic, oregano, thyme, fennel, red pepper flakes, and ¼ teaspoon of salt and sauté for about 4 minutes. Pour in ½ cup of the broth to deglaze the pot and cook until the liquid is reduced by half.

Add the remaining 7½ cups broth, the tomatoes, and the beans and bring to a boil, then lower the heat and simmer for 20 minutes.

Stir in the chard and another ¼ teaspoon salt and cook for 3 minutes more. Stir in the pasta and the parsley. Serve topped with Basil Lemon Drizzle and a sprinkling of Parmesan.

VARIATIONS: This soup is the ultimate "clean out the refrigerator" dish. All of those slightly aged vegetables you thought you were going to eat will find a nice home in this pot of yum. During the winter, substitute diced delicata or butternut squash for the zucchini. You can bump up the nutritional value and anticancer properties even more by adding that leftover cabbage I know you have in the back of your fridge.

STORAGE: Store in an airtight container in the refrigerator for up to 5 days or in the freezer for up to 2 months.

PER SERVING: Calories: 300; Total Fat: 6 g (0.5 g saturated, 3 g mono-unsaturated); Carbohydrates: 55 g; Protein: 12 g; Fiber: 13 g; Sodium: 600 mg

SERVES: 6
PREP TIME: 20 minutes
COOK TIME: 35 minutes

2 tablespoons extra-virgin olive oil

1 cup finely diced yellow onion

Sea salt

1 cup peeled and finely diced carrot

1 cup finely diced celery

1 cup finely diced zucchini

½ teaspoon finely chopped garlic

½ teaspoon dried oregano

¼ teaspoon dried thyme

¼ teaspoon fennel seeds, crushed

Pinch of red pepper flakes

8 cups Magic Mineral Broth (page 49), Chicken Magic Mineral Broth (page 50), or store-bought organic stock

1 (14-ounce) can crushed tomatoes

2 cups cooked red kidney beans, or 1 (15-ounce) can, rinsed, drained, and mixed with a spritz of fresh lemon juice and a pinch of salt

2 cups stemmed and finely chopped Swiss chard

4 ounces whole grain pasta, cooked

¼ cup finely chopped fresh parsley

Basil Lemon Drizzle (page 175), for garnish (optional)

Grated organic Parmesan cheese, for garnish

Thai It Up Chicken Soup

SERVES: 6

PREP TIME: 15 minutes

COOK TIME: 45 to 55 minutes

6 cups Chicken Magic Mineral Broth (page 50), Magic Mineral Broth (page 49), or store-bought organic stock

2 shallots, or 1 small red onion, peeled and halved

6 (1-inch) pieces of unpeeled fresh ginger

1 stalk lemongrass, bruised and cut into chunks

2 makrut lime leaves, or 1 teaspoon lime zest

½ teaspoon sea salt

1 (15-ounce) can coconut milk

3½ ounces rice noodles, broken into 2-inch pieces

1 cup peeled and finely diced carrot

Pinch of cayenne (optional)

1 organic chicken breast half, cut into ⅛-inch-thick diagonal slices

2 tablespoons freshly squeezed lime juice

¼ cup chopped fresh cilantro, for garnish

2 tablespoons sliced scallion, cut thinly on the diagonal, for garnish

Many people think that Thai food is hot, hot, hot. Well, maybe not, not, not. True, some Thai food can set off smoke detectors. But real Thai cooking emphasizes distinctive flavor combinations regardless of the heat. This soup, a takeoff on traditional Thai *tom kha gai* (a chicken soup), uses coconut milk, which is very soothing to the nerves. The ginger aids digestion, while the lime brightens up the overall flavor. The result is a soup guaranteed to jump-start even the most jaded taste buds.

Combine the broth, shallots, ginger, lemongrass, lime leaves, and ¼ teaspoon of the salt in a soup pot over high heat and bring to a boil. Lower the heat to medium-low and simmer for 20 minutes.

Using a slotted spoon, scoop out all of the solids and discard. Stir in the coconut milk and continue to simmer, being careful not to boil, for another 10 minutes.

Meanwhile, put the rice noodles into a bowl of hot water and soak until tender, about 10 minutes. Drain and set aside.

Stir the carrot and cayenne into the soup, simmer for 3 minutes, then add the chicken and simmer for an additional 7 minutes, until the chicken is tender and thoroughly cooked. Stir in the noodles, lime juice, and the remaining ¼ teaspoon salt, then taste; you my want to add a bit more salt. Serve garnished with the cilantro and scallion.

VARIATION: For an extra immune booster, add 1 cup of stemmed and sliced shiitake mushrooms when you add the chicken. Want to Thai it up vegetarian style? Use Magic Mineral Broth and add thin strips of tofu in place of the chicken.

COOK'S NOTE: For an easy way to slice raw chicken, place it in your freezer for 20 to 30 minutes to firm up. Slicing it straight out of the freezer will be a breeze!

STORAGE: Store in a covered container in the refrigerator for 3 to 5 days or in the freezer for up to 2 months.

PER SERVING: Calories: 290; Total Fat: 15.5 g (13.5 g saturated, 0.7 g mono-unsaturated); Carbohydrates: 35 g; Protein: 6 g; Fiber: 4 g; Sodium: 420 mg

Bella's Carrot, Orange, and Fennel Soup

Here's where a cook learns to ad lib. For years, I've made carrot ginger soup for my cancer patients when their tummies are a little off. One day, I came home to find my husband, Gregg, in a similar state; he felt a little foo in the belly, but nonetheless hungry. I went to the pantry to whip up some soup, only to find there was no ginger to be had. But there was fennel. "Fennel is good for the stomach," thought I, and into the pot it went. Gregg soon sat down, took one taste, and started raving. A few weeks and tweaks later, I found that adding cumin, cinnamon, and allspice really brought this soup home. I named this recipe after my dog, Bella, because she's quite possibly the only dog on the planet who prefers carrots to bacon; for every four carrots that went into making this soup, one went into Bella's mouth. Otherwise she howled. (Sigh.)

Heat the olive oil in a soup pot over medium heat, then add the onion, fennel, and a pinch of salt and sauté until golden, about 4 minutes. Stir in the carrots, orange zest, cumin, cinnamon, allspice, red pepper flakes, and ¼ teaspoon of salt and sauté until well combined. Pour in ½ cup of the broth and cook until the liquid is reduced by half.

Add the remaining 7½ cups broth and another ¼ teaspoon salt and cook until the carrots are tender, about 20 minutes.

In a blender, puree the soup in batches until very smooth, each time adding the cooking liquid first and then the carrot mixture. If need be, add additional liquid to reach the desired thickness.

Return the soup to the pot over low heat, stir in the orange juice, lemon juice, maple syrup, and a pinch of salt, and gently reheat slowly. Taste. Does it need a squeeze of lemon, a pinch or two of salt, or a drizzle of maple syrup? Serve garnished with a drizzle of the Cashew Cream.

COOK'S NOTE: Put liquid ingredients in the blender first, and then add the solids to blend more efficiently. The pressure builds up when blending hot liquids and can blow the lid right off the blender chamber, so always place a dishtowel over the blender lid before you hit the power button to prevent spin art on your kitchen wall (and possibly burns).

STORAGE: Store in an airtight container in the refrigerator for up to 4 days or in the freezer for up to 2 months.

PER SERVING: Calories: 215; Total Fat: 5.5 g (0.8 g saturated, 3.4 g monounsaturated); Carbohydrates: 40 g; Protein: 4 g; Fiber: 10 g; Sodium: 405 mg

SERVES: 6
PREP TIME: 30 minutes
COOK TIME: 35 minutes

2 tablespoons extra-virgin olive oil

1 cup chopped yellow onion

1 cup chopped fennel

Sea salt

3 pounds carrots, cut into 1-inch pieces

1 teaspoon orange zest

½ teaspoon ground cumin

¼ teaspoon ground cinnamon

¼ teaspoon ground allspice

Pinch of red pepper flakes

8 cups Magic Mineral Broth (page 49)

1 tablespoon freshly squeezed orange juice

2 teaspoons freshly squeezed lemon juice

¼ teaspoon maple syrup

Cashew Cream (page 178), for garnish

Cooling Cucumber Avocado Soup

SERVES: 6

PREP TIME: 15 minutes

COOK TIME: 2 hours in the refrigerator

2 cups water

2 pounds English cucumbers, peeled, seeded, and cut into chunks

2 ripe avocados, pitted and peeled

3 tablespoons freshly squeezed lime juice

¼ teaspoon maple syrup

Sea salt

Pinch of cayenne

1 tablespoon finely chopped fresh mint

1 tablespoon finely chopped fresh cilantro

Those of you into cool or room-temperature soups will embrace the clean, fresh feel of this blend. Avocado lovers will go ga-ga over the taste, while those with swallowing difficulties or mouth sores will delight in the creamy texture. Avocados are one of those great superfoods, full of good fats and vitamins. They're fun to work with, and the great shades of green in this soup are like painting a beautiful, edible watercolor.

Pour 1 cup of the water into the blender, then add the cucumbers, avocados, lime juice, maple syrup, ¼ teaspoon of salt, and the cayenne. Blend until extremely smooth, gradually adding more water until you reach the desired consistency. Taste and adjust the amount of salt, adding as much as ¾ teaspoon more.

Chill for at least 2 hours, then stir in the mint and cilantro and serve.

COOK'S NOTE: English cucumbers, which are usually wrapped in plastic in the produce section of the grocery store, really make a difference in this recipe. They're less watery than standard cucumbers and will add more substance to the soup.

STORAGE: Store in an airtight container in the refrigerator for up to 2 days.

PER SERVING: Calories: 95; Total Fat: 7.2 g (1 g saturated, 4.5 g mono-unsaturated); Carbohydrates: 8 g; Protein: 2 g; Fiber: 4 g; Sodium: 105 mg

Rockin' Black Bean Soup

A staple of Latin cuisine, this black bean soup rocks because it's a nutritional powerhouse. Black beans are rich in protein and dietary fiber. As for taste, I guarantee your taste buds will say, "More, please!"

Place the dried beans in a pan or bowl with water to cover and soak overnight, or for at least 8 hours. Drain the beans from their soaking water prior to cooking. Skip this step if you're using canned beans.

Heat the olive oil in a soup pot over medium heat, then add the onions and a pinch of salt and sauté until the onions are translucent, about 4 minutes. Add the bell pepper, jalapeño, minced garlic, oregano, cumin, cinnamon, and ¼ teaspoon of salt and sauté for 1 minute. Pour in ½ cup of the broth to deglaze the pot and cook until the liquid is reduced by half.

Add the remaining 7½ cups broth, along with the black beans, smashed garlic, kombu, cinnamon stick, and bay leaf. Bring to a boil over high heat, then simmer, partially covered, for 1 hour.

Test a bean, and once they are at least halfway cooked, add another ¼ teaspoon salt. (If too much salt is added too early, it will inhibit the softening of the beans.) Continue to simmer for another 30 minutes, until the beans are nice and soft.

Meanwhile, preheat the oven to 350°F. Cut the corn tortillas into strips and arrange them in a single layer on a sheet pan. Bake for 5 minutes, until slightly golden.

Using a slotted spoon, fish out and discard the kombu, cinnamon stick, and bay leaf, then remove half of the cooked beans and set aside. Puree the remaining beans and the broth in a blender, in batches if need be, blending until the beans are as smooth as velvet.

Return the soup to the pot over low heat, stir in the reserved beans, and gently reheat. Do a FASS check, and if it needs a little extra pop, add another ¼ teaspoon of salt and the lime juice.

Serve garnished with the tortilla strips, a sprinkling of cilantro, and a dollop of the Avocado Cream.

COOK'S NOTE: If you use canned beans, rinse, spritz with lemon juice, and sprinkle with salt. Add them just after sautéing the vegetables.

STORAGE: Store in an airtight container in the refrigerator for up to 5 days or in the freezer for up to 2 months.

PER SERVING: Calories: 390; Total Fat: 5.6 g (0.8 g saturated, 3.4 g monounsaturated); Carbohydrates: 70 g; Protein: 16 g; Fiber: 11 g; Sodium: 300 mg

SERVES: 6
PREP TIME: 15 minutes (after soaking the beans overnight)
COOK TIME: 1 hour 45 minutes

2 cups dried black beans, or 1 (15-ounce) can black beans

2 tablespoons extra-virgin olive oil

2 cups diced yellow onions

Sea salt

1 cup finely diced red bell pepper

1½ teaspoons seeded and finely diced jalapeño pepper

1 tablespoon minced garlic

1½ teaspoons dried oregano

½ teaspoon ground cumin

¼ teaspoon ground cinnamon

8 cups Magic Mineral Broth (page 49)

4 cloves garlic, smashed

1 (6-inch) strip of kombu

1 cinnamon stick

1 bay leaf

2 teaspoons lime juice (optional)

3 corn tortillas, for garnish

¼ cup fresh cilantro, chopped, for garnish

Avocado Cream (page 177), for garnish

Curry Cauliflower Soup

SERVES: 6

PREP TIME: 10 minutes

COOK TIME: 35 minutes

1 head cauliflower, cut into florets

3 tablespoons extra-virgin olive oil

Sea salt

1 cup finely diced yellow onion

2 carrots, peeled and diced small

1 cup finely diced celery

2 teaspoons curry powder

½ teaspoon ground cumin

½ teaspoon ground coriander

¼ teaspoon ground cinnamon

6 cups Magic Mineral Broth (page 49)

½ teaspoon lemon juice (optional)

Apricot Pear Chutney (page 172), for garnish

Cauliflower is a wonderful vegetable that's full of excellent cancer-fighting enzymes. Maybe that's why it's riding a wave of unprecedented popularity. Now, some people I know avoid cauliflower because, when steamed, it makes the kitchen smell like a stink bomb detonated. But here's a neat trick: roasting cauliflower eliminates that sulfur smell and produces an unbelievably sweet flavor. Give it a try. I promise your taste buds will jump for joy.

Preheat the oven to 400°F and line a baking sheet with parchment paper.

Toss the cauliflower with 1 tablespoon of the olive oil and ¼ teaspoon of salt, then spread it in an even layer on the prepared pan. Bake until the cauliflower is tender, about 25 minutes.

While the cauliflower is roasting, heat the remaining 2 tablespoons olive oil in a sauté pan over medium heat, then add the onion and a pinch of salt and sauté until translucent, about 3 minutes. Add the carrots, celery, and ¼ teaspoon salt and sauté until the vegetables begin to brown, about 12 minutes.

Add the curry powder, cumin, coriander, cinnamon, and another ½ teaspoon of salt and stir until the spices have coated the vegetables. Pour in ½ cup of the broth to deglaze the pan and cook until the liquid is reduced by half. Remove from the heat.

Pour 3 cups of the remaining broth into a blender, then add half of the sautéed vegetables and roasted cauliflower. Blend until smooth, then pour the mixture into a soup pot and repeat the process with the remaining 2½ cups broth and the remaining vegetables and cauliflower. (For a thinner consistency, add another cup of broth.)

Gently reheat the soup over low heat, then taste. You may want to add a spritz of fresh lemon juice and another ¼ teaspoon salt.

Serve garnished with a dollop of Apricot Pear Chutney, which undoubtedly will take you to the land of yum!

STORAGE: Store in an airtight container in the refrigerator for up to 4 days or in the freezer for up to 2 months.

PER SERVING: Calories: 165; Total Fat: 7.5 g (1.1 g saturated, 5.1 g mono-unsaturated); Carbohydrates: 23 g; Protein: 5 g; Fiber: 7 g; Sodium: 260 mg

Spiced Sweet Potato Soup

SERVES: 6

PREP TIME: 10 minutes

COOK TIME: 55 minutes

3 pounds sweet potatoes, peeled and diced into 1-inch cubes

2 tablespoons unrefined virgin coconut oil, melted, or extra-virgin olive oil

½ teaspoon sea salt

½ teaspoon ground cinnamon

½ teaspoon ground allspice

¼ teaspoon ground cardamom

⅛ teaspoon freshly grated nutmeg

6 to 8 cups Magic Mineral Broth (page 49)

Thank heavens that sweet potatoes are no longer relegated just to Thanksgiving. For years bodybuilders, seeking to repair their muscles after workouts, have feasted on sweet potatoes because of their outstanding nutritional content, ease of digestion, and pleasant flavor. Chock-full of beta-carotene, vitamin A, and other body boosters, sweet potatoes are also extremely anti-inflammatory, meaning they fight cancer. As a cook, I like sweet potatoes because they make a wonderful creamy canvas for warming, healing spices such as cinnamon and ginger. This soup is a great meal for people with a lingering metallic taste in their mouth due to chemotherapy. It's delicious served with a dollop of Apricot Pear Chutney (page 172).

Preheat the oven to 400°F and line a baking sheet with parchment paper.

Toss the sweet potatoes with the coconut oil until they're evenly coated. In a small bowl, combine ¼ teaspoon of the salt with the cinnamon, allspice, cardamom, and nutmeg and stir until well combined. Sprinkle the spice mixture over the potatoes and toss again until evenly coated.

Place the sweet potatoes in a single layer on the prepared pan and roast for 40 minutes, until tender.

Pour ⅓ cup of the broth into a blender, add one-third of the roasted potatoes, and blend until smooth, adding more liquid as needed. Transfer to a soup pot over low heat and repeat the process two more times. Stir in any remaining broth, along with the remaining ¼ teaspoon salt, before serving.

COOK'S NOTE: These roasted spiced sweet potatoes are fantastic on their own. Consider making half a recipe of soup and saving the remaining sweet potatoes for a delicious side dish or a quick and easy snack.

STORAGE: Store in a covered container in the refrigerator for 5 to 7 days or in the freezer for up to 2 months.

PER SERVING: Calories: 280; Total Fat: 4.8 g (4 g saturated, 0.3 g mono-unsaturated); Carbohydrates: 57 g; Protein: 5 g; Fiber: 9 g; Sodium: 465 mg

Summer's Best Zucchini Soup

I like the way nature balances her books. In summertime, everyone gets hot and sweats out water. So what does Mother Earth do? She produces an abundance of summer squash. It's full of water, making it an ideal vegetable to combat dehydration. I think of zucchini as the perfect party guest. It's mild and mixes well with a crowd. The key with zucchini is good prep, so that the flesh stays somewhat firm and tasty.

Heat the olive oil in a sauté pan over medium heat, then add the onion and a pinch of salt and sauté until golden, about 5 minutes. Add the garlic, potato, and ¼ teaspoon of salt and continue to sauté for about 8 minutes, until the potatoes begin to get tender, adding 1 tablespoon of broth if they begin to stick or the pan gets too dry. Add the zucchini, oregano, red pepper flakes, and another ¼ teaspoon of salt and sauté for 4 minutes. Pour in ½ cup of the broth to deglaze the pan and cook until the liquid is reduced by half. Remove from the heat.

Pour 2 cups of the broth into a blender, add one-third of the zucchini sauté, and blend until smooth. Transfer to a soup pot over low heat, and repeat the process two more times. Stir in the grated zucchini and lemon juice, then taste and adjust the seasoning if needed until you have achieved yum.

Serve garnished with the Pistachio Cream, parsley, and mint.

STORAGE: Store in an airtight container in the refrigerator for up to 3 days or in the freezer for up to 2 months.

PER SERVING: Calories: 130; Total Fat: 4.1 g (0.7 g saturated, 2.6 g mono-unsaturated); Carbohydrates: 23 g; Protein: 4 g; Fiber: 5 g; Sodium: 175 mg

SERVES: 8
PREP TIME: 10 minutes
COOK TIME: 20 minutes

2 tablespoons extra-virgin olive oil

1 cup finely diced yellow onion

Sea salt

2 cloves garlic, chopped

1 Yukon gold potato, peeled and diced small

6½ cups Chicken Magic Mineral Broth (page 50), Magic Mineral Broth (page 49), or store-bought organic stock

3½ pounds zucchini, quartered lengthwise, then cut crosswise into ½-inch pieces

1 teaspoon dried oregano

Pinch of red pepper flakes

1 cup grated zucchini

3 teaspoons freshly squeezed lemon juice

Pistachio Cream (page 179), for garnish

1 tablespoon chopped fresh parsley, for garnish

1 tablespoon chopped fresh mint, for garnish

Roasted Red Roma Tomato Soup

For many people, tomato soup is a familiar and beloved comfort food. In this version, the soup benefits from roasting the tomatoes in the oven, which lessens their acidity while adding sweetness. Just be aware that extra-juicy tomatoes may need to be drained into a bowl during the roasting process. Using the pan juices as the broth creates supercharged taste! Plus, the roasted tomatoes blend beautifully (and colorfully) with the carrots. This soup is equally delicious served hot, at room temperature, or chilled.

Preheat the oven to 400°F. Gently squeeze the tomatoes by hand to remove excess seeds, then put them in a bowl and toss with 1 tablespoon of the olive oil and ½ teaspoon of salt until evenly coated. Place the tomatoes, cut side down, in a single layer on sheet pans and roast for 20 to 30 minutes, until their skins are just browning and the juices are bubbly. Let cool for 5 minutes, then lift off the skins with a fork.

Meanwhile, heat the remaining 1 tablespoon olive oil in a soup pot over medium heat, then add the onion and a pinch of salt and sauté until golden, about 4 minutes. Add the carrots, garlic, and ¼ teaspoon of salt and continue to sauté until the carrots are just tender, about 5 minutes.

In a blender, puree the tomatoes with their juice and the carrot mixture until smooth. You may need to add some broth at the end of the blending process, depending on the juiciness of the tomatoes. Add 1 cup at a time until you have the desired thickness.

Return the soup to the pot and gently reheat over medium-low heat. Stir in another ¼ teaspoon of salt, then taste. Tomatoes can sometimes be acidic, so you may want to add a bit of maple syrup and another pinch or two of salt.

Serve topped with the Parsley Basil Drizzle, if desired, and a sprinkling of Parmesan cheese.

VARIATION: If fresh tomatoes aren't available, you can substitute two 28-ounce cans of plum tomatoes.

STORAGE: Store in an airtight container in the refrigerator for 5 days or in the freezer for 2 months.

PER SERVING: Calories: 135; Total Fat: 5.4 g (0.8 g saturated, 3.4 g mono-unsaturated); Carbohydrates: 21 g; Protein: 4 g; Fiber: 6 g; Sodium: 280 mg

SERVES: 6
PREP TIME: 20 minutes
COOK TIME: 35 minutes

4 pounds Roma tomatoes, halved

2 tablespoons extra-virgin olive oil

Sea salt

1 onion, diced small

3 carrots, scrubbed and diced small

1 clove garlic, chopped

Up to 2 cups Magic Mineral Broth (page 49) or store-bought vegetable stock, as needed

½ teaspoon maple syrup (optional)

Parsley Basil Drizzle (page 187), for garnish (optional)

Grated organic Parmesan cheese, for garnish (optional)

Velvety Red Lentil Dal

SERVES: 6

PREP TIME: 15 minutes (with canned tomatoes)

COOK TIME: 45 minutes

2 tablespoons unrefined virgin coconut oil or extra-virgin olive oil

1½ teaspoons cumin seeds

1½ teaspoons black or brown mustard seeds

1 onion, diced small

1 tablespoon minced fresh ginger

2 teaspoons turmeric

2 teaspoons ground cumin

Sea salt

2 cups chopped tomatoes, or 1 (14-ounce) can diced tomatoes, drained

8 cups Magic Mineral Broth (page 49)

2 cups red lentils, rinsed well

1 cinnamon stick

1 teaspoon freshly squeezed lime juice

½ teaspoon maple syrup

¼ cup finely chopped fresh cilantro or mint, for garnish

Tomato Mint Chutney (page 173), for garnish

I was working at the Chopra Center when an Indian saint stopped in. Her entourage laid down some pretty strict rules: No talking to the saint. No approaching the saint. And whatever you do, don't touch the saint. But after eating her bowl of dal, this little imp of a holy woman motioned me over and then . . . proceeded to kiss me on the forehead! The Chopra folks (and I guess the saint as well) like their dal chunky, but it's just as enjoyable blended and smooth. So blend the dal a bit if you want something a little easier to swallow or digest. Small amounts of this dal are wonderful for someone who isn't particularly hungry, as the cumin is an appetite stimulant.

Heat the coconut oil in a soup pot over medium heat. Add the cumin and mustard seeds and sauté until they begin to pop, then quickly add the onion, ginger, turmeric, ground cumin, and a pinch of salt and sauté for about 3 minutes. Add the tomatoes and ¼ teaspoon of salt and sauté for 2 minutes more. Pour in ½ cup of the broth to deglaze the pan and cook until the liquid is reduced by half.

Add the red lentils and stir well, then add the remaining 7½ cups broth and the cinnamon stick. Bring to a boil over high heat, then lower the heat, cover, and simmer for about 30 minutes, until tender.

Add another ¼ teaspoon of salt and simmer, for another 5 minutes. Remove the cinnamon stick and stir in the lime juice and maple syrup.

In a blender, puree the soup in batches until very smooth, adding additional broth or water if you'd like a thinner soup. Return the soup to the pot and gently reheat.

Serve garnished with the chopped cilantro and a dollop of Tomato Mint Chutney.

COOK'S NOTE: If you're in the mood for a heartier meal, skip the blender and just eat the dal atop brown basmati rice, topped with a dollop of chutney. Or, blend half of the dal until smooth, then add the unblended dal to your velvety mixture.

STORAGE: Store in an airtight container in the refrigerator for 5 days or in the freezer for 2 months.

PER SERVING: Calories: 365; Total Fat: 7 g (4.1 g saturated, 0.6 g mono-unsaturated); Carbohydrates: 58 g; Protein: 20 g; Fiber: 14 g; Sodium: 300 mg

Creamy Broccoli and Potato Soup

A lot of people have only had a close-up encounter with broccoli as raw crudités or boiled until it's gray and limp, which is unappetizing and often difficult to digest. Here sautéing the broccoli in olive oil, infusing it with broth, and then blending releases all of its sweetness and cancer-fighting properties and helps everything go down nice and easy.

Heat the olive oil in a large sauté pan over medium heat, then add the onion and sauté until lightly golden, about 3 minutes. Stir in the garlic and then the potatoes, along with a generous ¼ teaspoon of the salt. Sauté until the potatoes are just tender, about 5 minutes.

Meanwhile, cut the broccoli florets into bite-size pieces. Trim and peel the stems and cut them into bite-size pieces as well. Pour in ½ cup of broth to deglaze the pan, turn down the heat to medium-low, and cook until the liquid is reduced by about half. Add the broccoli and the remaining ¼ teaspoon salt, cover, and cook until the broccoli is bright green and just tender, 3 to 4 minutes.

Pour 2 cups of the remaining broth into a blender, add half of the broccoli mixture, and blend until smooth. Pour the mixture into a soup pot, then repeat the process with the remaining 2 cups broth and the remaining vegetables. Stir in the nutmeg.

Gently reheat the soup over low heat, then taste; you may want to add additional salt, a grinding of pepper, and the lemon juice.

Serve garnished with a sprinkle of the cheese.

STORAGE: Store in an airtight container in the refrigerator for up to 4 days.

PER SERVING: Calories: 155; Total Fat: 5.1 g (0.8 g saturated, 3.4 g monounsaturated); Carbohydrates: 26 g; Protein: 4 g; Fiber: 4 g; Sodium: 330 mg

SERVES: 6

PREP TIME: 20 minutes

COOK TIME: 20 minutes

2 tablespoons extra-virgin olive oil

1 cup finely diced onion

2 cloves garlic, chopped

2 cups peeled and finely diced Yukon gold potatoes

½ teaspoon sea salt

¾ pound broccoli

4½ cups Chicken Magic Mineral Broth (page 50), Magic Mineral Broth (page 49), or organic store-bought stock

3 shavings of nutmeg

Freshly ground pepper

½ teaspoon lemon juice (optional)

Shredded organic Cheddar cheese, for garnish (optional)

CHAPTER 3

Vital Vegetables

Vegetables joyfully talk to me—really! Oh, they were shy at first, and who can blame them? It takes time to learn their hidden language, which they speak only when they're really, really fresh. When they're at their peak of flavor, nutrition, and color (which, not surprisingly, all happens at the same time), my God! It sounds like a cacophony at the farmers' market: "Pick me! Pick me! Please!"

I'm here to tell you that you, too, can learn to hear the siren call of veggies, and more than that, *all* plant foods, which include the explosion of herbs and spices you'll find in these recipes. That alluring voice is so important to pick up on, because all the important, empowering nutritional qualities that take on cancer—those anti-inflammatories, antioxidants, high-quality fats, and tumor-pathway inhibitors—are found in veggies and other plant foods.

So how do we make veggies irresistible? Fantastic taste is the ultimate long-term motivator, but you also need a great warm-up act to get people psyched for the show. That comes by speaking first to sight and smell, as those senses energize our appetites before we even take that initial bite. Light up those senses, and victory—by which I mean a plate regularly filled with scrumptious, nutritious fruits and veggies—is suddenly within anyone's grasp.

Vegetables, when bought fresh, are like an edible watercolor. They're *incredibly* visually stimulating, and cover the visible spectrum like a Pantone color wheel. I think vision is a sense that's often overlooked, but if you think about people whose appetite is on a precipice, lovely looking fruits and vegetables can entice them off the ledge and back to the table. As for smells, have you ever been near a kitchen when a sweet potato covered in cinnamon is baking?

A lot of my friends laugh at my enthusiasm over vegetables. I like to tell them that while soups bring out my warm, loving side, vegetables bring out my passion. They are so breathtakingly alive. Steaming, roasting, sautéing, the aforementioned baking . . . there are so many quick and simple ways to make these delights delicious, and it's so important that people in treatment get the incredible bounty of anticancer properties that these veggies willingly offer up, with their heartfelt thanks.

How do I know? They told me so.

Basil Broccoli

An awesome emerging area of food research involves so-called "food synergies." That's where two foods eaten at the same meal enhance the body's ability to absorb more anticancer nutrients. This is most often seen in vegetables (such as broccoli) with fat-soluble vitamins. By bringing a little fat to the table (hello, extra-virgin olive oil!), you're giving your gut the best chance to assimilate broccoli's antioxidant punch. But that's not the only food synergy in this recipe. When researchers combined tomato and broccoli, prostate tumors in mice shrank at a higher rate than what either veggie could accomplish on its own. All this, and it tastes great, too!

Bring a large pot of water to a boil. Cut the broccoli florets off the stalks, then peel the stems and cut them into bite-size pieces. Add a pinch of salt and the broccoli florets and stems to the pot of water and blanch for 30 seconds. Drain the broccoli, then run it under cold water to stop the cooking process; this will retain its lush green color.

Heat the olive oil in a sauté pan over medium heat, then add the garlic and red pepper flakes and sauté for 30 seconds, just until aromatic. Add the cherry tomatoes and a pinch of salt and sauté for an additional minute. Stir in the broccoli florets and ¼ teaspoon of salt and sauté for 2 minutes; the broccoli should still be firm. Gently stir in the lemon juice, lemon zest, and basil and serve immediately.

COOK'S NOTE: No skimping on the basil! Not only does it contain powerful antioxidant properties, but basil, combined with the broccoli and the tomatoes or bell pepper, really takes the flavor over the top. The combination of the bright green of the broccoli and the red of the other veggies is beautiful, making this dish a feast for the eyes. Be sure to add the lemon juice and zest just before serving, as the lemon will dampen the color of the broccoli if it sits for more than a few minutes.

STORAGE: Store in an airtight container in the refrigerator for 5 to 7 days.

PER SERVING: Calories: 125; Total Fat: 7.7 g (1.1 g saturated, 5.4 g monounsaturated); Carbohydrates: 13 g; Protein: 5 g; Fiber: 5 g; Sodium: 125 mg

SERVES: 4
PREP TIME: 10 minutes
COOK TIME: 5 minutes

---

1 bunch of broccoli

Sea salt

2 tablespoons extra-virgin olive oil

1 tablespoon finely chopped garlic

Pinch of red pepper flakes

½ cup halved cherry tomatoes or diced red bell pepper

1 tablespoon freshly squeezed lemon juice

2 teaspoons lemon zest

¼ cup fresh basil, finely chopped

Baby Bok Choy with Yam and Ginger

SERVES: 6

PREP TIME: 15 minutes

COOK TIME: About 5 minutes

4 heads baby bok choy

2 tablespoons light sesame oil

2 scallions, white part only, thinly sliced

2 tablespoons minced fresh ginger

1 cup peeled and finely diced Garnet sweet potato or yam

Sea salt

1 tablespoon tamari

1 teaspoon maple syrup

1 tablespoon freshly squeezed lime juice, plus more to taste

¼ teaspoon toasted sesame oil (optional)

Like most cooks, I really enjoy watching and learning from other cooks as they go through their creative process. Case in point: I observed one of my favorite cooks, Claire Heart, working with bok choy at a Commonweal Cancer Help Program retreat. Bok choy is a great vegetable, but tends to be bitter. Claire completely solved that problem by pairing it with sweet potatoes to create a dish that tasted like a vegetarian Chinese Thanksgiving. It was a completely unique and delicious combo, with the colors blowing me away as well. I went home and decided to play around with her concept, adding a little ginger for zing and digestion and a few more Asian-style flavors. Thank you, Claire!

Trim the bases off the bok choy and discard. Trim the leaves from the stems and cut both crosswise into bite-size pieces, keeping the stems and leaves separate.

Heat the light sesame oil in a sauté pan over medium heat, then add the scallions and ginger and sauté for 30 seconds. Add the sweet potato and a pinch of salt and sauté for an additional minute. Add the bok choy stems, tamari, and maple syrup and sauté for 2 minutes more. Add the bok choy leaves, lime juice, ¼ teaspoon of salt, and the toasted sesame oil. Cook until the bok choy is just wilted, about 2 minutes, then taste: you may want to add a squeeze of lime if desired. Serve immediately.

STORAGE: Store in a covered container in the refrigerator for 3 days.

PER SERVING: Calories: 150; Total Fat: 6 g (0.9 g saturated, 2.2 g monounsaturated); Carbohydrates: 19 g; Protein: 9 g; Fiber: 6 g; Sodium: 595 mg

Green Beans with Brazil Nuts and Basil

Green bean recipes are a little like socks; everybody has a few. I came across a website boasting 471 green bean recipes. By the time I linked to it seconds later, they were up to 472. Clearly, green beans are a popular vegetable. This dish is dairy free and delicious. Instead of a common cheese topping, I use finely ground Brazil nuts, which you'll swear taste like Parmesan cheese. Why Brazil nuts? Because they're an amazing source of the mineral selenium, which some research suggests lessens chemotherapy's toxic effects on healthy hair, kidney, and GI tract cells.

Bring a generous amount of water (about 8 cups) to a boil. Add ¼ teaspoon of salt and the green beans and cook until tender but still crisp, 3 to 6 minutes. Drain the green beans, then run them under cold water to stop the cooking process.

Heat the olive oil in a large sauté pan over medium heat, then add the shallot and a pinch of salt and sauté until translucent, about 1 minute. Stir in the beans, add ¼ teaspoon of salt, and cook, stirring occasionally, until heated through, about 2 minutes. Remove from the heat and add several grinds of pepper, a spritz of the lemon juice, and the nuts. Toss with the basil and lemon zest before serving.

VARIATION: If you don't have Brazil nuts, Maple-Glazed Walnuts (page 137) make a great substitute.

STORAGE: Store in an airtight container in the refrigerator for 2 days.

PER SERVING: Calories: 320; Total Fat: 8.3 g (1.1 g saturated, 4.1 g mono-unsaturated); Carbohydrates: 47 g; Protein: 18 g; Fiber: 12 g; Sodium: 110 mg

SERVES: 6
PREP TIME: 15 minutes
COOK TIME: 10 minutes

Sea salt

1 pound green beans, trimmed

2 tablespoons extra-virgin olive oil

2 tablespoons chopped shallot

Freshly ground pepper

Freshly squeezed lemon juice

2 tablespoons finely ground Brazil nuts or walnuts

2 tablespoons finely chopped fresh basil

½ teaspoon lemon zest

Emerald Greens with Orange

SERVES: 4

PREP TIME: 10 minutes

COOK TIME: 10 minutes

---

2 tablespoons extra-virgin olive oil

1 teaspoon minced garlic

Pinch of red pepper flakes

2 tablespoons dried cranberries

¼ cup freshly squeezed orange juice

6 cups stemmed and chopped Swiss chard, in bite-size pieces

¼ teaspoon sea salt

½ teaspoon orange zest

¼ teaspoon maple syrup

I remember the first time I brought home a bunch of Swiss chard. I laid those big, leafy stalks on my counter and thought to myself, "Should I just put these in a vase and stare at them?" I was a bit intimidated. So are many people. And that's a shame, because the phytochemicals in greens are phenomenal cancer fighters. Actually, greens are easy to work with if you do a quick rip and strip (I'm talking the chard, not your clothes) as soon as you get them home. That's the first step. The second is ridding the greens of their often naturally bitter taste. The simple fix is a quick bath in olive oil over a little heat. Sautéing makes the flavor and consistency much more palate friendly. Adding orange to the mix makes these greens especially yummy. Believe me, even kids approve!

Heat the olive oil in a large sauté pan over medium heat, then add the garlic, red pepper flakes, cranberries, and orange juice and sauté for 30 seconds, just until aromatic. Add the chard, salt, and orange zest and sauté until the color of the chard begins to darken and intensify. Use a slotted spoon to transfer the greens to a bowl, then bring the liquid in the pan to a boil. When the liquid shrinks in from the sides of the pan and thickens a bit, stir the greens back in, then stir in the maple syrup. Do a FASS check. You may want to add another pinch of salt. Serve immediately.

VARIATION: To make this a real jewel of a dish, omit the cranberries and sprinkle 2 tablespoons of gorgeous ruby red pomegranate seeds over the greens just before serving.

COOK'S NOTES: The flavor of this dish is greatly intensified by reducing the liquid in the pan. Take the time to perform this step. Your taste buds will be rewarded.

One trick to preparing greens is ripping them off their tough stems. This makes them easier to eat and digest. You can chop the chard stems into small pieces and add them to the pan earlier so they have a chance to cook more.

STORAGE: Store in an airtight container in the refrigerator for 5 to 7 days.

PER SERVING: Calories: 90; Total Fat: 7.2 g (1 g saturated, 5 g mono-unsaturated); Carbohydrates: 7 g; Protein: 1 g; Fiber: 1 g; Sodium: 260 mg

Gregg's Stuffed Acorn Squash with Quinoa, Cranberries, and Swiss Chard

I know I'm on to something when a confirmed, dyed-in-the-wool meat eater starts claiming a vegetable dish as his favorite meal of all time. So says my husband, Gregg, and believe me, he's an honest food critic. I've noticed that lots of normally veggie-adverse people gravitate to this dish. It could be because it's colorful or comes in its own organic bowl, but I believe the hearty taste elicits a comfort food response. Squash is easy to digest and has numerous nutritional elements—anti-inflammatory, antioxidant, and immune-boosting—that make it a boon for anyone dealing with cancer. Squash is also a natural vessel for all sorts of wonderful fillings. And if you aren't in the mood for roasting squash, this quinoa filling makes for a delectable dish all on its own.

Preheat the oven to 350°F and line a sheet pan with parchment paper.

To make the squash, cut the tops off the squash and scoop out the strings and seeds. Also cut the pointy ends off the bottoms of the squash so they'll stand up once they're stuffed.

Stir the olive oil, salt, allspice, ginger, cinnamon, and red pepper flakes together in a bowl. Use a brush to spread the spice mixture over the inside of the squash. Place the squash, top side down, on the prepared pan and roast for 20 to 25 minutes, until tender. Check after 20 minutes by touching the top of a squash with your finger. Once it's soft, remove the squash from the oven and cover with foil until you're ready to fill them.

Meanwhile, make the filling. Put the quinoa in a fine-mesh sieve and rinse well under running cold water.

Heat the 2 teaspoons of olive oil in a saucepan over medium heat. Add the shallot and fennel and sauté until soft, about 3 minutes. Stir in the cumin and coriander, then stir in the quinoa. Stir in the broth and ¼ teaspoon of the salt, cover, and bring to a boil, then lower the heat and simmer for 15 to 20 minutes, until the quinoa has absorbed all of the liquid. Remove from the heat, and fluff with a fork.

continued

SERVES: 4

PREP TIME: 25 minutes

COOK TIME: 45 minutes

SQUASH

4 acorn squash

2 tablespoons extra-virgin olive oil

¼ teaspoon sea salt

¼ teaspoon ground allspice

¼ teaspoon ground ginger

¼ teaspoon ground cinnamon

Pinch of red pepper flakes

FILLING

1 cup quinoa

1 tablespoon plus 2 teaspoons extra-virgin olive oil

1 tablespoon finely diced shallot

3 tablespoons finely diced fennel

¼ teaspoon ground cumin

¼ teaspoon ground coriander

2 cups Magic Mineral Broth (page 49) or water

½ teaspoon sea salt

2 cloves garlic, minced

Pinch of red pepper flakes

½ cup dried cranberries or raisins

6 cups stemmed and chopped Swiss chard or kale, in bite-size pieces

Freshly squeezed lemon juice

Gregg's Stuffed Acorn Squash with Quinoa, Cranberries, and Swiss Chard, *continued*

While the quinoa is cooking, heat the 1 tablespoon of olive oil in a large sauté pan over medium heat, then add the garlic, red pepper flakes, and cranberries. Stir for 10 seconds, then add the chard and the remaining ¼ teaspoon salt. Sauté until the greens are tender, about 3 minutes for chard, 5 minutes for kale. Remove from the heat and stir in a squeeze of the lemon juice.

To assemble the dish, spoon the quinoa mixture into the squash, then top each squash with a scoop of the greens.

STORAGE: Store in an airtight container in the refrigerator for 3 days or in the freezer for 1 month.

PER SERVING: Calories: 530; Total Fat: 16.3 g (2.3 g saturated, 9.9 g mono-unsaturated); Carbohydrates: 93 g; Protein: 11 g; Fiber: 13 g; Sodium: 650 mg

The Best Offense Is a Good Defense

Here's a reason to eat organic that I bet you've never heard before: compared to their commercially raised cousins, organics are natural-born fighters. And here's the really cool part: they're able to pass their survival skills on to those who eat them. Integrative oncologist Dr. Donald Abrams explains: "If a vegetable is grown indoors or in a hothouse, it doesn't have to do anything to protect itself from its environment. Whereas if you grow, say, a tomato organically outdoors, it needs to protect itself from insects and other predators. So it produces chemicals to protect itself. And it turns out, for the most part, those are the phytonutrients that are beneficial to people." A little symbiotic survival: that's what I call a win-win!

Mashed Cinnamon Butternut Squash

To the uninitiated, winter squash can be a bamboozling vegetable. Sure, it tastes delicious, but being so hard and funny-looking, it's a bit befuddling when whole. The first time I got one home, I felt like I was working with a tree stump. How was I going to get to all of that delicious flesh in the middle? Machete? Chainsaw? Actually, a good sharp chef's knife is all you need. Then again, most supermarkets now sell precut squash. If you've ever worked with pumpkin, taking on squash isn't all that different. Only there's no trick here, just treat. (I'm a fan of cutting squash in half lengthwise, then prebaking it so I can easily scoop out the middle, but that's just me.)

Preheat the oven to 400°F and line a baking sheet with parchment paper.

Toss the squash with the olive oil, cinnamon, ginger, and ¼ teaspoon of salt until the squash is well coated, then spread it in a single layer on the prepared pan. Roast for 25 to 30 minutes, until soft and tender.

Transfer the squash to a food processor, add the maple syrup, nutmeg, and a pinch of salt, and process until smooth and creamy. Taste. If you think it needs a little extra punch, try adding 1 teaspoon of fresh lemon juice.

STORAGE: Store in an airtight container in the refrigerator for 3 days.

PER SERVING: Calories: 160; Total Fat: 7.2 g (1.1 g saturated, 5 g mono-unsaturated); Carbohydrates: 25 g; Protein: 2 g; Fiber: 4 g; Sodium: 155 mg

SERVES: 4
PREP TIME: 15 minutes
COOK TIME: 35 minutes

1 butternut squash, peeled and cut into 1-inch cubes, or one package of precut butternut squash

2 tablespoons extra-virgin olive oil

¼ teaspoon ground cinnamon

¼ teaspoon ground ginger, or 1 teaspoon grated fresh ginger

Sea salt

¼ teaspoon maple syrup

⅛ teaspoon freshly grated nutmeg

1 teaspoon lemon juice (optional)

Kale with Sweet Potatoes and Pecans

SERVES: 4

PREP TIME: 15 minutes

COOK TIME: 10 minutes

2 tablespoons extra-virgin olive oil or unrefined virgin coconut oil

1 teaspoon minced fresh ginger

1 cup peeled and finely diced Garnet sweet potato

⅛ teaspoon ground cinnamon

¼ cup Magic Mineral Broth (page 49) or water

3 cups cleaned, stemmed, and chopped dinosaur kale, in bite-size pieces

¼ teaspoon sea salt

2 tablespoons golden raisins

¼ teaspoon maple syrup

2 tablespoons ground pecans, for garnish

If there's a safe haven in the vegetable kingdom, it's sweet potatoes. I mean, what's not to love? Sweet taste, beautiful color, and fantastic nutrition, not to mention a creamy texture that allows you to introduce chopped greens in a nonthreatening manner. Here, I've added kale, which has outstanding anticancer properties, and some zippy ginger, which aids digestion.

Heat the oil in a large sauté pan over medium heat, then add the ginger and sauté for 30 seconds, just until aromatic. Add the sweet potato, cinnamon, and broth and sauté for about 1 minute. Add the kale, salt, and raisins and sauté until the kale is a darker shade of green and the sweet potatoes are tender, about 5 minutes. Stir in the maple syrup, then taste; you might want to add another pinch of salt if desired.

Serve garnished with the ground pecans.

COOK'S NOTE: The ground pecans have the same texture as a sprinkling of finely grated cheese. If you'd like something crunchier, place ¼ cup of pecans on a baking sheet and toast at 350°F for 7 to 10 minutes, until aromatic and slightly browned. Chop coarsely before sprinkling on this beautiful dish.

STORAGE: Store in a covered container in the refrigerator for 5 days.

PER SERVING: Calories: 160; Total Fat: 10.1 g (1.3 g saturated, 6.6 g mono-unsaturated); Carbohydrates: 17 g; Protein: 3 g; Fiber: 3 g; Sodium: 200 mg

Kale with Carrots

SERVES: 4

PREP TIME: 5 minutes

COOK TIME: 35 minutes

4 cups stemmed and chopped Tuscan kale, in bite-size pieces

2 tablespoons extra-virgin olive oil

1 red onion, cut into half moons

Sea salt

2 carrots, peeled and diced small

3 cloves garlic, minced

1 teaspoon minced fresh ginger

2 tablespoons freshly squeezed lemon juice

Remember those days, growing up, when iceberg lettuce was the only green you could find in the grocery store? Thankfully, that's changed dramatically over the last generation. Romaine rolled in, then—*gasp!*—mesclun, and now there are endless varieties of field greens, baby greens, micro greens, and even micro sprouts available. Which brings us to kale. People sometimes steer away from kale because it's slightly bitter, but I've found that using carrots and ginger tastefully balances kale's right-out-of-the-earth taste. Greens are vital for maintaining health during treatment, and this recipe will help you learn to love their flavor. For a decadently delicious touch, sprinkle Maple-Glazed Walnuts (page 137) over the greens just before serving.

Cover the kale with cold water and set aside. Heat the olive oil in a large, deep sauté pan over medium-high heat, then add the onion and a pinch of salt and sauté for 3 minutes. Decrease the heat to low and cook slowly until the onions are caramelized, about 20 minutes.

Increase the heat to medium, add the carrots, garlic, ginger, and a pinch of salt, and sauté for 3 to 4 minutes, until the carrots are tender. Drain the kale and add it to the pan along with a scant ¼ teaspoon of salt. Sauté until the greens turn bright green and wilt, about 3 minutes. Test the greens; you may need to add 1 tablespoon of water and continue cooking, covered, until they become just a little more tender, 2 to 3 minutes. Drizzle on the lemon juice and stir gently. Serve immediately.

COOK'S NOTES: The longer the lemon just sits on the greens, the more the greens will lose their beautiful color. Wait to add the lemon juice until just before serving.

No Tuscan kale at the market? No worries! Any kale will do, or substitute spinach, Swiss chard, collard greens, mustard greens, or any other leafy green.

STORAGE: Store in a covered container in the refrigerator for 3 days.

PER SERVING: Calories: 120; Total Fat: 7.6 g (1.1 g saturated, 5 g mono-unsaturated); Carbohydrates: 14 g; Protein: 3 g; Fiber: 3 g; Sodium: 125 mg

Broccoli with Garlic and Ginger

Think of this dish as the Three Tenors of the anti-inflammatory world. Broccoli, garlic, and ginger harmonize wonderfully both on the plate and in the body, synergistically bringing an Asian flavor to the palate while delivering vital anticancer nutrients across our biological landscape. And it comes together super-fast! An added taste/body bonus: the hit of extra-virgin olive oil carries flavors around the tongue while allowing for greater absorption of broccoli's fat-soluble vitamins.

Bring a large pot of water to a boil. Add the salt. Add the broccoli and blanch for 30 seconds. Drain the broccoli, then run it under cold water to stop the cooking process; this will retain its lush green color.

Heat the oil in a sauté pan over medium heat. Add the ginger and garlic and sauté for 30 seconds, just until aromatic. Stir in the broccoli and a pinch of salt and sauté for 2 minutes; the broccoli should still be firm. Serve immediately.

COOK'S NOTE: Here's a time-saving tip. When you bring your broccoli home from the market, cut it up into florets, and follow the first step of this recipe. Once you have blanched broccoli in the fridge, you can use it in all sorts of dishes, and it will cut your cooking time in half.

STORAGE: Store in an airtight container in the refrigerator for 4 days.

PER SERVING: Calories: 70; Total Fat: 4 g (0 g saturated, 2 g mono-unsaturated); Carbohydrates: 6 g; Protein: 2 g; Fiber: 2 g; Sodium: 323 mg

SERVES: 4
PREP TIME: 10 minutes
COOK TIME: 5 minutes

½ teaspoon sea salt

1 large bunch broccoli, cut into florets, stems peeled and cut into bite-size pieces

1 tablespoon extra-virgin olive oil or coconut oil

1 tablespoon grated ginger

2 garlic cloves, chopped

Arugula with Edamame, Radish, and Avocado

Arugula is a newbie to the cancer "superfoods" group. Researchers only recently discovered that arugula rivals its cruciferous cousins—such as kale and broccoli—in the amount of cancer-fighting sulfur compounds it contains. Normally, these sulfur-rich foods naturally taste a little bitter, but arugula tends toward a more peppery taste. Overall, this wonderful salad has a zesty feel, thanks to the Cilantro Lime Vinaigrette and radish. A friend of mine calls radish the sorbet of vegetables because of its ability to clean and brighten the palate. One taste, and I predict you'll agree. Edamame, by the way, is just another name for soybeans.

Combine the arugula or mixed greens with the edamame, radishes, and avocado in a large bowl. Add the vinaigrette and toss to combine before serving.

STORAGE: If you must store the salad, don't add the dressing. Store the greens and veggies in an airtight container in the refrigerator for 1 day at most.

PER SERVING: Calories: 160; Total Fat: 11.2 g (1.4 g saturated, 6.7 g monounsaturated); Carbohydrates: 12 g; Protein: 5 g; Fiber: 5 g; Sodium: 200 mg

SERVES: 4
PREP TIME: 15 minutes
COOK TIME: Not applicable

6 cups arugula or mixed salad greens

1 cup fresh or frozen shelled edamame, mixed with a spritz of fresh lime juice and a pinch of sea salt

4 radishes, trimmed and sliced

1 avocado, spritzed with fresh lime juice and sprinkled with sea salt (so it doesn't discolor)

¼ cup Cilantro Lime Vinaigrette (page 180)

Baked Sweet Potatoes with Assorted Toppings

SERVES: 4

PREP TIME: 10 minutes

COOK TIME: 45 to 60 minutes

4 orange-fleshed sweet potatoes

4 teaspoons olive oil or coconut oil

I always think of baked sweet potatoes as little rafts of nutritious delight. Unto themselves, they're quite tasty and full of fiber, a wonderful blood sugar regulator. But what they're best at, at least when they're baked and the top is slit open, is carrying numerous other healthy ingredients along for the ride. Chopped herbs, chutneys, veggies, nut creams, yogurt . . . all are great variations (see following). Many people gravitate toward a sweet potato when they feel like eating but aren't over-the-top hungry. I like the simplicity with which they can be prepared. Bake four, eat one, put the rest in an airtight container, and they reheat in a flash. A great go-to food!

Preheat the oven to 400°F and line a baking sheet with parchment paper.

Scrub the sweet potatoes well and dry them off with a clean towel. Brush the skin of each potato with 1 teaspoon of oil. Pierce each potato a several times with a fork. Place the potatoes on the prepared pan and bake for 45 minutes to an hour or until tender.

Make a slit in the top of each sweet potato and add a tablespoon of your favorite topping.

TOPPING OPTIONS:
- *Basic:* sea salt, freshly ground pepper, with 1 tablespoon butter, ghee, coconut oil, olive oil, yogurt, or nut butter.
- *Add:* 1 tablespoon chopped fresh mint, parsley, or cilantro
- *Add:* ¼ teaspoon ground cinnamon, ½ teaspoon turmeric
- *Add:* 2 teaspoons chopped walnuts or pecans

OTHER TOPPING IDEAS:
- ¼ cup Basil Broccoli (page 75)
- ¼ cup Emerald Greens with Orange (page 78)
- ¼ cup Kale with Carrots (page 86)
- 1 tablespoon Apricot Pear Chutney (page 172)
- 1 tablespoon Cashew Cream (page 178)
- 1 tablespoon Moroccan Pesto (page 186)
- 1 tablespoon Herbed and Spiced Yogurt (page 188)

STORAGE: Store in an airtight container in the refrigerator for 4 days.

PER SERVING (FOR BASIC OPTION): Calories: 152; Total Fat: 4.75 g (0.7 g saturated, 3.7 g monounsaturated); Carbohydrates: 26 g; Protein: 2 g; Fiber: 3.9 g; Sodium: 122 mg

Roasted Root Vegetables with Rosemary and Thyme

SERVES: 6

PREP TIME: 20 minutes

COOK TIME: 40 minutes

---

2 pounds root vegetables (such as potatoes, sweet potatoes, carrots, parsnips, turnips, rutabagas), peeled and cut into 1-inch cubes

2 tablespoons extra-virgin olive oil

½ teaspoon sea salt

½ teaspoon freshly ground pepper

1 tablespoon chopped fresh rosemary, or ¼ teaspoon dried

1½ tablespoons chopped fresh thyme, or ½ teaspoon dried

1 tablespoon freshly squeezed lemon or orange juice (optional)

2 tablespoons chopped fresh parsley, for garnish

Eating veggies all the time is a good thing. Eating green veggies all the time? Okay, that may be asking a little too much. Fortunately, vegetables come in all colors of the rainbow and offer all kinds of anticancer benefits. Root vegetables, such as parsnips, rutabagas, and butternut squash, are especially rich in carotenoids, which fight the oxidative stress on which cancer cells thrive. I always like having a tray of cut-up root vegetables primed for roasting. They'll last a week in the fridge, preroast, and taste great, post-roast, either on their own or as a side dish for entrées such as Orange Ginger Roasted Chicken (page 109).

Preheat the oven to 400°F and line a large baking sheet with parchment paper.

In a large bowl, toss the vegetables with the olive oil, salt, pepper, rosemary, and thyme until evenly coated. Spread the vegetables in a single layer on the prepared pan (using two pans if need be). Bake for 30 to 40 minutes, or until tender. Transfer to a bowl or platter and spritz with the lemon juice, if desired, and sprinkle with the parsley. Serve immediately.

COOK'S NOTE: Here are some other ideas for spicing up your roots: Replace the rosemary and thyme with ½ teaspoon cumin, ¼ teaspoon ginger, ¼ teaspoon ground cinnamon.

STORAGE: Store in an airtight container in the refrigerator for 4 days.

PER SERVING: Calories 130 g; Total Fat: 3.7 g (0.5 g saturated, 2.8 g mono-unsaturated); Carbohydrates: 15.5 g; Protein: 1.7 g; Fiber: 4 g; Sodium: 145 mg

Stir-Fried Baby Bok Choy with Shiitake Mushrooms

I love Asian fare, but I can also see why people stay away from it in their kitchens. It can be a bit daunting, especially all of those veggies with exotic names that most of us didn't grow up with and don't have the faintest idea how to prepare. But I'm here to take you over those culinary hurdles, and it's important, because most Asian vegetables have loads of health-supportive phytochemicals. Here I've combined two powerhouses, bok choy and shiitake mushrooms. I prefer baby bok choy, as bok choy gets more bitter as it matures.

Trim the bases off the bok choy and discard. Trim the leaves from the stems and cut both crosswise into bite-size pieces, keeping the stems and leaves separate.

Heat the light sesame oil in a sauté pan over medium heat, then add the scallions, ginger, garlic, mushrooms, and a pinch of salt and sauté for 30 seconds. Add the water, tamari, and the bok choy stems and sauté for 2 minutes. Add the bok choy leaves, lime juice, toasted sesame oil, and a pinch of salt and sauté until the bok choy is just wilted, about 2 minutes. Taste and add another squeeze of lime if you like. Sprinkle with the toasted sesame seeds and serve immediately.

COOK'S NOTE: To toast seeds or nuts, preheat the oven or toaster oven to 350°F and line a baking sheet with parchment paper. Spread the seeds or nuts in an even layer on the prepared pan and toast until aromatic and slightly browned, 5 to 7 minutes. Check frequently, as they can burn easily.

STORAGE: Store in a covered container in the refrigerator for 3 days.

PER SERVING: Calories: 150; Total Fat: 7.8 g (1 g saturated, 2.6 g monounsaturated); Carbohydrates: 16 g; Protein: 10 g; Fiber: 6 g; Sodium: 585 mg

SERVES: 6
PREP TIME: 15 minutes
COOK TIME: 5 minutes

4 heads baby bok choy

2 tablespoons light sesame oil

2 scallions, white parts only, thinly sliced

2 tablespoons minced fresh ginger

2 cloves garlic, minced

½ pound shiitake mushrooms, stemmed and sliced ¼ inch thick

Sea salt

2 tablespoons water

1 tablespoon tamari

1 tablespoon freshly squeezed lime juice

1½ teaspoons toasted sesame oil

1 tablespoon toasted sesame seeds

Shredded Carrot and Beet Salad

One of my favorite gatherings is the Center for Mind Body Medicine's annual Food as Medicine training program, where hundreds of nutritionally minded physicians, nurses, and other wellness professionals share knowledge and great food. I cook for the attendees, and they often inspire me. Take Dr. Joel Evans. He's a proponent of the school of thought (and emerging science) that the more vibrant a food's color, the more nutrition it's likely to contain. As an ode to Joel, I set out to create the most colorful salad I could, using red beets, orange carrots, and fresh mint. If, as a kid, I'd had a vegetable crisper instead of a box of crayons, this salad would have been the result. You can substitute lemon or lime juice for the orange juice.

Whisk the orange juice, lemon juice, olive oil, ginger, and salt together until thoroughly combined. Put the carrots in a mixing bowl, drizzle with half of the dressing, and toss until evenly coated. Place the carrots on one side of a shallow serving bowl. Put the beets in the mixing bowl, drizzle with the remaining dressing, and toss until evenly coated. Place the beets in the serving bowl next to the carrots for a beautiful contrast of red and orange. Top with the chopped mint before serving.

STORAGE: Store in an airtight container in the refrigerator for 3 to 5 days.

PER SERVING: Calories: 50; Total Fat: 2.5 g (0.4 g saturated, 1.7 g monounsaturated); Carbohydrates: 7 g; Protein: 1 g; Fiber: 2 g; Sodium: 195 mg

SERVES: 4
PREP TIME: 10 minutes
COOK TIME: Not applicable

2 tablespoons freshly squeezed orange juice

2 teaspoons freshly squeezed lemon juice

2 teaspoons extra-virgin olive oil

½ teaspoon minced fresh ginger

¼ teaspoon sea salt

1 cup peeled and shredded carrot

1 cup peeled and shredded red beet

2 tablespoons chopped fresh mint

Warm and Toasty Cumin Carrots

SERVES: 4

PREP TIME: 10 minutes

COOK TIME: 5 minutes

½ teaspoon cumin seeds

2 tablespoons extra-virgin olive oil

1 teaspoon minced fresh ginger

1½ cups peeled and sliced carrots, cut ¼ inch thick

¼ teaspoon sea salt

2 tablespoons water

1 teaspoon freshly squeezed lemon juice

1 teaspoon maple syrup

Chopped fresh parsley, for garnish

Toasting cumin releases its aromatic, flavorful, and incredibly healthy oils. As the seeds heat up, they begin popping like popcorn, which is how you know they're done.

Toast the cumin seeds in a dry sauté pan over medium heat, shaking the pan back and forth until they start to pop and become aromatic. Immediately add the olive oil and ginger and sauté for 1 minute. Stir in the carrots and salt, then turn down the heat to medium-low, add the water, cover, and cook for about 2 minutes, until just barely tender. Stir in the lemon juice and maple syrup. Garnish with the parsley and serve immediately.

STORAGE: Store in an airtight container in the refrigerator for 3 days.

PER SERVING: Calories: 85; Total Fat: 7.2 g (1 g saturated, 5.1 g mono-unsaturated); Carbohydrates: 6 g; Protein: 0 g; Fiber: 1 g; Sodium: 180 mg

Warm Napa Cabbage Slaw

When I was growing up, coleslaw was one-dimensional—cold cabbage drowned in mayo with a few slivers of carrot for coloring. These days, slaw has gotten an extreme makeover, and myriad versions now call to the senses. This concoction is both warm and sweet and serves as a great base for salmon, chicken, tofu, or tempeh. Sautéing the onion, red cabbage, and carrots in a little rice vinegar, tamari, and ginger makes it easy to eat and mighty flavorful.

Whisk the vinegar, tamari, maple syrup, and ginger together in a bowl.

Heat the sesame oil in a large sauté pan over medium heat, then add the onion and a pinch of salt and sauté until the onion is translucent, about 3 minutes. Add the napa cabbage, red cabbage, carrots, and a pinch of salt and sauté until the cabbage is slightly wilted, about 2 minutes. Stir in the vinegar mixture and cook until the liquid is reduced by half and coats the vegetables. Remove from the heat and stir in the cilantro.

VARIATION: Add some protein to this dish by stirring in 1½ cups of shredded roasted chicken, tofu, or tempeh when you add the vinegar. This is a delicious addition and can turn a side dish into a meal.

COOK'S NOTE: You may be wondering how to take on cabbage, the bocce ball of vegetables. Place the cabbage on a cutting board with the stem side down. Using a sharp chef's knife, cut the cabbage in half from top to bottom. Use the tip of your knife to remove the core. To shred cabbage by hand, hold the cabbage on the cutting board at an angle and give it a shave by making a thin slice down the flat (cut) side of the cabbage.

STORAGE: Store in an airtight container in the refrigerator for 3 to 5 days.

PER SERVING: Calories: 85; Total Fat: 3.7 g (0.5 g saturated, 1.5 g mono-unsaturated); Carbohydrates: 11 g; Protein: 2 g; Fiber: 2 g; Sodium: 610 mg

SERVES: 4
PREP TIME: 10 minutes
COOK TIME: 10 minutes

2 tablespoons rice vinegar

2 tablespoons tamari

1 teaspoon maple syrup

1 tablespoon minced fresh ginger

1 tablespoon light sesame oil

1 cup thinly sliced red onion

Sea salt

2 cups shredded napa cabbage

1 cup shredded red cabbage

1 cup peeled and shredded carrots

¼ cup fresh cilantro leaves

CHAPTER 4

Protein-Building Foods

Proteins are the Incredible Hulks of nutrients, vital for repairing the body. This is doubly so for people in treatment. Chemotherapy and other treatments break down cells and tissues; as a result, the body requires 50 to 70 percent more protein just to get back to equilibrium. Fortunately, extra protein is easy to get into your diet. Eggs, fish, chicken, beans, and seafood all deliver much-needed protein, and all are featured in this chapter.

Each of these proteins is unique. Eggs and chicken (which came first?) are considered "complete" proteins, containing enough of the nine essential amino acids needed to create a whole protein. They're kind of like putting ultra-premium gas in your car. Veggie protein sources—beans, legumes, seeds—have different amounts and combinations of those essential amino acids, so you have to mix 'em up (for example, have some nuts at noon and a chickpea burger later in the day) to properly utilize those protein makers. Fish protein—notably from cod, which is generally easy to digest—increases insulin sensitivity in humans. That may be helpful for people receiving chemotherapy and/or steroids that can increase blood sugar and promote insulin resistance.

These delicious, protein-dense meals mean you don't have to eat a lot to get those essential amino acids. No half-pound burgers here! Four ounces of fish or meat delivers between 29 and 39 grams of protein, nearly half the daily protein needs of a healthy 120-pound woman. I've also made sure these proteins are easily and enjoyably accessible. The chicken and fish recipes are all marinated or tenderized. That maximizes flavor while breaking down the proteins, which makes them easier to eat and digest. Marinating also adds moisture, which people dealing with dry mouth or throat issues will appreciate.

It's vital that you use the highest-quality proteins, as in wild fish and organic eggs and chicken. I fully realize they often cost more, but their nutritional profiles are far, far superior to commercially raised products. Commercial chickens often are treated with antibiotics, while some commercial cattle are injected with hormones. That's the last thing you need to ingest. As for fish, wild versus farm-raised fish generally have much better omega-3 fatty acid profiles; this may lessen the inflammation linked to possible chemotherapy resistance.

Easy Eggs in a Cup

SERVES: 4

PREP TIME: 10 minutes

COOK TIME: 20 minutes

1 tablespoon extra-virgin olive oil

½ cup finely diced red onion

1 teaspoon minced garlic

4 cups tightly packed baby spinach, washed and dried

Sea salt

Pinch of freshly grated nutmeg

¼ cup crumbled organic feta cheese (optional)

4 organic eggs

Pinch of freshly ground pepper

Baked or shirred (pronounced "sheared") eggs have been around forever. In this recipe, baking eggs over a little sautéed spinach with feta cheese and a shaving of nutmeg creates a dish that looks and tastes beautiful. Just the sight of these eggs nestled in colorful ramekins is enough to bring even the most reluctant eater back to the table. To further enhance the yum factor, serve topped with Basil Lemon Drizzle (page 175).

Preheat the oven to 375°F.

Heat the olive oil in a sauté pan over medium heat, then add the onion and sauté until translucent, about 3 minutes. Stir in the garlic and sauté for an additional 30 seconds, then stir in the spinach and a pinch of salt and cook until wilted and tender, about another 30 seconds. Remove from the heat and stir in the nutmeg.

Lightly grease 4 small ramekins with olive oil. For each ramekin, spoon in one-fourth of the spinach mixture, then sprinkle on 1 tablespoon of the cheese. Gently crack 1 egg on top of the cheese, then sprinkle the pepper and a pinch of salt over all 4 ramekins.

Bake for 12 to 14 minutes, until very little liquid remains and moves around when you shake the ramekins.

Let cool for 3 minutes, then run a knife or an offset spatula around the inside edge of each ramekin to loosen the eggs. Using your knife or spatula to help support the eggs, carefully transfer to a plate and serve immediately.

COOK'S NOTE: To avoid a watery end product, make sure the spinach is well dried prior to adding it to the sauté pan. Spinach naturally gives off moisture when it cooks, so you don't want to add even more by cooking it when it's wet. A salad spinner works miracles to dry spinach quickly and efficiently. For a time-saver, buy prewashed organic bagged spinach from the market.

STORAGE: Store in an airtight container in the refrigerator for 2 days.

PER SERVING: Calories: 120; Total Fat: 8.5 g (2.1 g saturated, 4.4 g mono-unsaturated); Carbohydrates: 5 g; Protein: 7 g; Fiber: 1 g; Sodium: 185 mg

Simple Scrambled Eggs with Kale

You know the feeling: it's late, you've had a long day, you're a tad hungry, but you're really not up for anything more than a kitchen drive-by. What's easy, fast, tasty, and healthy? Scrambled eggs! I always suggest a quick scramble because eggs are a great platform for adding anything you like. Here, I've chosen kale, but chopped herbs or leafy greens such as chard, spinach, or arugula work just as well. But here's the key to the whole thing: Cook your eggs *low* and *slow* and they'll come out perfect (ignore this advice at your own rubbery egg peril). I heat the pan first, drizzle in the oil or melt the butter, then turn down the flame and pour in the eggs (sometimes I even take the pan off the flame altogether for the egg-pouring and initial whipping phase). Do it right, and your eggs will have that perfect velvety feel.

In a medium bowl, crack the eggs, then add the salt, turmeric, pepper, and water and beat well with a whisk or a fork until the egg mixture becomes foamy.

Heat a 10-inch skillet over medium heat, then add the olive oil. When the olive oil begins to shimmer, add the egg mixture and turn down the heat to medium-low. Add the eggs to the pan and cook, stirring frequently with a wooden spoon. After a minute or two, the eggs will begin to form curds. Add the greens and keep stirring continuously until the eggs are soft and shiny. Remove the mixture from the heat and serve immediately.

COOK'S NOTE: Keep in mind that the eggs continue to cook in the hot pan, so remove from the heat 30 seconds before you think you should to prevent overcooking.

STORAGE: Not applicable.

PER SERVING: Calories: 132; Total Fat: 10 g (2.25 g saturated, 5.2 g mono-unsaturated); Carbohydrates: 5.25 g; Protein: 8.2 g; Fiber: 0.1 g; Sodium: 300 mg

SERVES: 2
PREP TIME: 10 minutes
COOK TIME: 5 minutes

4 organic eggs

¼ teaspoon sea salt

1 teaspoon turmeric (optional)

¼ teaspoon freshly ground pepper

1 tablespoon water

2 teaspoons olive oil

1 cup kale, stemmed and chopped into bite-size pieces

Nana's Egg Salad

SERVES: 2

PREP TIME: 5 minutes

COOK TIME: Not applicable

2 organic eggs, hard-boiled

1 teaspoon mayonnaise or Vegenaise

¼ teaspoon Dijon mustard

⅛ teaspoon sea salt

⅛ teaspoon paprika

Pinch of cayenne

¼ teaspoon freshly squeezed lemon juice

People going through treatment often want to eat familiar foods, and for many folks egg salad fits the bill. What I did here was take my Nana's egg salad and adapt it so all that great protein was easier to nosh. Instead of German-style chunky egg salad, I opted for a lighter, creamier texture that works great on crackers, in a pita or wrap, or on top of salad greens. Adding a pinch of cayenne and a little lemon gives this egg salad a bit more zip. Nana would have approved.

Put the eggs in a mini food processor and pulse just 4 times or so, until they're broken down into small pieces. Alternatively, place them in a bowl and use the back of a fork to break them up. Add the mayonnaise, mustard, salt, paprika, cayenne, and lemon juice and process or stir until combined. Taste; you may want to add additional salt and lemon juice if needed. Serve immediately.

COOK'S NOTES: Fresh basil makes a wonderful addition; add about 1 teaspoon, finely chopped.

I learned how to make a perfect hard-boiled egg from my mother, who learned the secret from my culinary hero, Julia Child. Place the eggs in 4 cups of cold water in a high rather than wide pot. Cover and bring the eggs just to a boil, then immediately remove from the heat. Once the water has cooled to the touch, about 15 minutes, the eggs will have a perfectly cooked yolk.

STORAGE: Store in an airtight container in the refrigerator for 2 to 3 days.

PER SERVING: Calories: 80; Total Fat: 5.5 g (1.6 g saturated, 2 g mono-unsaturated); Carbohydrates: 1 g; Protein: 6 g; Fiber: 0 g; Sodium: 240 mg

Poached Eggs with Basil Lemon Drizzle

Here's all you need to know about poached eggs: Ira Gershwin said his songwriting career wouldn't be complete until he got his beloved poached eggs into one of his songs, which he eventually did ("I'm a poached egg . . . without a piece of toast; Yorkshire pudding . . . without a beef to roast."). I guess Ira felt like so many of us do: sometimes the best little meal is the simplest. In this case, I've enhanced the yum factor by topping this comfort food with Basil Lemon Drizzle. The result is a very light sauce, which the fat from the yolk takes on a trip all around your mouth. Hmm . . . yummmm.

Pour 6 inches of water into a large saucepan and place over medium-high heat. When it's almost boiling, add the vinegar, then crack each egg open in a small dish and gently slide the egg into the water. Maintain the water temperature at just below a simmer, turning the heat down to low if necessary. Cook until the egg whites are set and the centers are still soft, about 3 minutes. Remove with a slotted spoon and place on a paper towel to drain off excess water.

Serve immediately, sprinkling each egg with a pinch of sea salt and topping with 2 teaspoons of Basil Lemon Drizzle.

COOK'S NOTES: Like your yolks firmer? Let them cook for an extra 30 to 60 seconds.

Go the extra mile and prepare this take on eggs Benedict. It's worth it! Put four pieces of sprouted grain bread on a cutting board and use a cookie cutter or the mouth of a large glass to punch out circle shapes. Toast the circles, then drizzle with a bit of extra-virgin olive oil and sprinkle lightly with sea salt. Place a poached egg on top of each piece of toast, then top with 2 teaspoons of Basil Lemon Drizzle.

STORAGE: Not applicable.

PER SERVING: Calories: 70; Total Fat: 5 g (1.6 g saturated, 1.9 g mono-unsaturated); Carbohydrates: 0 g; Protein: 6 g; Fiber: 0 g; Sodium: 145 mg

SERVES: 4
PREP TIME: 2 minutes
COOK TIME: 5 minutes

1 tablespoon vinegar

4 organic eggs

Sea salt

Basil Lemon Drizzle (page 175), for garnish

Curried Chicken Salad

SERVES: 6
PREP TIME: 15 minutes
COOK TIME: Not applicable

1½ pounds roasted organic chicken

1 Granny Smith apple, diced into ¼-inch pieces

¼ cup raisins or currants

¼ cup minced scallions, green part only

2 stalks celery, diced small

½ cup organic plain Greek-style yogurt

¼ cup mayonnaise

1 tablespoon freshly squeezed lime juice

1 tablespoon curry powder

½ teaspoon ground ginger

½ teaspoon sea salt

6 butter lettuce leaves, washed and dried

¼ cup slivered toasted almonds (see page 93), for garnish

¼ cup chopped fresh cilantro, for garnish (optional)

This salad was inspired by those gorgeous, colorful Bollywood flicks that offer a feast of singing, dancing, and romance. I love Indian food, as it was my first real introduction to all things curry. Only much later did I learn that turmeric, a typical curry spice that gives curries a yellow tint, has tremendous antitumor and anti-inflammatory properties. And to think, I loved it just for its taste! Here, I was hankering for a swirl of flavors with an Indian feel. The chicken makes a great starting point because it's full of protein and amenable to all sorts of accessorizing. In this case, the apple and raisins play delightfully off the curry spices.

Chop the chicken into ½-inch pieces and put them in a bowl. Stir in the apple, raisins, scallions, and celery. Separately, whisk together the yogurt, mayonnaise, lime juice, curry powder, ginger, and salt. Add the yogurt mixture to the chicken and stir gently until thoroughly combined. Serve atop the lettuce leaves, garnished with the almonds and cilantro, if desired.

VARIATION: Making pita pocket sandwiches is a fantastic way to get much-needed nutrients into your body and fill your belly while you're running errands, waiting for a doctor's appointment, or otherwise on the go. Place a pita on a flat work surface and cut a 2-inch section off the top using a knife. With the pita lying flat, insert ¼ cup of salad greens, then carefully spread ½ cup of the chicken salad on top of the greens, making certain to spread it around the entire cavity of the pita.

COOK'S NOTE: Save time by using store-bought organic roast chicken or, better yet, the leftovers from Orange Ginger Roasted Chicken (page 109).

STORAGE: Store in an airtight container in the refrigerator for 3 days.

PER SERVING: Calories: 300; Total Fat: 11.3 g (3.1 g saturated, 3.8 g mono-unsaturated); Carbohydrates: 15 g; Protein: 34 g; Fiber: 2 g; Sodium: 375 mg

Chicken and Broccoli Stir-Fry with Cashews

SERVES: 6

PREP TIME: 25 minutes

COOK TIME: 10 minutes

Juice of 1 lime

½ teaspoon sea salt

4 organic skinless, boneless chicken thighs, cut into bite-size pieces

2 teaspoons kudzu root powder

¼ cup cold water

2 tablespoons sesame or grapeseed oil

½ pound broccoli, cut into florets

½ cup toasted cashews, for garnish

SAUCE

¼ cup tamari

¼ cup water

1 tablespoon maple syrup

2 tablespoons freshly squeezed lime juice

1 tablespoon rice vinegar

2 teaspoons minced garlic

2 teaspoons minced fresh ginger

Pinch of cayenne

There's something about a chicken and broccoli stir-fry that screams "Chinese take-out!" But this is a healthier and tastier recipe than your standard MSG-fest, so let's call it "Chinese take-in." The dark meat's slightly higher fat content makes for a flavorful, moist dish, so people with throat or mouth issues may find it easier to chew and swallow (though if you prefer, you can substitute an equivalent amount of breast meat). The dish is thickened with kudzu root, a phenomenal anticancer plant, which is a lot more desirable than the cornstarch found in most carry-out fare. Plus, the sauce blend of tamari, lime juice, ginger, and maple syrup is so delicious that you'll be able to take that Chinese restaurant off speed dial.

Stir the lime juice and salt together. Add the chicken to the blend and marinate for 20 minutes in the refrigerator.

In a small bowl, whisk the kudzu root powder with the ¼ cup cold water until completely dissolved, making a slurry.

Meanwhile, make the sauce. Combine the tamari, ¼ cup water, maple syrup, lime juice, vinegar, garlic, ginger, and the cayenne together in a bowl.

Remove the chicken from the refrigeratior and pat it dry with a paper towel.

Heat a wok or large, heavy sauté pan over high heat for 2 minutes. Add the oil and swirl to coat the pan. Add the chicken and toss or stir constantly for 2 minutes. Add the broccoli and stir-fry until bright green, about 2 minutes. Pour in the kudzu slurry and toss until well combined. Add the sauce and stir-fry for another 30 seconds, tossing constantly.

Serve immediately, garnished with the cashews.

COOK'S NOTE: For a vegetarian version, use tofu or tempeh in place of the chicken.

STORAGE: Store in an airtight container in the refrigerator for 4 days.

PER SERVING: Calories: 250; Total Fat: 12.8 g (2.3 g saturated, 6 g mono-unsaturated); Carbohydrates: 20 g; Protein: 13 g; Fiber: 1 g; Sodium: 415 mg

Cozy Comfy Chicken and Rice

This has always been my personal comfort dish, a meal I make from leftovers after roasting a chicken on the weekend. One day a friend was in the kitchen when I was making it, and she started asking innocuous questions: "Say, how much of the shallot are you using?" "Was that a half cup of olives?" I was so busy cooking that I didn't really pay attention to what she was doing with the answers. She figured out the recipe and started making it for friends, who loved it and wanted the recipe too. I guess I wasn't meant to hold on to this one. That's okay. It's really, really good, and I hope you get as much pleasure out of it as I do.

Bring the broth to a boil in a large saucepan. (If it's been frozen, give it a spritz of lemon juice.) Pour the broth into a small heatproof bowl, add the saffron, and let it infuse the broth. Using the same saucepan, heat the olive oil over medium-high heat, then add the onion and a pinch of salt and sauté until soft, about 2 minutes. Add the shallot and ¼ teaspoon of salt and sauté until just golden, about 1 minute. Add the rice and stir until mixed well, about 1 minute, to slightly toast the rice.

Stir in the broth and ¼ teaspoon of salt and give the rice a quick stir. Bring the rice to a boil, then lower the heat, cover, and simmer for 12 minutes.

Stir in the chicken, olives, pimiento, and lemon juice. Cover, remove from the heat, and let stand for 12 minutes.

Fluff with a fork, then serve garnished with the parsley.

VARIATION: For those who would rather avoid chicken, try this as a rice dish using Magic Mineral Broth (page 49) . . . it's delicious!

COOK'S NOTES: Sautéing the rice with the onion and shallot gives this dish a little more depth of flavor.

As a time-saver, you can purchase an already roasted organic chicken from the store for this dish.

My favorite type of olives for this dish is an Italian variety called Cerignola. They're more buttery and mellow than many varieties. If you can't find them, Kalamata olives are also wonderful here. Just make sure you give them a good rinse before adding them to the dish.

STORAGE: Store in an airtight container in the refrigerator for 5 days.

PER SERVING: Calories: 225; Total Fat: 6.2 g (1.2 g saturated, 3.7 g mono-unsaturated); Carbohydrates: 26 g; Protein: 16 g; Fiber: 2 g; Sodium: 320 mg

SERVES: 4
PREP TIME: 15 minutes
COOK TIME: 30 minutes

2¼ cups Chicken Magic Mineral Broth (page 50) or store-bought organic chicken stock

¼ teaspoon finely chopped saffron threads

1 tablespoon extra-virgin olive oil

2 tablespoons finely diced yellow onion

Sea salt

1 tablespoon finely diced shallot

1 cup ~~jasmine~~ *Brown* rice, rinsed

1¼ cups chopped or shredded roasted organic chicken

3 tablespoons chopped olives

~~1 to 2 tablespoons diced pimiento~~ peppers

Spritz of fresh lemon juice

½ cup chopped fresh flat-leaf parsley, for garnish

Orange Ginger Roasted Chicken

Roasted chicken is a staple for many people, though they often bemoan the all-too-frequent bland, dry results. Not here. This is a moist, zippy take. I've replaced the run-of-the-mill rosemary-thyme rub with ginger, orange zest, and cinnamon, which are also appetite stimulants. Rubbing the spices under the skin, filling the cavity with more aromatics and orange juice, and then roasting the whole shebang makes for one succulent bird! Drizzle with Moroccan Pesto (page 186) or add a dollop of Apricot Pear Chutney (page 172).

Use disposable kitchen gloves to handle the bird more easily and keep things sanitary.

Preheat the oven to 400°F.

Pat the chicken dry with paper towels. Stir the paprika, coriander, and ground cinnamon together, then divide the mixture in half and stir 1 teaspoon of the salt into half. Rub the salted spice mixture all over the outside of the chicken. Sprinkle the remaining ½ teaspoon salt inside the chicken.

With your palm facing downward, use your first three fingers to gently lift the skin on both sides of the breast to loosen it from the meat. Rub the remaining spice mixture, the orange zest, and the grated ginger under the skin of each breast, massaging them lightly into the meat. Place the garlic, cinnamon sticks, ginger pieces, and orange rind inside the cavity along with half of the orange juice.

Place the chicken on a roasting rack in a glass or ceramic baking dish, breast side up. Roast until a meat thermometer reads 160°F when inserted in the thigh and the juice from the meat runs clear, about 1 hour.

Let the chicken rest for at least 10 minutes before carving. Just before serving, pour the remaining orange juice over the chicken.

COOK'S NOTE: Leftovers, anyone? Using leftover roasted chicken will save time and add flavor to any recipe calling for roasted or shredded chicken, such as Curried Chicken Salad (page 104), Cozy Comfy Chicken and Rice (page 107), Lemony Greek Chicken Soup (page 53), and Thai It Up Chicken Soup (page 58).

STORAGE: Store in a covered container in the refrigerator for 3 to 5 days.

PER SERVING: Calories: 215; Total Fat: 5.1 g (1.3 g saturated, 1.5 g mono-unsaturated); Carbohydrates: 4 g; Protein: 35 g; Fiber: 1 g; Sodium: 715 mg

SERVES: 6
PREP TIME: 20 minutes
COOK TIME: 1 hour

1 (4½- to 5-pound) organic chicken

1 teaspoon paprika

¼ teaspoon ground coriander

¼ teaspoon ground cinnamon

1½ teaspoons sea salt

Juice and zest of 1 orange, rind reserved

1 teaspoon grated fresh ginger, plus 1 finger-length piece of unpeeled fresh ginger, halved lengthwise

3 cloves garlic

2 cinnamon sticks

My Family's Favorite Chicken

SERVES: 4

PREP TIME: 20 minutes
(plus 30 minutes for marinating)

COOK TIME: 15 minutes

4 organic skinless, boneless chicken breast halves

2 tablespoons freshly squeezed lemon juice

1 tablespoon extra-virgin olive oil

¼ teaspoon sea salt

¼ teaspoon red pepper flakes

3 cloves garlic, minced

1 tablespoon lemon zest

1 tablespoon chopped fresh thyme, or ¼ teaspoon dried thyme

¼ cup chopped fresh parsley, for garnish

Parsley Basil Drizzle (page 187), for garnish (optional)

My Grandma Doris was a real piece of work. And, boy, did she have class! Doris was allergic to kitchens, so she used to take my brother and me out to fine restaurants whenever we visited. She loved one French restaurant in particular, always ordering chicken paillard with potato puree. It seemed so exotic, so chic, that Jeff and I always followed suit and loved it. It wasn't until I was in cooking school years later that I learned it was just a fancy name for pounded chicken with mashed potato. You gotta love the French! But it's still my favorite chicken dish, and it's great for people who are having trouble eating. That's because pounding the chicken flat makes it quick to cook and very easy to chew.

Place the chicken in several layers of parchment paper and pound each with a meat pounder until nice and thin, approximately ¼ inch thick.

Combine the lemon juice, olive oil, salt, red pepper flakes, garlic, lemon zest, and thyme and whisk until thoroughly blended. Pour the mixture over the chicken and marinate in the refrigerator for 30 minutes.

Heat a grill or grill pan to high heat. Remove the chicken from the marinade and pat each breast dry with paper towels. Grill for 1 to 2 minutes on each side, until firm to the touch or the juices run clear. Serve garnished with the parsley and the Parsley Basil Drizzle.

COOK'S NOTE: Like snowflakes, no two pieces of chicken are alike. Some will be thicker and require a little extra pounding. Don't get carried away with your mallet though, as the thinner parts of the chicken will tear if they're pounded too much. Or here's a time-saving tip: Ask the butcher to pound the chicken for you. They're usually happy to provide this service.

STORAGE: Store tightly wrapped in the refrigerator for 2 days.

PER SERVING: Calories: 170; Total Fat: 5 g (0.9 g saturated, 2.9 g monounsaturated); Carbohydrates: 2 g; Protein: 28 g; Fiber: 0 g; Sodium: 225 mg

Tuscan Farro and Bean Salad

Here's a great example of what I call culinary architecture, which entails building on a great foundation. In this case, I'm playing off what Middle Easterners call tabouli, a wonderful salad with a fantastic fresh taste that's incredibly easy to make (and impossible to mess up). The base of any tabouli is a grain, lemon juice, parsley, and mint. Then we add the ornamentation, which emphasizes form and function. The beans create a complete protein, the bell pepper offers up a pleasing crunch and a whole bunch of antioxidants, while olives add a little healthy salt. Like any powerful piece of architecture, it's the combination of simplicity and tasteful elegance that makes this salad so enjoyable and memorable.

Put the beans, farro, bell pepper, olives, parsley, mint, lemon zest, lemon juice, olive oil, and salt in a large bowl and stir until thoroughly combined. Chill for 1 hour. Before serving, taste; you may need to add another pinch of salt or a dash of lemon juice. Serve with the feta cheese sprinkled over the top.

COOK'S NOTE: This is a particularly nice vegetarian dish that provides complete protein while also being high in fiber and low in fat. Because of the low fat and high fiber content, it would appeal to breast and prostate cancer patients.

You can certainly substitute canned beans in this recipe. Use about half of a 15-ounce can and, as usual, drain and rinse, then refresh the beans with a spritz of fresh lemon juice and a pinch of sea salt.

STORAGE: Store in an airtight container in the refrigerator for 5 to 7 days.

PER SERVING: Calories: 255; Total Fat: 11.1 g (1.6 g saturated, 7.9 g mono-unsaturated); Carbohydrates: 32 g; Protein: 8 g; Fiber: 6 g; Sodium: 580 mg

SERVES: 6
PREP TIME: 15 minutes
COOK TIME: Not applicable

1 cup cooked cannellini beans

2 cups Simple Tuscan Farro (page 147)

¼ cup finely diced red bell pepper

3 tablespoons pitted Kalamata olives, rinsed and sliced thin

1 cup finely chopped and loosely packed fresh flat-leaf parsley

1 cup finely chopped and loosely packed fresh mint

Zest of 1 lemon

¼ cup freshly squeezed lemon juice

¼ cup extra-virgin olive oil

½ teaspoon sea salt

2 ounces organic feta cheese, crumbled (optional)

Middle Eastern Chickpea Burgers

MAKES: 17 patties
PREP TIME: 15 minutes
COOK TIME: 25 minutes

2 cups cooked chickpeas, or
1 (15-ounce) can, drained, rinsed,
and mixed with a spritz of fresh
lemon juice and a pinch of
sea salt

½ teaspoon sea salt

½ teaspoon turmeric

½ teaspoon paprika

¼ teaspoon ground cumin

¼ teaspoon ground coriander

⅛ teaspoon ground cinnamon

2 teaspoons minced garlic

1 teaspoon minced fresh ginger

1 organic egg, beaten

3 tablespoons extra-virgin
olive oil

2 tablespoons freshly squeezed
lemon juice

2½ cups cooked brown
basmati rice

3 tablespoons finely diced
red bell pepper

¼ cup loosely packed minced
fresh flat-leaf parsley

These chickpea burgers are similar to a Middle Eastern falafel. This isn't like the Americanized version of falafel that resembles carnival food deep-fried in some unhealthy oil. That's a culinary crime, because falafel done right is so delicious and nutritious. It's all in the blend. Here the secret ingredient is basmati rice, which holds the chickpea mixture together and creates a complete protein. I love the mini-burger concept; the whole wheat bun is like putting falafel in a top hat and tails, perfect for folks who like the taste of beans when they're broken down and combined with heady herbs and spices. Gently pan-seared or baked, these burgers are bountiful bites of health, especially topped with a dollop of Tomato Mint Chutney (page 173).

Preheat the oven to 375°F and line a baking sheet with parchment paper.

Combine the chickpeas, salt, turmeric, paprika, cumin, coriander, cinnamon, garlic, ginger, egg, olive oil, and lemon juice in a food processor and process until smooth and well combined, scraping the sides occasionally. Transfer the mixture to a bowl and fold in the rice, bell pepper, and parsley.

Moisten your hands to keep the mixture from sticking, then shape the mixture into ¼-inch-thick patties about 2½ inches in diameter. Place them on the prepared pan and bake for 22 to 25 minutes, until the patties start to get dry and crisp on the outside. They will firm up as they cool.

VARIATIONS: For a crispy burger, heat 2 teaspoons of olive oil in a skillet over medium heat and cook the patties for about 3 minutes on each side, until golden brown. For a vegan burger, substitute 1 tablespoon tahini for the egg.

COOK'S NOTE: If you want to cook just a few patties, pop them in your toaster oven. To freeze these burgers, either cooked or uncooked, stack them up with parchment paper between the burgers, then wrap first in plastic wrap, then in foil. The parchment paper makes it easy to remove the desired number of burgers from the bundle. Once thawed, cooked burgers can be reheated at 350°F for 15 minutes, and uncooked burgers can be baked as directed here, at 375°F for 22 to 25 minutes.

STORAGE: Store in a covered container in the refrigerator for 3 to 5 days. Burgers can also be frozen in cooked or uncooked form for 2 months (see Cook's Note).

PER SERVING: Calories: 100; Total Fat: 3.5 g (0.5 g saturated, 2 g mono-unsaturated); Carbohydrates: 15 g; Protein: 3 g; Fiber: 3 g; Sodium: 223 mg

Lemon Mustard Salmon Salad

All salmon are not created equal. This recipe features wild Alaskan sockeye. Wild salmon are far higher in omega-3s than their farm-raised brethren, and omega-3s have been linked to a host of cancer-fighting benefits. You don't even have to go fishing or handle a salmon fillet to make this dish; there are great brands of wild sockeye that come in cans (see Resources). That said, you can also make this with an equal amount of leftover home-cooked salmon. Either way, this salad is easy to prepare: all it takes is a quick stir with a few choice ingredients, and there you go—a nice, filling dish that's rich in protein, yummy, and versatile. Serve it in a pita, wrap it in a tortilla, or pile it atop salad greens.

Put the salmon in a bowl and break it into small pieces with a fork. Stir in the mustard, lemon juice, olive oil, cayenne, salt, celery, and parsley, then taste. If needed, adjust the flavors with lemon juice and a pinch of salt before serving.

VARIATIONS: Add capers or chopped radishes to this dish—they will not disappoint!

Or combine just the salmon and celery with 2 tablespoons of Basil Lemon Drizzle (page 175) or 1 tablespoon of Moroccan Pesto (page 186); both are great dressings to try with this salmon recipe.

STORAGE: Store in an airtight container in the refrigerator for 2 days.

PER SERVING: Calories: 180; Total Fat: 8.5 g (0.7 g saturated, 3.4 g monounsaturated); Carbohydrates: 1 g; Protein: 27 g; Fiber: 0 g; Sodium: 670 mg

SERVES: 2
PREP TIME: 5 minutes
COOK TIME: Not applicable

1 (7½-ounce) can boneless, skinless, sockeye salmon, drained, or leftover Poached Salmon with Moroccan Pesto (page 116)

3 teaspoons Dijon mustard

2 teaspoons freshly squeezed lemon juice

2 teaspoons extra-virgin olive oil

Pinch of cayenne

Pinch of sea salt

3 tablespoons finely chopped celery

2 tablespoons finely chopped fresh flat-leaf parsley

Poached Salmon with Moroccan Pesto

SERVES: 4

PREP TIME: 10 minutes

COOK TIME: 20 minutes
(plus 20 minutes to marinate)

Juice of 1 lemon

½ teaspoon sea salt

4 (4-ounce) salmon fillets,
pin bones removed

4 cups Magic Mineral Broth
(page 49)

Moroccan Pesto (page 186),
for serving

I like to pan-sear or broil salmon, but poaching is a great way to enjoy a fillet without having to endure a lot of the cooking smells. Most people associate poaching with eggs, and the concept is the same here. By briefly dunking the fillet in a simmering liquid, it quickly becomes moist and tender. Poaching isn't boiling, and thank goodness, because that kind of long immersion is a sure way to give fish the consistency of a hockey puck. Here, the poaching liquid is Magic Mineral Broth, which infuses the salmon with even more nutrients—and more yum. Moroccan Pesto is a snazzy topping for this dish, but the possibilities are endless. See the variations for a few more suggestions.

Stir the lemon juice and salt together, then add the salmon and turn to coat thoroughly. Marinate in the refrigerator for 20 minutes.

In a large straight-sided sauté pan or a low-sided pot just wide enough to hold the salmon in a single layer, bring the broth to a slow boil over medium heat. Slide the salmon into the broth and poach for 7 to 9 minutes, just until the fish is tender and an instant-read thermometer inserted into the center of each fillet registers 127°F.

Garnish each with a generous dollop of Moroccan Pesto and serve immediately.

VARIATIONS: There are many toppings you can dollop on poached salmon, including Basil Lemon Drizzle (page 175), Olive and Caper Relish (page 185), and Parsley Basil Drizzle (page 187).

COOK'S NOTE: Usually it's best to buy your fish the same day you're preparing it. However, life doesn't always work that way. If you must store the fish longer, put it in a resealable plastic bag in the coldest part of your refrigerator, which is usually the back of the bottom shelf. It should hold for an extra two days. Put a note on the fridge to remind you that the fish is there. You know that old saying: "Out of sight, out of mind."

STORAGE: Store in an airtight container in the refrigerator for 2 days.

PER SERVING: Calories: 245; Total Fat: 10.9 g (1.7 g saturated, 4.9 g monounsaturated); Carbohydrates: 12 g; Protein: 24 g; Fiber: 2 g; Sodium: 530 mg

Triple-Citrus Ginger Black Cod

Black cod is chock-full of anti-inflammatory omega-3 fatty acids, which makes it a very forgiving fish that retains its moisture when cooked. If it were in a band, it would be the bass player—steady, meaty, but not much of a soloist. It benefits from some jazzy front men and especially likes to swing with citrus high notes. You'll find plenty of those riffs in this dish. You can substitute wild salmon, halibut, or sea bass for the black cod with excellent results.

In a small bowl or glass measuring cup, whisk together the orange juice, lime juice, lemon juice, olive oil, orange zest, lemon zest, ginger, and cayenne. Place the cod in a baking dish and season each piece with ⅛ teaspoon of the salt. Pour half of the orange juice mixture over the cod and turn to coat well. Cover and marinate in the refrigerator for 30 minutes.

Preheat the oven to 400°F.

Remove the cod from the refrigerator, uncover, and add 2 tablespoons of water to the bottom of the dish. Bake just until the fillets are tender and an instant-read thermometer inserted into the center of each fillet registers 137°F; this will take 10 to 15 minutes, depending on the thickness of the fillets.

Meanwhile, combine the remaining orange juice mixture and the mustard in a small saucepan over medium heat and simmer until the liquid is reduced by half. Pour the reduction over the fillets, sprinkle with the parsley, and serve immediately.

COOK'S NOTE: Shopping for fish can be a bit harrowing. Maybe it's the fact that half of them are staring at you from behind the counter, as if to say, "Jeez, how did I end up here?" So, if you're going to do them—and yourself—justice, here's how to rustle up a fine, fresh fillet. Use your eyes and nose. Look for a cut with moist, glistening flesh, with no flat, brown edges. If the fish looks dull, give it a pass. Same goes for any fillet with a fishy or ammonia smell. Don't be shy about asking your fishmonger a few questions, like when the fish came in and from where. Most stores have regular shipments; knowing that schedule in advance can help you plan when to have fish.

STORAGE: Store tightly wrapped in an airtight container in the refrigerator for 1 to 2 days.

PER SERVING: Calories: 130; Total Fat: 4.3 g (0.7 g saturated, 2.6 g monounsaturated); Carbohydrates: 5 g; Protein: 18 g; Fiber: 0 g; Sodium: 370 mg

---

SERVES: 4
PREP TIME: 15 minutes
COOK TIME: 20 minutes
(plus 30 minutes to marinate)

½ cup freshly squeezed orange juice

2 tablespoons freshly squeezed lime juice

2 tablespoons freshly squeezed lemon juice

1 tablespoon extra-virgin olive oil

Zest of 1 orange

Zest of 1 lemon

½ teaspoon minced fresh ginger

Pinch of cayenne

4 (3.5-ounce) black cod fillets, pin bones removed

½ teaspoon sea salt

1 teaspoon Dijon mustard

¼ cup coarsely chopped fresh flat-leaf parsley or mint

Baked Citrus Halibut with Signora's Tomato Sauce

SERVES: 4

PREP TIME: 25 minutes (including marinating)

COOK TIME: 15 minutes

---

2 tablespoons freshly squeezed lemon juice

¼ teaspoon sea salt

4 (6-ounce) halibut fillets

1 teaspoon extra-virgin olive oil

1 cup Signora's Tomato Sauce (page 189)

¼ cup Olive and Caper Relish (page 185)

Sometimes creating a recipe is like trying to solve a Rubik's Cube. You twist it this way and that and get real close to figuring it out, only to realize you're not quite there yet. Such was the case here. Halibut is a great fish for health, but left to its own devices it can be rather bland. So I toyed, I tinkered, and I went through more fish than Shamu until—*hallelujah!*—I got it right. If you aren't in the mood for this southern Italian version, try the south-of-the border variation.

Preheat the oven to 400°F and lightly oil an ovenproof pan large enough to accommodate all of the fillets in a single layer.

Stir the lemon juice and salt together, then coat the halibut in the mixture and refrigerate for 15 minutes.

Pat the fillets dry with paper towels and place them in the prepared pan. Brush each fillet with ¼ teaspoon of the olive oil and top with ¼ cup of the tomato sauce.

Bake for 12 to 15 minutes, until the fish is opaque and flakes easily. To be certain the fish is done, push a two-pronged kitchen fork straight down into the flesh. If you feel no resistance, the fish is cooked; if not, return the fish to the oven for another minute or two.

Top each fillet with 1 tablespoon of the relish before serving.

VARIATION: For a totally different taste sensation, marinate the halibut in Cilantro Lime Vinaigrette (page 180) for 30 minutes. Pat the fillets dry with paper towels. Sprinkle each fillet with a pinch of salt and a pinch of cayenne, and bake as directed.

STORAGE: Store in an airtight container in the refrigerator for 2 days.

PER SERVING: Calories: 380; Total Fat: 28 g (4.7 g saturated, 17.4 g mono-unsaturated); Carbohydrates: 5 g; Protein: 26 g; Fiber: 1 g; Sodium: 450 mg

Turkey Patties with Apple and Arugula

Why a pattie and not a burger? You can shape these into a poultry puck if you like, but they're ideal in bite-size proportions. They're perfect for steak-and-egg types who prefer a morning protein rush. Apple—which is commonly added to sausage links—adds a pleasant, sweet taste that isn't overpowering. These are fast and simple to make and store well in the freezer.

In a large bowl, combine the turkey, arugula, apple, onion, fennel seeds, cumin, salt, pepper, and lemon juice and mix well. Form into desired sizes of patties.

To grill, preheat a grill pan and brush with oil. Grill the patties over medium heat until browned on both sides. Continue grilling until cooked through. Or, in a sauté pan, add just enough oil to coat a hot pan. Sauté over medium heat for about 4 minutes on each side, until brown, then add a tablespoon of water and cover to steam until cooked through.

Serve as a burger in a bun, with breakfast, or take for lunch.

COOK NOTE: When mixing the turkey with other ingredients, use a light hand. If you over work the turkey, the patties will be tough.

STORAGE: Store in an airtight container in the refrigerator for 3 days or individually wrapped in the freezer for 3 months.

PER SERVING: Calories: 160; Total Fat: 3 g (1 g saturated, 2 g mono-unsaturated); Carbohydrates: 3 g; Protein: 23 g; Fiber: 0 g; Sodium: 245 mg

SERVES: 6
PREP TIME: 15 minutes
COOK TIME: 10 minutes

1½ pounds ground dark-meat organic turkey

1 cup tightly packed arugula or spinach leaves, finely chopped

1 cup peeled, diced apple

½ cup finely chopped red onion

1 teaspoon crushed fennel seeds

½ teaspoon ground cumin

½ teaspoon sea salt

½ teaspoon freshly ground pepper

Spritz of fresh lemon juice

Olive oil to coat the pan or grill

Chapter 5

Anytime Foods

People pride themselves on eating at regular intervals, like clockwork, but dealing with cancer often disrupts that timing. The disease and/or treatments can depress appetite by making eating or digestion difficult, or because the brain's hunger center becomes impaired. Also, many common chemotherapies and steroids take the blood sugar on a roller-coaster ride, further throwing off normal eating patterns. Those three square large meals you're used to? Well, they're possible, but as often as not, you'll need to get your nutrition *whenever* you're hungry. That's regardless of the hour, or whether you just ate a half hour ago.

That's why these anytime foods are so important: whenever a craving hits, these desirable morsels are ready to eat, easily accessible, and nutrient dense. Ounce for ounce, there are no wasted calories here; every bite carries a flood of macronutrients to get you through the day. Remember the story of the tortoise and the hare? Mr. Slow and Steady had the right idea: a small but consistent effort at eating can have wonderful cumulative effects. Ideally, you're shooting to get in six small meals or snacks a day. That's best accomplished by concentrating on how *often* you eat, rather than how *much*. The goal is to stay nourished throughout the day, which is the purpose of these recipes. They're designed to be portable and storable—and, of course, they'll blow your mind with their taste.

Somewhere in this wide array of anytime foods, I hope you'll discover a few that remind you of your favorite snacks. Dips, salads, wraps—they're all designed to provide long-lasting energy with each bite. For example, toasted nuts are really a no-brainer, tiny taste sensations requiring just a little prep. You can eat them straight or use them as a topping for salads, oatmeal, and other dishes. Either way, they'll provide extra nutrition and a big dose of yum. They're also the perfect snack anytime you're on the road. And speaking of portable, at the end of the chapter you'll find two recipes that I like to think of as "wrap, roll, and carry." These easy and delicious mobile meals are packed with protein.

In a very real sense, these anytime foods allow you to engage in high-performance eating, just like athletes or hikers who eat high-energy foods with a sense of purpose. By noshing throughout the day, you're providing your body with the nutrients it needs to stay strong!

Anytime Bars

You never know when hunger will strike, but when it does, take advantage of those moments to nourish yourself. That's the whole idea behind these Anytime Bars. My clients often take these portable packets of pleasure to chemo sessions. Many people actually want to eat during a treatment, and these bars are delicious, healthy alternatives to the bowls of sweets often found around infusion centers. You can change the ingredients in this recipe to fit your taste preferences. Split the batter and make half with currant and cranberries and the other half with walnuts or whatever you'd like. These bars come together very quickly with a food processor, but if you don't have one, hand-chopping the fruit and nuts works well.

Preheat the oven to 350°F and line a baking sheet with parchment paper. Lightly oil a 9-inch square pan.

Spread the pecans in a single layer on the prepared baking sheet and toast for 7 to 10 minutes, until aromatic and slightly browned. Watch them carefully, as they can burn easily. Repeat this process for the almonds. Turn down the oven to 325°F.

Combine the flour, flaxseeds, salt, baking powder, and baking soda in a food processor and process for 5 seconds to combine. Add the pecans and almonds and pulse 5 times to coarsely chop the nuts. Add the oats, dates, and apricots and pulse 10 to 15 times, until the mixture is well chopped but still coarse.

In a large bowl, whisk the egg, maple syrup, and vanilla together until thoroughly combined. Add the fruit and nut mixture and use your hands to mix thoroughly, being sure to separate any clumps of fruit. Spread the mixture in the oiled baking pan in an even layer and bake for 25 to 30 minutes, until set and golden brown; don't overbake, or the bars will be too dry. Let cool on a wire rack for 5 minutes, then cut into 25 squares. Leave the bars in the pan until completely cool so they'll hold together when you remove them.

continued

MAKES: 25 bars
PREP TIME: 15 minutes
COOK TIME: 30 minutes

1 cup raw pecan halves

1 cup whole raw almonds

4 tablespoons brown rice flour or gluten-free flour mix, or coconut flour

2 tablespoons finely ground flaxseeds

¼ teaspoon sea salt

⅛ teaspoon baking powder

⅛ teaspoon baking soda

¼ cup old-fashioned rolled oats

1 cup pitted dates (preferably Medjool), quartered

1 cup unsulfured dried apricots, cut in half

1 organic egg

5 tablespoons maple syrup

1 teaspoon vanilla extract

Anytime Bars, *continued*

VARIATIONS: When it comes to changing up the mixture, the only limit is your imagination. Here are a few ideas to get you started:

- Use walnuts instead of pecans.

- Add ¼ cup dried cranberries, cherries, blueberries, raisins, or currants when mixing together at the end.

- Add 1 tablespoon of grated orange zest when mixing together at the end.

- Add 2 tablespoons of sesame seeds when mixing together at the end.

- Add ¼ cup of unsweetened shredded coconut when mixing together at the end.

COOK'S NOTE: While oats don't contain gluten, they're often processed alongside wheat, so if your sensitivity to gluten is extreme, be sure to use Bob's Red Mill gluten-free oats (see Resources, page 211).

STORAGE: Store in an airtight container at room temperature for 5 to 7 days or in the freezer for 2 months.

PER SERVING: Calories: 120; Total Fat: 6.5 g (0.6 g saturated, 3.7 g monounsaturated); Carbohydrates: 14 g; Protein: 2 g; Fiber: 2 g; Sodium: 35 mg

Beyond Just Good Cornbread

Cornbread is a food that lends itself to passionate opinions, as in, "Nobody makes cornbread as good as my [momma, grammy, Uncle Algernon . . . fill in the blank]." Not only that, but once someone gets a beloved piece of that cornbread in their hands, well, as one writer said, "If you try to take my cornbread, there will be consequences and repercussions." I think of cornbread as a bit like barbecue: Nearly every region of the country has its variation, which, as if ordained from above, is simply the best. Cornbread, cornpone, johnnycakes, hush puppies—the names and approaches differ, but not the devotion. My version is California-style, as in we keep all of that awesome taste while using healthier ingredients. Some spelt flour helps, as does just a bit of organic maple syrup as a sweetener and extra-virgin olive oil in place of butter. The lemon zest allowed me to put the word "beyond" into the title of this recipe. If you'll allow me to play yenta, I'd match the cornbread with Rockin' Black Bean Soup (page 63). They make for a very happy couple.

Preheat the oven to 400°F and lightly oil an 8-inch square baking pan.

Combine the cornmeal, flours, baking powder, baking soda, and salt and stir with a wire whisk until well combined.

In a small bowl, whisk together the egg, buttermilk, maple syrup, olive oil, and lemon zest until well combined, then pour into the dry ingredients and whisk just until the batter is evenly moistened and no large lumps remain; don't overmix, or the cornbread will be tough and dry.

Scrape the batter into the prepared pan and bake until lightly browned and just beginning to pull away from the edges of the pan, 20 to 25 minutes. Let cool on a wire rack for about 10 minutes, then cut into 16 squares and serve warm.

COOK'S NOTES: Cornbread is one of those foods that's best served warm, so when you pull leftovers out of the fridge, warm them in an oven or toaster oven.

STORAGE: Store tightly wrapped in the refrigerator for 4 days or in the freezer for 2 months.

PER SERVING: Calories: 115; Total Fat: 5 g (1 g saturated, 3 g mono-unsaturated); Carbohydrates: 16 g; Protein: 3 g; Fiber: 2 g; Sodium: 200 mg

MAKES: 16 pieces
PREP TIME: 10 minutes
COOK TIME: 30 minutes

1 cup cornmeal

½ cup spelt flour

½ cup whole wheat flour

2 teaspoons baking powder

½ teaspoon baking soda

½ teaspoon sea salt

1 organic egg

1 cup organic buttermilk

¼ cup maple syrup

¼ cup extra-virgin olive oil

1 tablespoon lemon zest

Best Oatmeal Ever

SERVES: 2

PREP TIME: 5 minutes (after soaking the oats overnight)

COOK TIME: 15 minutes

1 cup rolled or steel-cut oats

1½ tablespoons freshly squeezed lemon juice

¼ teaspoon sea salt

½ teaspoon ground cinnamon

¼ teaspoon ground ginger, or 1 teaspoon grated fresh ginger

⅛ teaspoon ground cardamom

1 teaspoon maple syrup

¼ cup almond milk (optional)

Chopped toasted almonds or walnuts (see page 93), for garnish (optional)

Blueberry Compote (page 182), Dried Fruit Compote (page 183), or Seasonal Stewed Fruit (page 184), for garnish (optional)

Ever notice how the consistency of most oatmeal falls somewhere between wall plaster and grout? As a result, we often resort to the culinary equivalent of wallpapering, covering up the abomination with butter and brown sugar. This is sooooo unnecessary, because oatmeal just needs a little love to deliver a heartwarming, nutritious meal. The best oatmeal recipe is akin to a two-part harmony, pairing solid prep with inspiring spices to yield a joyous anytime song. Part of the trick is to soak the oats overnight. Top this with fruit compote or nuts, and you'll never again be tempted to use oatmeal as an all-purpose adhesive.

Place the oats in a pan or bowl with the lemon juice and water to cover and soak overnight.

Drain the oats in a fine-mesh sieve and rinse well under cold running water. Combine the oats, 2 cups water, and salt in a saucepan and bring to a boil over medium-high heat. Lower the heat, stir in the cinnamon, ginger, and cardamom, and cover. Continue cooking, stirring occasionally, for 10 minutes. The oatmeal will become very creamy as the water evaporates. For less-moist oatmeal, leave the lid off for the last 3 to 4 minutes of cooking. Stir in the maple syrup and almond milk and serve garnished with toasted nuts or a dollop of compote if you like.

COOK'S NOTE: Our ancestors had it right. Before they cooked their oatmeal, they soaked it overnight in a bowl of water and lemon juice. Why lemon juice? Because its acids help break down the outer shell of the oats. This makes their nutrients more available and also gives them a creamier texture. For the best taste and nutrition, go with organic rolled oats or organic steel-cut oats, which are popular in Ireland and Scotland. For extra calories, add a tablespoon of extra-virgin coconut oil or nut butter.

STORAGE: Store in an airtight container in the refrigerator for 3 days.

PER SERVING: Calories: 220; Total Fat: 2.7 g (0 g saturated, 0 g mono-unsaturated); Carbohydrates: 42 g; Protein: 7 g; Fiber: 5 g; Sodium: 295 mg

Black Bean Hummus

Navy Bean and
Sun-Dried Tomato Dip

Cannellini Bean Dip
with Kalamata Olives

Curried Hummus

Edamame Avocado Dip
with Wasabi

Edamame Avocado Dip with Wasabi

Wasabi is rich in chemicals that research suggests may keep certain cancer cells from replicating. The combination of wasabi and ginger might be a bit much for those with swallowing difficulties, but for everyone else this concoction's creamy coolness makes it perfect for slathering on rice crackers or as a dip for vegetables, especially jicama.

Combine all of the ingredients in a food processor. Process until smooth; taste. Add additional lime juice or salt if needed before serving.

COOK'S NOTE: If you're up for it, go the extra mile and add some additional heat! Another ¼ teaspoon of wasabi powder will turn up the wow factor in this dip. This gorgeous dip is very versatile. Use it like a condiment, spread on sandwiches or wraps. Yum!

STORAGE: Store in an airtight container in the refrigerator for 2 days.

PER SERVING: Calories: 130; Total Fat: 10.3 g (1.3 g saturated, 6.1 g mono-unsaturated); Carbohydrates: 8 g; Protein: 4 g; Fiber: 5 g; Sodium: 115 mg

SERVES: 6
PREP TIME: 10 minutes
COOK TIME: Not applicable

1 cup fresh or frozen shelled edamame, mixed with a spritz of fresh lime juice and a pinch of sea salt

2 avocados, peeled, pitted, and spritzed with fresh lime juice and a pinch of salt

1 tablespoon minced fresh ginger

½ teaspoon minced garlic

¼ cup water

4 tablespoons freshly squeezed lime juice

1 tablespoon extra-virgin olive oil

¾ teaspoon salt

2 teaspoons wasabi powder

1 tablespoon chopped fresh mint

Cannellini Bean Dip with Kalamata Olives

The creamy white beans provide a nutritious canvas that blends well with the purplish black kalamatas. The beans are high in protein, which keeps the body in fighting shape during treatment.

Combine all of the ingredients in a food processor and process until smooth. Do a FASS check before serving and add a pinch or two of salt if needed to balance out the lemon.

STORAGE: Store in an airtight container in the refrigerator for 5 days.

PER SERVING: Calories: 195; Total Fat: 8.5 g (1.2 g saturated, 6.1 g mono-unsaturated); Carbohydrates: 22 g; Protein: 8 g; Fiber: 6 g; Sodium: 715 mg

SERVES: 6
PREP TIME: 10 minutes
COOK TIME: Not applicable

2 cups cooked cannellini beans or 1 (15-ounce) can, drained, rinsed, and mixed with a spritz of fresh lemon juice and a pinch of sea salt

½ teaspoon minced garlic

3 tablespoons extra-virgin olive oil

2 tablespoons water

2 tablespoons freshly squeezed lemon juice

½ teaspoon sea salt

Pinch of cayenne

¼ cup pitted Kalamata olives, rinsed

¼ cup chopped fresh basil

Navy Bean and Sun-Dried Tomato Dip

2 cups cooked navy beans, or 1 (15-ounce) can, drained, rinsed, and mixed with a spritz of fresh lemon juice and a pinch of sea salt

¼ cup oil-packed sun-dried tomatoes, rinsed

¼ cup chopped fresh parsley

½ teaspoon minced garlic

3 tablespoons extra-virgin olive oil

2 tablespoons freshly squeezed lemon juice

2 tablespoons water

½ teaspoon sea salt

The creaminess of navy beans makes a great base for spreads and dips, which I've supercharged by adding sun-dried tomatoes. Use it as a sandwich spread or a dollop on veggies.

Combine all of the ingredients in a food processor and process until smooth. Do a FASS check before serving, and add another spritz of lemon juice or a pinch of salt if needed.

STORAGE: Store in an airtight container in the refrigerator for 5 to 7 days.

PER SERVING: Calories: 195; Total Fat: 8.2 g (1.1 g saturated, 5.5 g monounsaturated); Carbohydrates: 24 g; Protein: 8 g; Fiber: 9 g; Sodium: 635 mg

Black Bean Hummus

2 cups cooked black beans, or 1 (15-ounce) can, drained, rinsed, and mixed with a spritz of fresh lemon juice and a pinch of sea salt

½ teaspoon chopped garlic

2 tablespoons water

1 tablespoon tahini

1 tablespoon freshly squeezed lemon juice

½ teaspoon ground cumin

¼ teaspoon sea salt

¼ teaspoon paprika

⅛ teaspoon cayenne

⅛ teaspoon ground cinnamon

1 tablespoon extra-virgin olive oil

¼ cup finely chopped fresh cilantro (optional)

I used black beans in this recipe because I love their taste and nutritional profile—lots of antioxidants. Pureeing the beans makes them more digestible.

Combine the beans, garlic, water, tahini, lemon juice, cumin, salt, paprika, cayenne, and cinnamon in a food processor and process until smooth. Add the olive oil and process to combine. Do a FASS check and add a spritz of lemon and an additional pinch of salt if needed. Serve garnished with the cilantro, if desired.

COOK'S NOTE: If you really want to put this dip over the top, place a dollop of Avocado Cream (page 177) on top, or for a quick fix, a few slices of avocado will do.

STORAGE: Store in an airtight container in the refrigerator for 5 days.

PER SERVING: Calories: 145; Total Fat: 4 g (1 g saturated, 3 g monounsaturated); Carbohydrates: 21 g; Protein: 7 g; Fiber: 9 g; Sodium: 525 mg

Curried Hummus

Sometimes I feel like the United Nations is meeting in my kitchen. This time around it's Sri Lanka, India, and Lebanon at the table. It sounds exotic, but this is really just a nice, simple hummus (that's the Lebanese part) with a zingy curry buzz (hello, India). Chickpeas are rich in protein and essential amino acids for keeping the body strong, while the tahini's sesame seeds have high levels of anticancer phytochemicals. The seeds are ground into a paste that's easy to digest.

Place the currants in a small bowl of hot water to soak and plump up. Combine the chickpeas, water, lemon juice, tahini, olive oil, curry powder, ginger, and salt in a food processor and process until smooth. Transfer to a mixing bowl and do a FASS check. Add a spritz of lemon if it needs a little extra zing.

Before serving, drain the currants thoroughly and stir them into the hummus.

COOK'S NOTE: For a time-saving trick, buy a 16-ounce container of premade organic hummus at the market and add curry powder, ginger, lemon juice, and currants, as directed. This is a wonderful way to spice up a store-bought snack.

STORAGE: Store in an airtight container in the refrigerator for 5 to 7 days.

PER SERVING: Calories: 180; Total Fat: 5.7 g (0.7 g saturated, 2.6 g mono-unsaturated); Carbohydrates: 27 g; Protein: 7 g; Fiber: 7 g; Sodium: 630 mg

SERVES: 6
PREP TIME: 10 minutes
COOK TIME: Not applicable

¼ cup currants

2 cups cooked chickpeas, or 1 (15-ounce) can, drained, rinsed, and mixed with a spritz of fresh lemon juice and a pinch of sea salt

2 tablespoons water

2 tablespoons freshly squeezed lemon juice

1 tablespoon tahini

1 tablespoon extra-virgin olive oil

1 teaspoon curry powder

1 teaspoon ground ginger

½ teaspoon sea salt

Creamy Polenta

SERVES: 6

PREP TIME: 5 minutes

COOK TIME: 15 minutes

4 cups Magic Mineral Broth (page 49), Chicken Magic Mineral Broth (page 50), or store-bought organic stock

½ teaspoon sea salt

Spritz of fresh lemon juice

1 cup polenta

2 tablespoons extra-virgin olive oil

¼ cup grated organic Parmesan cheese (optional)

Polenta is the frequent flier of the cornmeal set. Just about anywhere there's an airport, you're likely to find some version of this staple. Hungarians call it *puliszka*, the Turks *mamalika*, and us Americans—well, we just say, "Grits, please." Polenta amiably morphs itself into many dishes. I've seen it prepared with tomato sauce, different cheeses, various oils, garlicky greens, you name it. This version is somewhat similar to oatmeal (think thin oatmeal, not the stuff that doubles as spackle) using Magic Mineral Broth to add taste and nutritional value far beyond that of water.

Bring the broth to a boil in a saucepan over high heat. Stir in the salt and lemon juice, then very slowly add the polenta in a steady stream, whisking all the while. Immediately decrease the heat to low, switch to a wooden spoon, and stir until smooth. Add the olive oil and stir constantly for about 15 minutes. Stir in the cheese, if desired, and serve immediately.

VARIATIONS: Top your polenta with a serving of Emerald Greens with Orange (page 78), Signora's Tomato Sauce (page 189), simple poached eggs (see page 103), or Basil Lemon Drizzle (page 175).

You can also use Creamy Polenta for a breakfast cereal. Use water in place of the broth, omit the cheese, and add ½ teaspoon of maple syrup toward the end. Top with Blueberry Compote (page 182) and Maple-Glazed Walnuts (page 137).

Make polenta rounds. Pour the polenta onto a sheet pan and allow it to cool and firm up. Once the polenta is firm, cut it into rounds using a cookie cutter or a glass. Try using polenta rounds instead of toast with a poached egg, or for a nosh with your favorite dollop.

COOK'S NOTE: For easy polenta cleanup, use cold water to clean the pan, as warm or hot water will make a sticky mush.

STORAGE: Store in an airtight container in the refrigerator for 4 days. Polenta circles can be wrapped and frozen in a resealable plastic bag for 1 month.

PER SERVING: Calories: 190; Total Fat: 7 g (1.4 g saturated, 3.3 g mono-unsaturated); Carbohydrates: 28 g; Protein: 4 g; Fiber: 3 g; Sodium: 535 mg

Coconut Ginger Lime Rice with Cilantro

The American Institute for Cancer Research loves brown rice. In fact, they just named it as one of their go-to grains for fighting cancer. But let's face it: brown rice needs a little kitchen love to excite the taste buds. Here it gets that with some fantastic costars. Ginger and lime add super high notes and great anti-inflammatory properties, while coconut milk bathes the rice in all its enticing glory. Coconut milk has an antiviral fat, lauric acid, that's found in mother's milk. It's also high in selenium, a mineral shown to lower chemotherapy side effects including hair loss and abdominal pain in ovarian cancer patients.

SERVES: 6

PREP TIME: 5 minutes

COOK TIME: 20 to 25 minutes

1 (15.5-ounce) can coconut milk

1¼ cups water

½ teaspoon sea salt

1 inch unpeeled fresh ginger, thinly sliced into rounds

1 cup brown jasmine or basmati rice, rinsed until the water runs clear

2 teaspoons freshly squeezed lime juice

¼ cup coarsely chopped fresh cilantro or mint

In a pot with a tight-fitting lid, combine the coconut milk, water, and salt. Smash the ginger pieces with the flat side of your knife to release their flavor, then add them to the pot. Bring to a rolling boil over medium heat. Add the rice and stir well. Return the water to a boil, cover, and decrease the heat to low. Simmer for 20 to 25 minutes, or until the water is fully absorbed and there are steam holes on the top. Uncover and remove and discard the ginger. Add the lime juice and herbs and gently toss with a fork. Taste; you may want to add another squeeze of lime juice or another pinch of salt, before serving.

COOK'S NOTES: If you want to make the brown rice easier to digest, soak the grain in cool water and the juice of half a lemon for 8 hours or overnight before cooking; this will make its nutrients more available and decrease the cooking time. If you don't have time to soak the rice, add an extra ¼ cup of liquid and cook for an additional 15 minutes.

This recipe will work in a pressure cooker or rice cooker, and it is easy to double so you have leftovers. Use a 15.5-ounce can of coconut milk and adjust the quantity of water and the remaining ingredients.

STORAGE: Store in an airtight container in the refrigerator for 3 days.

PER SERVING: Calories: 165; Total Fat: 6 g (5 g saturated, 0 g mono-unsaturated); Carbohydrates: 24 g; Protein: 3 g; Fiber: 1 g; Sodium: 396 mg

Spiced Toasted
Almonds

Maple-Glazed Walnuts

Maple-Glazed Walnuts

In Celtic folklore, the walnut tree—and the nuts that fall from it—are associated with an unrelenting passion for life's challenges. Maybe that's why I'm so crazy for this treat. Or maybe it's because I love crunchy maple goodies. Someone laughingly said to me that these delicious nuts are like peanut brittle without the chewy toffee epoxy. I'll vouch that these are a delight for lovers of crispy snacks. Plus, walnuts are high in omega-3s and heart-healthy, and they may help slow memory loss. Eat these straight up or sprinkled on cereal, salad, or anything you like for extra flavor and crunch.

MAKES: ½ cup
PREP TIME: 5 minutes
COOK TIME: 10 minutes

½ cup raw walnuts

2 teaspoons maple syrup

Pinch of salt

Pinch of cayenne

Preheat the oven to 350°F and line a sheet pan with parchment paper.

Toss the walnuts with the maple syrup, salt, and cayenne until evenly coated, then spread them evenly on the prepared sheet pan. Bake for 7 to 10 minutes, until aromatic and slightly browned. Let cool to room temperature, then use a metal spatula to loosen the nuts.

VARIATIONS: For an extra kick, add some ginger and ¼ teaspoon of orange zest.

If you'd prefer a savory variation, substitute ¼ teaspoon olive oil for the maple syrup.

If you aren't a walnut fan, substitute ½ cup sliced almonds or pecans.

STORAGE: Store in an airtight container in the refrigerator for 2 weeks or in the freezer for 2 months.

PER SERVING: Calories: 90; Total Fat: 8.2 g (0.8 g saturated, 1.1 g mono-unsaturated); Carbohydrates: 4 g; Protein: 2 g; Fiber: 1 g; Sodium: 75 mg

Spiced Toasted Almonds

MAKES: 2 cups

PREP TIME: 5 minutes

COOK TIME: 10 minutes

2 cups raw almonds

1 teaspoon extra-virgin olive oil

½ teaspoon maple syrup

¼ teaspoon sea salt

1 teaspoon ground cinnamon

¼ teaspoon ground ginger

Sometimes I think that if we could get cars to run on almonds, you wouldn't need more than a handful to go from San Francisco to L.A. Yeah, they have that much energy—twenty nuts are more than enough to get anyone through a hunger rush—and they're nutrient dense, so the body can put every calorie to work. It's easy to prep a whole bunch of these; all it takes is a little olive oil, some seasoning, and a few minutes in the oven and they're ready to rock. I tell my clients to leave little bowls of these around the house so they're constantly tempted to grab a healthy nibble.

Preheat the oven to 350°F.

Toss the almonds with the olive oil, maple syrup, salt, cinnamon, and ginger until evenly coated, then spread them evenly on a sheet pan. Bake for 7 to 10 minutes, until aromatic and slightly browned. You know they're done when you can smell them. The almonds will become crispy as they cool.

VARIATIONS: While I was scuttling around the Commonweal Retreat Center's kitchen, I came up with the following mix of tasty morsels that everyone seemed to love. To 2 cups of toasted almonds, add 1 tablespoon of dark chocolate chips, ¼ cup of dried cherries, and ¼ cup of pumpkin seeds.

If you're looking for a more savory flavor, swap out the cinnamon and ginger for ¼ teaspoon each of dried rosemary, sage, and thyme.

COOK'S NOTE: When in doubt, take them out (of the oven)! Nuts will continue to roast after they have been removed from the oven.

STORAGE: Store in an airtight container in the refrigerator for 2 weeks or in the freezer for 2 months.

PER SERVING: Calories: 105; Total Fat: 9.1 g (0.7 g saturated, 5.7 g mono-unsaturated); Carbohydrates: 4 g; Protein: 4 g; Fiber: 2 g; Sodium: 40 mg

Curried Kale Chips

Funny, when I first introduced people to kale chips more than a dozen years ago, it was like I had stepped off a spaceship from another planet. "Kale? Chips? You're kidding?!" was a common response to the then-unknown crunch. Now? There are bags galore at the local supermarket, usually selling for six bucks and up. These are better. The olive oil and baking remove kale's natural bitterness, with the curry doing what curry does best—making you reach for the chips even before they're off the baking pan. Plus, extensive research on curcumin, which is in curry powder's turmeric, shows promise in protecting against inflammation-linked diseases including cancer.

Preheat the oven to 300°F. Line a rimmed baking sheet with parchment paper.

Place the kale in a large bowl and add the olive oil, salt, and curry powder and combine until the leaves are well coated. Place the kale on the prepared baking sheet in a single layer. Bake for 10 minutes, or until the kale becomes nice and crisp. Remove from the oven and allow it to rest for 5 minutes.

COOK'S NOTE: Some ovens run very cool, so it may take more than 10 minutes for the kale to get crisp. If your kale isn't crisp after 10 minutes, bake in 5-minute increments until it crisps up.

STORAGE: Store in an airtight container at room temperature for 3 days.

PER SERVING: Calories: 81; Total Fat: 4.25 g (.6 g saturated, 2.8 g monounsaturated); Carbohydrates: 10.2 g; Protein: 3.35 g; Fiber: 2.1 g; Sodium: 243 mg

SERVES: 4 (makes approximately 6 cups)
PREP TIME: 5 minutes
COOK TIME: 10 minutes

1 bunch kale, stemmed and torn into 2-inch pieces

1 tablespoon extra-virgin olive oil

½ teaspoon sea salt

½ teaspoon curry powder

Orange Pistachio Quinoa

Quinoa is its own little ecosystem, containing all of the essential amino acids that we must obtain through the diet. Put another way, quinoa brings some good nutrients to the table that the body needs to begin repairing itself. Its mild taste makes it a perfect backdrop for this nicely layered crunchy/chewy portable dish, in which olive oil, citrus, vitamin-rich pistachios, and raisins dance delightfully on the taste buds, and herbs (mint, cumin, and coriander) provide a huge hit of taste and anticancer nutrients.

Preheat the oven to 325°F.

Spread the pistachios in an even layer on a sheet pan and bake for 7 to 10 minutes, until aromatic and slightly browned. Let cool.

Place the quinoa in a fine-mesh strainer and rinse well under cold running water to remove all the resin.

In a pot, bring the broth and 1 teaspoon salt to a boil. Add the quinoa and cover. Decrease the heat and simmer for 15 minutes. Transfer from the heat and fluff with a fork. Spread mixture out on a sheet pan and "rake" with a fork occasionally until cooled.

Transfer the quinoa from the sheet pan to a large bowl. Stir in the cumin, coriander, salt, and pepper. Add the mint, scallions, orange juice, orange zest, olive oil, lemon juice, toasted pistachios, and raisins. Mix well and taste; you may need a pinch of salt, a squeeze of lemon, or a dash of olive oil.

VARIATION: Make this a meal in a bowl by adding 1 cup of cooked chickpeas when you stir everything together.

COOK'S NOTES: Rinse, rinse, and rinse again! Quinoa is naturally coated with a bitter-tasting resin. To get rid of the resin, put the grain in a bowl of cool water, swish it around with your hand, then drain it in a fine-mesh sieve.

Quinoa is gluten free, which makes sense when you consider that botanically, it isn't a grain at all; it's more closely related to beets.

STORAGE: Store in an airtight container in the refrigerator for 4 days.

PER SERVING: Calories: 265; Total Fat: 10.3 g (1.3 g saturated, 5.9 g mono-unsaturated); Carbohydrates: 40 g; Protein: 7 g; Fiber: 6 g; Sodium: 435 mg

SERVES: 6
PREP TIME: 15 minutes
COOK TIME: 15 minutes

½ cup raw pistachios

1½ cups quinoa

2½ cups Magic Mineral Broth (page 49) or water

1 teaspoon sea salt

1 teaspoon cumin

½ teaspoon coriander

⅛ teaspoon freshly ground pepper

½ cup chopped fresh mint

2 scallions, both green and white parts, finely chopped

⅛ cup freshly squeezed orange juice

Zest of 1 orange

1½ tablespoons olive oil

1½ tablespoons freshly squeezed lemon juice

½ cup raisins

Quinoa Porridge with Walnut Cream

SERVES: 6
PREP TIME: 10 minutes
COOK TIME: 20 minutes

WALNUT CREAM

1 cup walnuts

1 cup water

1 teaspoon freshly squeezed lemon juice

1 teaspoon maple syrup (use a little more if you want a slightly sweeter cream)

½ teaspoon sea salt

QUINOA

1 cup quinoa

2 cups water

¼ teaspoon sea salt

2 tablespoons freshly squeezed orange juice

1 tablespoon maple syrup

1 teaspoon ground cinnamon

½ teaspoon ground ginger

⅛ teaspoon ground nutmeg or freshly grated nutmeg

1½ to 2 cups fresh blueberries, blackberries, raspberries

¾ cup toasted coarsely chopped walnuts

Protein is really important for staying strong during and after treatment, and quinoa is an excellent vegetable protein source. If you're a fan of oatmeal, millet, or buckwheat, you'll find that the slightly nutty, somewhat crunchy taste and texture of quinoa is right in your wheelhouse. It's versatile, perfect for storing a batch in the fridge and dolloping it up in numerous ways. Here, quinoa benefits from the fat in the walnut cream, which adds a luscious coating to this flavorful porridge. With cinnamon, nutmeg, and a cup of fresh berries (blue, black, or raspberry—take your pick!), this could well turn into one of your favorite warming treats.

To make the walnut cream, put the walnuts in a bowl, add water to cover, and let stand overnight. The next day, preheat the oven to 350°F. Drain the walnuts well and spread on a baking pan. Toast for 8 to 10 minutes or until they're lightly browned and aromatic, then cool completely.

Put the toasted walnuts, 1 cup water, and the lemon juice, maple syrup, and salt in a blender. Blend on high speed until creamy and smooth, 1 to 2 minutes. Transfer the cream to a bowl or jar.

To prepare the quinoa, rinse it in a strainer and drain it well. In a medium saucepan, bring the quinoa, water, and salt to a boil over high heat. Turn the heat to low, then cover and simmer until the water is absorbed, about 15 minutes. Set aside off the heat to cool for a few minutes, then fluff the quinoa up with a fork.

When you are ready to serve, stir ½ cup of the prepared walnut cream and the orange juice, maple syrup, cinnamon, ginger, and nutmeg into the cooked quinoa. Serve the quinoa in bowls, and top each serving with a dollop of the remaining walnut cream, a small handful of blueberries, and a sprinkling of toasted walnuts.

STORAGE: Store in an airtight container in the refrigerator for 4 days.

PER SERVING: Calories: 370; Total Fat: 24g (2.5 g saturated, 3.5 g mono-unsaturated); Carbohydrates: 33 g; Protein: 10 g; Fiber: 5 g; Sodium: 240 mg

Kathie Swift's "Ciao Bella" Chia Pudding

Think of chia seed as flaxseed's first cousin. Both have outstanding anti-inflammatory omega-3 fatty acids and high fiber for better blood sugar regulation. Chia seeds do a cute magic trick when placed overnight in water: They plump up, taking on a tapioca-like texture. Here, I've borrowed a chia pudding recipe from my friend, the outstanding integrative dietitian Kathie Madonna Swift, MS. She adds some coconut milk, vanilla, and a few spices to the chia and—*Bazinga!*— we have pudding, Houston. Kathie says that adding kefir—a fermented milk—is fantastic for maintaining the "good" bacteria that your gut microbiome (environment) needs to properly function. This pudding is great for breakfast or as a quick snack to keep you rolling through your day.

In a 1-quart sealable glass jar, add the kefir, chia seeds, maple syrup, vanilla, and cinnamon. Seal the jar and shake well until evenly mixed. Place the jar in the refrigerator and chill for at least 3 hours or overnight.

Serve topped with the blueberries and slivered almonds.

VARIATION: Cocoa Cinnamon Chia Pudding—add ½ teaspoon ground cinnamon and ½ teaspoon unsweetened cocoa powder when you add the vanilla extract. Serve with chopped walnuts and banana slices.

COOK'S NOTE: I like to take a fun parfait-type glass and add a scoop of chia pudding, then layer with blueberries and repeat, topping off it off with the slivered almonds. If the pudding gets too stiff, I add a little almond milk to loosen it up.

STORAGE: Store in an airtight container in the refrigerator for 3 days.

PER SERVING: Calories 203; Total Fat: 10.6 g (0.7 g saturated, 0.5 g mono-unsaturated); Carbohydrates: 20 g; Protein: 7.4 g; Fiber: 8 g; Sodium: 58 mg

SERVES: 2

PREP TIME: 5 minutes (plus 3 hours or overnight chill time)

COOK TIME: Not applicable

---

1 cup plain, unsweetened kefir or nondairy kefir such as coconut or almond kefir

¼ cup chia seeds

2 teaspoons maple syrup

1 teaspoon vanilla extract

1 teaspoon ground cinnamon

½ cup fresh or frozen blueberries

1 tablespoon slivered almonds

Mediterranean Lentil Salad

SERVES: 6

PREP TIME: 10 minutes

COOK TIME: 25 minutes

1 cup dried lentils, preferably Le Puy green lentils, rinsed well

1 clove garlic, peeled and smashed

½ teaspoon dried oregano

Sea salt

2 bay leaves

1 cinnamon stick, or ¼ teaspoon ground cinnamon

¼ cup extra-virgin olive oil

2 tablespoons freshly squeezed lemon juice

1 teaspoon lemon zest

½ teaspoon ground cumin

1 red bell pepper, seeded and diced small

1 small cucumber, seeded and diced small

¼ cup pitted Kalamata olives, rinsed and sliced

3 tablespoons chopped fresh mint

3 tablespoons chopped fresh flat-leaf parsley

Freshly ground pepper

2 ounces organic feta cheese, crumbled (optional)

I should have called this Lentil Inside-Out Salad. Here's why: With most salads, you pour on the dressing on at the end and coat the dish from the outside in. But in this salad, the lentils cool off in the fridge in a bath of dressing—in this case, olive oil, lemon, and cumin. They absorb all those wonderful flavors, which are heightened by the addition of red bell pepper, Kalamata olives, parsley, and mint. This Mediterranean delight is like vacationing on the island of Crete without leaving your home. Resilient Le Puy lentils hold their shape well throughout the cooking process, making them perfect for a salad.

Combine the lentils, garlic, oregano, ¼ teaspoon salt, bay leaves, and cinnamon stick in a saucepan and cover with water by 2 inches. Bring to a boil, then cover, lower the heat, and simmer until the lentils are tender, 20 to 25 minutes. Drain the lentils thoroughly and discard the whole spices.

In a separate bowl, whisk the olive oil, lemon juice, lemon zest, cumin, and ¼ teaspoon salt together. Toss the lentils with the vinaigrette, then refrigerate for 20 minutes.

Stir in the bell pepper, cucumber, olives, mint, and parsley and combine, then taste. Season as needed with another pinch of salt, a few grinds of pepper, or lemon juice. Serve with the feta cheese sprinkled over the top, if desired.

STORAGE: Store in an airtight container in the refrigerator for 3 to 5 days.

PER SERVING: Calories: 210; Total Fat: 11.6 g (1.5 g saturated, 7.8 g mono-unsaturated); Carbohydrates: 21 g; Protein: 7 g; Fiber: 5 g; Sodium: 195 mg

Forbidden Rice Salad

SERVES: 4

PREP TIME: 5 minutes (after soaking the rice overnight)

COOK TIME: 35 minutes

---

2 cups water

2 (½-inch) slices rinsed, unpeeled fresh ginger, plus 1 teaspoon minced fresh ginger

2 pods star anise (optional)

Sea salt

1 cup forbidden rice, soaked overnight and rinsed

1 tablespoon freshly squeezed lime juice

1 tablespoon unseasoned rice vinegar

2 tablespoons finely chopped fresh cilantro, basil, or mint

2 tablespoons finely diced red bell pepper

This recipe is like one of those beautiful American heritage quilts where every colorful swatch—or in this case ingredient—has a wonderful backstory. Forbidden rice, also called emperor's rice, was so named because its deep purple hue is reminiscent of a royal cloak. As with many grains and vegetables, the rich color of forbidden rice signifies high levels of antioxidants and phytochemicals. Star anise also has anticancer properties and a light licorice flavor that's immensely appealing.

Bring the water, sliced ginger, star anise, and ¼ teaspoon of salt to a boil, then stir in the rice. Cover, lower the heat, and simmer for 30 minutes, then check to see if the rice is tender.

Whisk the lime juice, rice vinegar, and minced ginger, and a pinch of salt together in a mixing bowl. Add the rice and toss to combine, then stir in the cilantro and bell pepper. Serve immediately.

STORAGE: Store in an airtight container in the refrigerator for 5 to 7 days.

PER SERVING: Calories: 185; Total Fat: 1.9 g (0.5 g saturated, 0.6 g mono-unsaturated); Carbohydrates: 40 g; Protein: 5 g; Fiber: 4 g; Sodium: 150 mg

Simple Tuscan Farro

If you believe the ancients had something on us, you'll like farro; it's been found in archaeological digs dating back nearly twenty thousand years. It was the staple that kept the Roman legions on the move. What I like about farro is that it's a whole grain, which nutritionally is far superior to refined white wheat. Some people who are sensitive to wheat can tolerate farro because it is lower in gluten.

Place the farro in a pan or bowl with the water and juice of 1 lemon and let soak overnight, or for at least 8 hours.

Drain and rinse the farro. Bring the broth and a pinch of salt to a boil in a large saucepan, add the farro, and return to a boil. Lower the heat, cover, and simmer for 20 to 30 minutes, until tender. If there's any excess liquid, drain it off, then stir in the olive oil and 1 tablespoon of lemon juice.

COOK'S NOTES: Farro is a drainable grain, so don't sweat the amount of liquid used to cook it. The texture of cooked farro is like barley, so when you taste for doneness, know that you can always drain out the excess water if it is finished cooking.

This is an excellent grain to freeze. Use it as a creative addition to the next soup you make.

STORAGE: Store in a covered container in the refrigerator for 2 days or in the freezer for 2 months.

PER SERVING: Calories: 275; Total Fat: 1.7 g (0.3 g saturated, 1.1 g monounsaturated); Carbohydrates: 56 g; Protein: 11 g; Fiber: 6 g; Sodium: 230 mg

SERVES: 6
PREP TIME: 5 minutes (after soaking the farro overnight)
COOK TIME: 30 minutes

2 cups farro

6 cups water

Juice of 1 lemon

6 cups Magic Mineral Broth (page 49) or water

Sea salt

2 teaspoons extra-virgin olive oil

1 tablespoon freshly squeezed lemon juice

Rice Paper Moo-Shu Rolls

SERVES: 6

PREP TIME: 10 minutes

COOK TIME: Not applicable

---

6 (8-inch) rice paper rounds

2 tablespoons Edamame Avocado Dip with Wasabi (page 131)

1½ cups Warm Napa Cabbage Slaw (page 97)

1½ cups roasted organic chicken, shredded

12 fresh mint leaves

One of my favorite ways of getting people to enjoy eating veggies is to wrap them in rice paper rolls. If you've ever enjoyed Vietnamese spring rolls, you're familiar with these delightful silky casings that hug veggies tight as a drum. They can be found in any Asian market or the Asian section of most grocery stores. In the package, rice paper rolls look delicate, like round sheets of frosted glass, but slip them into warm water for about a minute and they become soft and pliable. Put them back on the counter, add the ingredients, and wrap them just as you would a small burrito. It may take two or three tries, but I promise you'll get the knack (I've even taught the technique to kids). The result will be veggie heaven, as the rolls are easy to swallow and digest.

Fill a large, shallow bowl with warm water. Soak 1 rice paper round at a time in the water until pliable, generally 30 to 60 seconds, depending on water temperature and the rice paper. Place the softened rice paper on a work surface and carefully spread 1 teaspoon of the edamame dip on the bottom third of the rice paper, leaving 2½ inches between the dip and the edges of the paper. Place ¼ cup of the slaw on top of the dip and ¼ cup of the shredded chicken on top of the slaw, then lay 2 mint leaves over the filling. Fold the right and left sides of the paper in over the filling, compressing the filling slightly. Fold the bottom edge up and over the filling, then tightly roll the entire thing away from your body, pressing gently to make a compact roll.

Moisten your finger with warm water and run it along the inside edge of the flap that remains at the top of the roll, then press the moistened edge against the roll to seal. Repeat with the remaining ingredients. Cut the rolls in half on the diagonal with a sharp knife before serving.

COOK'S NOTE: When you take these to go, leave them whole and wrap tightly in wax paper. Eat right away or cut when you are ready to eat!

STORAGE: Store in a covered container in the refrigerator for 3 days.

PER SERVING: Calories: 140; Total Fat: 4.7 g (1 g saturated, 1.8 g mono-unsaturated); Carbohydrates: 11 g; Protein: 12 g; Fiber: 1 g; Sodium: 250 mg

Curried Hummus and Vegetable Pinwheels

These wraps are a quick, healthy pick-me-up. Curry is one of my favorite spices to use, and doubly so if I'm working with folks dealing with cancer. Turmeric and its subcomponent, curcumin, are common curry ingredients that have tumor-inhibiting and appetite-stimulating properties. Here, I'm using hummus to transport the curry because it's a great canvas for blending spices and veggies. The pinwheel turns this into a simple finger food, easy to prep, grab, and go. If you're wondering why I often add mango, just take a bite. And another. And another . . .

Place a tortilla on a flat work surface. Spread ¼ cup of the hummus over the tortilla, leaving a ¾-inch border all the way around. Lay one-fourth of the spinach, carrot, cucumber, and mango over the hummus, then roll up into a tube, sushi style. Glue down the top edge with a smear of hummus. Repeat with the remaining ingredients. Trim the ends, then slice the rolls in half on the diagonal or, alternatively, cut crosswise into 1-inch pinwheels before serving.

STORAGE: Store in a covered container in the refrigerator for 3 days.

PER SERVING: Calories: 340; Total Fat: 8.8 g (0.8 g saturated, 2.6 g mono-unsaturated); Carbohydrates: 53 g; Protein: 12 g; Fiber: 10 g; Sodium: 835 mg

SERVES: 4

PREP TIME: 10 minutes

COOK TIME: Not applicable

4 (8-inch) spelt or whole wheat tortillas or gluten-free tortillas

1 cup Curried Hummus (page 133)

2 cups baby spinach, washed and dried

¾ cup peeled and shredded carrot

¾ cup peeled, seeded, and grated cucumber

½ cup thinly sliced mango (optional)

Chapter 6

Tonics and Elixirs

There's something about reaching for a cold one that just works, yes? Whether you're playing softball, sitting on a sun-drenched porch, or coming in from working in the garden, a tall, ice-filled glass of a favorite beverage is guaranteed to slake your thirst and put a smile on your face. And, of course, the same goes for a mug of steaming liquid love on a frosty day. Pop a cinnamon stick in that tea, cider, or hot chocolate and you're halfway to a happy nap.

A choice libation chock-full of nutrients can be a real lifeline for people dealing with the head, neck, and mouth issues particular to certain cancers and treatments. I saw this firsthand with my father, as he battled and beat throat cancer. The radiation treatments left his throat so sore that he really couldn't eat solid foods. The only way for him to get nutrition was through the various smoothies that soothed his pain while delivering vital nutrients to his body.

These smoothie recipes are outstanding for getting delicious nourishment where it needs to go. They're nutrient dense, so those having a tough time with weight loss can benefit from just a few sips. They're also full of herbs and spices such as ginger (great for tummy aches) and cinnamon (a super blood sugar regulator). And they all taste wonderful, even including the ground flaxseeds that many nutritionists recommend for those in treatment.

Smoothies play several other important roles. Dehydration is a common but often hard-to-detect treatment side effect. By the time you feel the signs of serious dehydration—dizziness, nausea, cramps, impaired thinking—you could be headed for the hospital. Most folks think drinking water is enough to stay hydrated. Not necessarily. Water without added electrolytes and minerals passes quickly through the body, taking much-needed nutrients right out of the bloodstream. Also, anyone who is dealing with a metallic taste in his or her mouth is likely to find tap water extremely unpalatable. If you've ever tasted distilled water, you'll know what I mean.

Staying hydrated with the tonics and elixirs in this chapter can also lessen nausea, replenish nutrients lost because of diarrhea, and counteract the constipating effects of pain medications including opiates. Of course, they're also refreshing in the extreme. And if your doctor says to avoid cold drinks, fret not; these smoothies taste great at room temperature. Now that's worthy of a toast!

Turmeric and Cinnamon Masala Chai

SERVES: 1

PREP TIME: 5 minutes

COOK TIME: 10 minutes

1 ounce water

8 ounces almond milk

½ teaspoon turmeric

¼ teaspoon ground cinnamon

⅓ cup peeled fresh ginger, sliced ¼ inch thick

Pinch of freshly ground pepper

2 teaspoons dark amber maple syrup

Isn't your mouth watering already? Talk about an alluring recipe. Masala is Indian for a spice blend, most notably those used in teas (aka chai). This incredibly comforting libation heals both body and mind; the spices, notably turmeric and cinnamon, have outstanding anti-inflammatory properties. I recommend this chai to anyone whose appetite is waning or who finds him- or herself with a touch of indigestion. Added bonus: the almond milk, besides tasting great, is perfect for those of us who are lactose intolerant.

In a small saucepan, combine the water, almond milk, turmeric, cinnamon, ginger, and pepper. Allow the chai to gently cook over medium-low heat for 2 minutes, or until small bubbles start to appear. Cover, and simmer for another 3 minutes. Turn off the heat, stir in the maple syrup, and allow the chai to sit for 5 minutes, then pour into a cup to serve.

STORAGE: Not applicable.

PER SERVING: Calories 99; Total Fat: 2.75 g (0.5 g saturated, 0.2 g mono-unsaturated); Carbohydrates: 18 g; Protein: 1.3 g; Fiber: 1.1 g; Sodium: 149 mg

Annemarie's Calming Kudzu Elixir

MAKES: 1 cup

PREP TIME: 3 minutes

COOK TIME: 5 minutes

1½ tablespoons kudzu root powder

1 cup cold, unfiltered apple juice

⅛ teaspoon grated fresh ginger (optional)

1 teaspoon vanilla extract

¼ teaspoon ground cinnamon

My mentor, Annemarie Colbin, founded the cooking school I attended, the Natural Gourmet Institute for Health and Culinary Arts. She also authored *Food and Healing*, a bible for chefs who believe in health-supportive cooking. This recipe comes from her book; it's a stress-relieving elixir that uses kudzu, a vine, which is outstanding for controlling nausea and an upset stomach. The only thing I've done is add a little ginger and cinnamon. For those days when you need a hug pronto and there's no one around to soothe your body and soul, this concoction will do the trick.

In a small pot, mix the kudzu root powder into the cold apple juice, stirring until dissolved. Stir in the ginger, vanilla, and cinnamon and bring to a boil over medium-low heat, stirring constantly until the liquid thickens and becomes translucent. Serve hot or cold.

VARIATIONS: For a cozy and soothing pudding, follow Annemarie's original recipe, leaving out the ginger and cinnamon, and increase the amount of kudzu to 2 tablespoons.

For a more nutrient-dense pudding with extra protein, swirl 1 tablespoon of tahini into the mixture as soon as it thickens.

COOK'S NOTE: Kudzu is a wonderful thickening agent that can replace cornstarch in any recipe. If you are using it as a thickener in place of cornstarch, be sure you dilute the kudzu with 1 tablespoon of cold water first, then add it according to the recipe instructions.

STORAGE: Not applicable.

PER SERVING: Calories: 170; Total Fat: 0 g; Carbohydrates: 39 g; Protein: 0 g; Fiber: 0 g; Sodium: 30 mg

Commonweal's Most Nourishing and Healing Tea

You may have heard the slogan "You've tried the rest; now try the best." That's the way I feel about this tea recipe. It was developed ages ago by the fantastic folks at the Commonweal Cancer Help Program, a renowned retreat for patients and caregivers. They've kindly allowed me to share their recipe with you. When I cook at Commonweal, I make six quarts of it a day so I'll have some on hand for anyone coming through the door. Yes, it's *that* popular. The blend of ginger, cloves, cinnamon, and cardamom is like a backrub in a cup. It turns me into absolute mush, it's so good.

Combine the ginger and water in a saucepan and bring to a boil. Lower the heat, cover, and simmer for 30 minutes.

Add the coriander, cardamom, cinnamon, and cloves and continue to simmer for an additional 20 minutes.

Strain the tea through a fine-mesh sieve into a clean saucepan. (I recommend that you save the spices; see Cook's Notes.) Add the rice milk and maple syrup and gently reheat without boiling for 2 to 3 minutes, until warm. Stir in the vanilla, then taste. Add more milk or sweetener if you like. Serve hot or cold.

COOK'S NOTES: The tea will keep in the refrigerator for up to 2 weeks without the milk and sweetener, so you may want to set some aside prior to adding the milk and sweetener.

Recycle the spices that are strained out of the tea and use them to make another, smaller batch of tea. They'll keep in the refrigerator for 4 to 5 days. To make more tea, combine the spices and 6 cups of water and bring to a boil. Add 2 tablespoons peeled fresh ginger slices. Simmer for 30 minutes, then strain the tea and discard the spices. Add sweetener and milk to taste and reheat without boiling for 2 to 3 minutes. Remove from the heat and stir in the vanilla before serving.

STORAGE: Store in an airtight container in the refrigerator for 1 week.

PER SERVING: Calories: 40; Total Fat: 0.9 g (0 g saturated, 0.6 g monounsaturated); Carbohydrates: 8 g; Protein: 0 g; Fiber: 1 g; Sodium: 15 mg

MAKES: 8 cups
PREP TIME: 5 minutes
COOK TIME: 55 minutes

⅓ cup sliced peeled fresh ginger, cut ¼ inch thick

10 cups water

3 tablespoons coriander seeds

1½ tablespoons cardamom pods

4 cinnamon sticks

5 whole cloves

1½ cups rice milk or almond milk

1 to 3 tablespoons maple syrup

1 teaspoon vanilla extract

Ginger Peppermint Green Tea

MAKES: 4 cups
PREP TIME: 3 minutes
COOK TIME: 25 minutes

---

4 cups water

4 (½-inch) slices peeled fresh ginger

1 green tea bag

1 peppermint tea bag

1 tablespoon freshly squeezed lemon juice

1 teaspoon honey

This tea is a little like a mother's gentle belly rub for a child with a tummy ache, as both peppermint and ginger have qualities that relax the smooth muscles surrounding the intestine.

Bring the water and ginger to a boil in a saucepan, then lower the heat, cover, and simmer for 10 minutes. Remove from the heat, add the green and peppermint tea bags, and steep for 10 minutes.

Remove the tea bags and ginger, then stir in the lemon juice and honey. Serve hot, or chill for at least 1 hour before serving over ice.

STORAGE: Store, covered, in the refrigerator for 5 days.

PER SERVING: Calories: 10; Total Fat: 0 g; Carbohydrates: 2 g; Protein: 0 g; Fiber: 0 g; Sodium: 0 mg

Green Tea Ginger Lemonade

MAKES: 4 cups
PREP TIME: 3 minutes
COOK TIME: 25 minutes, plus 1 hour for chilling

---

4 cups water

4 (½-inch) slices peeled fresh ginger

2 green tea bags

1 tablespoon freshly squeezed lemon juice

2 teaspoons honey

Green tea is great for you, with many of its compounds linked to potential anticancer benefits. I love drinking green tea, but without a little help it can be astringent and bitter. Here, I've added ginger and lemon with honey to really knock out the bitterness. The result is a refreshing lemonade that's far healthier than the average store-bought blend. If you really want to amp up the sweetness, squeeze in the juice of a few oranges.

Bring the water and ginger to a boil in a saucepan, then lower the heat, cover, and simmer for 10 minutes. Remove from the heat, add the tea bags, and steep for 10 minutes.

Remove the tea bags and ginger, then stir in the lemon juice and honey. Chill for at least 1 hour before serving over ice.

STORAGE: Store, covered, in the refrigerator for 5 to 7 days.

PER SERVING: Calories: 15; Total Fat: 0 g; Carbohydrates: 3 g; Protein: 0 g; Fiber: 0 g; Sodium: 0 mg

Cinnamon Ginger Tea

I've been playing with ginger in various forms for years. From an Ayurvedic (traditional eastern Indian medicine) perspective, ginger "fires" the body's digestive hearth, making the stomach and colon more efficient in metabolizing food. Here, I've combined ginger with cinnamon's round, sweet flavor to create a modified chai tea with great health benefits. Cinnamon regulates blood sugar, while both ginger and cinnamon contain tumor inhibitors. This tea is a great way to wake up both your taste buds and your tummy.

MAKES: 4 cups
PREP TIME: 3 minutes
COOK TIME: 15 minutes

4 cups water

4 (½-inch) slices peeled fresh ginger

1 cinnamon stick

2 teaspoons honey

Bring the water, ginger, and cinnamon stick to a boil in a saucepan, then lower the heat, cover, and simmer for 10 minutes.

Remove the ginger and cinnamon stick, stir in the honey, and serve immediately.

STORAGE: Store, covered, in the refrigerator for 5 days.

PER SERVING: Calories: 13; Total Fat: 0 g; Carbohydrates: 3 g; Protein: 0 g; Fiber: 0 g; Sodium: 0 mg

Ginger Tea Spritzer

This cool, refreshing drink tastes wonderful and can help combat nausea.

MAKES: 1 cup syrup
PREP TIME: 3 minutes
COOK TIME: 20 minutes

3 ginger tea bags

2 cups boiling water

¼ teaspoon honey

¼ teaspoon freshly squeezed lemon juice

Sparkling water

Put the tea bags in a small saucepan, pour the boiling water over them, and steep for 15 minutes.

Put the saucepan over medium heat and cook until the tea is reduced by half. Stir in the honey and lemon juice, then let cool to room temperature.

For each serving, put 2 tablespoons of the ginger syrup in a glass and add sparkling water.

COOK'S NOTE: For a change, try making this recipe with both chamomile and ginger tea bags, or a chamomile-ginger blend, if you can find one.

STORAGE: Store the syrup, covered, in the refrigerator for 5 days.

PER SERVING: Calories: 0; Total Fat: 0 g; Carbohydrates: 0 g; Protein: 0 g; Fiber: 0 g; Sodium: 0 mg

Mouthwatering Watermelon Granita

My freezer ended up with warning notes all over it after I made this granita. I put the liquid into a shallow pan in the freezer, only to completely forget it was in there. Minutes later I opened the slide-out freezer drawer and was hit with a tidal wave of red. It wasn't quite like the elevator door opening in *The Shining*, but it was pretty bad. I figured, "Okay, fool me once, shame on you." I swabbed out the whole freezer, put the food back in, made another batch, put that in the freezer, and left the kitchen. A few minutes later my husband, Gregg, wandered into the kitchen. Pause. "Beccaaa!!" Okay, fool me twice, shame on me. Once I cleaned off Gregg and the freezer (in that order), I made a third batch, and up went the warning notes. Success!

Put the watermelon in a food processor or blender and process on high speed until smooth.

Add the lime juice and honey to the food processor or blender and pulse to combine. Transfer to a freezer-safe 8 by 10-inch pan with sides at least 2 inches high and freeze for 1 hour.

Use a fork to rake the mixture, breaking up the frozen parts into smaller chunks and pushing them toward the center, like a pile of leaves. Return the granita to the freezer and repeat the raking process twice more at 30-minute intervals until entirely frozen.

VARIATION: A fun variation on any granita is fruit drops, which I think of as a frozen version of Tootsie Pops, especially the part where you get to the sweet middle. Pour the liquid mixture into an ice cube tray, then stick a few blueberries into each of the compartments. They'll end up suspended in the middle after the liquid freezes. Put a toothpick or Popsicle stick into each while they freeze, and you can enjoy the fruit drops straight up, or skip the sticks and use them in beverages. Either way, these fruit drops are a treat for the eyes, and great for people with mouth sores or anyone who wants to stay hydrated.

STORAGE: Store in an airtight container in the freezer for 3 weeks.

PER SERVING: Calories: 20; Total Fat: 0 g; Carbohydrates: 7 g; Protein: 0 g; Fiber: 0 g; Sodium: 0 mg

SERVES: 6
PREP TIME: 8 minutes
COOK TIME: 2 hours in the freezer

---

2 cups chopped watermelon

2½ tablespoons freshly squeezed lime juice

2 teaspoons honey

Cantaloupe Granita with Mint

SERVES: 6

PREP TIME: 30 minutes

COOK TIME: 2 hours in the freezer

¼ cup boiling water

1 cup fresh mint leaves, loosely packed, plus 10 fresh mint leaves, finely chopped

6 cups chopped cantaloupe

2 teaspoons honey

2 tablespoons freshly squeezed lime juice

When treatment side effects dry out the body—a fairly common occurrence—granitas come to the rescue. Granitas are similar to Italian ices in consistency, making them great for people with mouth sores, and melons are full of rehydrating water. In fact, melons are a wonderful source of fluids and nutrients. One caveat: Melons should be eaten on an empty stomach, as they can cause a lot of tummy rumbling when combined with other foods. Consumed this way, they fast-track into the small intestine, allowing quick absorption of nutrients. And here's a fun fact: Cantaloupes are named after the Italian town Cantalupo, which means "howl of the wolf." No telling if there's a run on cantaloupes there whenever the moon is full . . .

Pour the boiling water over the 1 cup of mint leaves, cover, and steep for 30 minutes. Strain the liquid and discard the mint leaves.

Put the cantaloupe in a food processor or blender and process on high speed until smooth.

Add the honey, lime juice, mint infusion, and the 10 chopped mint leaves to the food processor or blender and pulse to combine. Transfer to a freezer-safe 8 by 10-inch pan with sides at least 2 inches high and freeze for 1 hour.

Use a fork to rake the mixture, breaking up the frozen parts into smaller chunks and pushing them toward the center, like a pile of leaves. Return the granita to the freezer and repeat the raking process twice more at 30-minute intervals until entirely frozen.

COOK'S NOTES: To make frozen fruit pops, see the Variation on page 161.

Use caution when opening the freezer door while the granita is freezing. You want to end up with this frozen delight in your belly and not on the bottom of the freezer!

STORAGE: Store in an airtight container in the freezer for 3 weeks.

PER SERVING: Calories: 95; Total Fat: 0.3 g (0.1 g saturated, 0 g monounsaturated); Carbohydrates: 20 g; Protein: 1 g; Fiber: 2 g; Sodium: 25 mg

Ginger Ale with Frozen Grapes

Ginger is one of your best friends during chemo. Its flavor can spark even the most jaded taste buds, while its antinausea properties help soothe an upset tummy. A lot of people think store-bought ginger ale will do the trick, but the actual ginger content in most commercial varieties is minimal. Plus, who wants a load of high-fructose corn syrup? Enter this recipe, which uses straight-up ginger syrup so you can control the amount of zing in your tonic. The frozen grapes serve the same purpose as your basic ice cubes, while sneaking a bunch of healthy minerals and phytochemicals into the brew.

Bring the water and ginger to a boil in a saucepan, then lower the heat, cover, and simmer for 1 hour. Uncover and continue to simmer for 30 minutes.

Strain the infusion through cheesecloth and discard the ginger. Stir in the lemon juice and honey and let cool to room temperature.

For each serving, add ¼ cup of the ginger syrup to a glass with frozen grapes, then fill the glass with sparkling water and garnish with a sprig of mint.

COOK'S NOTE: You can also use this ginger syrup to make a hot beverage. Just stir 3 tablespoons of the syrup into 1 cup of hot water, then add more honey or lemon if you like.

STORAGE: Store the ginger syrup in an airtight container in the refrigerator for 7 days. Store the grapes in a resealable plastic bag in the freezer for 3 months.

PER SERVING: Calories: 50; Total Fat: 0.2 g (0.1 g saturated, 0 g mono-unsaturated); Carbohydrates: 12 g; Protein: 0 g; Fiber: 1 g; Sodium: 5 mg

MAKES: About 2 cups syrup
PREP TIME: 5 minutes
COOK TIME: 1 hour 30 minutes

4 cups water

2 cups sliced unpeeled fresh ginger

2 tablespoons freshly squeezed lemon juice

2 tablespoons honey

Frozen seedless grapes

Sparkling water

Mint sprigs, for garnish

Peach Ginger Smoothie

MAKES: 4½ cups

PREP TIME: 5 minutes

COOK TIME: Not applicable

1¼ cups peach nectar

¾ cup organic plain yogurt

1 teaspoon minced fresh ginger

3 cups frozen peaches, or 3 cups fresh peaches, pitted and chopped

1 tablespoon finely ground flaxseeds

1½ teaspoons maple syrup

½ teaspoon vanilla extract

½ teaspoon freshly squeezed lime juice

When I was a kid, nothing compared to hearing the jingling bells of the ice cream man; it meant I got a Creamsicle. Looking for that taste again and to create something kids would adore, I came up with this recipe. One note: If you have a sensitive mouth or throat issues, omit the ginger to avoid irritation.

Combine the peach nectar, yogurt, ginger, and half of the peaches in a blender and process until smooth. Add the remaining peaches and the flaxseeds, maple syrup, vanilla, and lime juice and blend until smooth and creamy. Serve immediately.

VARIATIONS: Add 1 tablespoon of unrefined virgin coconut oil for additional healthy fat and calories.

For more protein, add a scoop of whey protein powder.

STORAGE: Store in an airtight glass container in the refrigerator for 2 days. Shake well before serving.

PER SERVING: Calories: 135; Total Fat: 2.4 g (1 g saturated, 0.6 g mono-unsaturated); Carbohydrates: 25 g; Protein: 3 g; Fiber: 1 g; Sodium: 27 mg

Peach Ginger
Smoothie

Triple Berry
Smoothie

Triple Berry Smoothie

A lot of people wonder why an otherwise decent-tasting smoothie's flavor gets destroyed when a healthy item like flaxseeds is added. The easy answer is the initial recipe wasn't designed to accommodate a nutritious fix. The normal response is to add a ton of sweetener, but I don't agree with that approach, especially in recipes for cancer patients. So I created this berry blast to play well with the vital flax and whey. The abundant antioxidants make this smoothie one for the books.

Combine the yogurt, water, and orange juice in a blender and process for a few seconds. Add the strawberries and process until well blended, then add the blueberries, raspberries, flaxseeds, and maple syrup and blend until smooth. Serve immediately.

VARIATIONS: Add 1 tablespoon of unrefined virgin coconut oil for additional healthy fat and calories.

For more protein, add a scoop of whey protein powder.

STORAGE: Store in an airtight glass container in the refrigerator for 2 days. Shake well before serving.

PER SERVING: Calories: 145; Total Fat: 4.6 g (1.8 g saturated, 1 g mono-unsaturated); Carbohydrates: 24 g; Protein: 4 g; Fiber: 5 g; Sodium: 40 mg

MAKES: 3¾ cups
PREP TIME: 5 minutes
COOK TIME: Not applicable

1 cup organic plain yogurt

1 cup water

¼ cup freshly squeezed orange juice

1 cup frozen strawberries

1½ cups frozen blueberries

½ cup frozen raspberries

1 tablespoon ground flaxseeds

1 teaspoon maple syrup

Chocolate Banana Smoothie

There was this old restaurant called Fields in my hometown of Baltimore. Every town has a place like this—or at least used to—with a soda counter, red plastic stools, and sweet-and-sour elderly waitresses in pink candy striper outfits. Going to Fields was like making a pilgrimage, except instead of seeking wisdom we desired to attain the perfect milkshake. I think this smoothie gives Fields a run for its money—without creating the world's largest sugar spike. A little almond butter is the secret ingredient, creating a creamy goodness that will make you want to twirl around in your seat.

Put all of the ingredients in a blender and process until smooth. Do a FASS check and add a few drops of lemon juice to perk up the flavor if needed. Serve immediately.

VARIATIONS: For a more chocolaty flavor, add 2½ tablespoons cocoa powder. Chocolate goodness!

Add 1 tablespoon of unrefined virgin coconut oil for additional healthy fat and calories.

For more protein, add a scoop of whey protein powder.

COOK'S NOTES: The ice cubes make a big difference in thickening up the smoothie. If this is the consistency you prefer, add the optional ice cubes along with the frozen bananas.

It's much easier to peel bananas before they're frozen. Once they're peeled, store them in a resealable plastic bag and pop them in the freezer. They're a delicious snack on their own, and great to have on hand for smoothies and frozen drinks. If you don't have frozen bananas on hand and want to make this shake right away, use room-temperature bananas and be sure to include the ice cubes.

STORAGE: Store in an airtight glass container in the refrigerator for 2 days. Shake well or blend again before serving.

PER SERVING: Calories: 165; Total Fat: 8 g (0.5 g saturated, 2.8 g mono-unsaturated); Carbohydrates: 22 g; Protein: 4 g; Fiber: 4 g; Sodium: 270 mg

---

MAKES: 3½ cups
PREP TIME: 5 minutes
COOK TIME: Not applicable

---

3 cups unsweetened almond milk or rice milk

2 frozen bananas

2 tablespoons unsweetened cocoa powder

1½ tablespoons almond butter

1 tablespoon finely ground flaxseeds

½ teaspoon maple syrup

¼ teaspoon vanilla extract

Pinch of sea salt

4 ice cubes (optional; see Cook's Notes)

Lemon juice (optional)

Chapter 7

Dollops of Yum!

I can see why people might look at the dollops that follow and think of them as the culinary equivalent of a jaunty chapeau peacock feather or a fabulous consignment store bling ring. Pistachio Cream? Basil Lemon Drizzle?! Tomato Mint Chutney?!? At first glance, they may seem like add-ons, albeit tasty ones. However, there's a whole lot more to these dollops of yum. For people in treatment—and especially those dealing with impaired taste buds—these recipes create the zing of taste and texture they absolutely need to be drawn to a dish.

Take vinaigrettes. They play an obvious role with salads, but they're also great as marinades for fish and meat. There's nothing like meat marinated until it's so tender that it practically dissolves in your mouth.

The drizzles are also useful. They ensure that the first thing that hits the tongue has an explosive burst of flavor. Without this coaxing, some people may not work their way through the more subtle flavors of the rest of the food—and its accompanying nutrients.

The dollops here also visually enhance the dishes they adorn and help carry their flavor. They're designed to move taste around in the mouth, seeking those islands of taste buds that are in the best shape to transmit maximum savoriness. When I recommend that dollop X—say, Tomato Mint Chutney—goes with dish Y—for example, Middle Eastern Chickpea Burgers—you can take it to the bank. Or the table.

Dollops also provide additional delicious, nutrient-dense calories, which is so important for people trying to keep weight on, so use them whenever you can. I've designed many of these dollops to go with multiple dishes. Apricot Pear Chutney complements five of the recipes in this book, and the Olive and Caper Relish plays nicely off another five. The Basil Lemon Drizzle is great over almost any fish dish or salad you can imagine. My advice? Always keep plenty of dollops on hand, which is easy to do because they last for a long time in the fridge and freezer. That way, you'll never have a dish go out half-dressed. I mean, what would the neighbors say?

Apricot Pear Chutney

MAKES: 4 cups
PREP TIME: 15 minutes
COOK TIME: 50 minutes

2 pounds pears, peeled, cored, and diced

1¼ cups chopped unsulfured dried apricots

½ teaspoon lemon zest

½ cup brown rice vinegar

¼ cup freshly squeezed lemon juice

¼ cup maple syrup

½ teaspoon minced garlic

½ teaspoon grated fresh ginger

½ teaspoon sea salt

½ teaspoon ground cinnamon

¼ teaspoon ground allspice

¼ teaspoon ground cardamom

¼ teaspoon red pepper flakes

1 pod star anise (optional)

Chutney is a relish, but believe me, it doesn't taste anything like ordinary relish. Here the pear's mellow sweetness plays perfectly against the apricot's tartness. The sweet-sour combo leaves those taste buds wanting more, kind of like delirious rock fans screaming for an encore, and they'll stay at the table until their demands are satisfied! This chutney is also a nutritious alternative to jam or jelly. Any pear will work for this recipe; some of my favorites are Bosc, brown Asian, or Anjou.

Combine all of the ingredients in a large saucepan and bring to a boil. Lower the heat to maintain a bubbly simmer and cook with the lid partially off, stirring occasionally, for 45 to 50 minutes, so that the liquid begins to evaporate. Once the pears are soft but not mushy and the liquid has reduced to a thick coating over the fruit, remove the chutney from the heat. Remove the star anise (you can save it for garnish, if you like). Serve warm or at room temperature.

GOES WITH: Curry Cauliflower Soup (page 64), Spiced Sweet Potato Soup (page 66), Velvety Red Lentil Dal (page 70), Orange Ginger Roasted Chicken (page 109), and Middle Eastern Chickpea Burgers (page 112).

COOK'S NOTE: This chutney is quite versatile. A dollop is a delicious addition to many soups, and it can also be served over roasted chicken. For a sophisticated snack, spread soft goat cheese on crackers and top with a bit of the chutney.

STORAGE: Store in an airtight container in the refrigerator for 7 days or in the freezer for 2 months.

PER SERVING: 2 tablespoons—Calories: 20; Total Fat: 0 g; Carbohydrates: 5 g; Protein: 0 g; Fiber: 1 g; Sodium: 20 mg

Tomato Mint Chutney

The flavors in this wonderful chutney make it a good choice for brightening just about any dish.

Heat the olive oil in a large, heavy skillet over medium-low heat, then add the shallots, red pepper flakes, cumin seeds, mustard seeds (if using), and cinnamon sticks and sauté until the shallots are golden brown, about 4 minutes. Stir in the tomatoes, maple syrup, and salt, then lower the heat and simmer for 15 to 20 minutes, until the tomato juices have evaporated.

Stir in the ginger and mint and serve warm or at room temperature.

GOES WITH: Velvety Red Lentil Dal (page 70), Basil Broccoli (page 75), My Family's Favorite Chicken (page 110), Middle Eastern Chickpea Burgers (page 112), poached salmon (see page 116), Triple-Citrus Ginger Black Cod (page 119), and just about any brown rice, polenta, or pasta dish.

COOK'S NOTES: The brown mustard seeds can be found in the bulk foods section of the market and add a delicious flavor.

For a less-spicy chutney, decrease the amount of ginger and red pepper flakes.

STORAGE: Store in an airtight container in the refrigerator for 3 to 4 days or in the freezer for 2 months.

PER SERVING: 2 tablespoons—Calories: 35; Total Fat: 1.9 g (0.3 g saturated, 1.3 g monounsaturated); Carbohydrates: 5 g; Protein: 0 g; Fiber: 1 g; Sodium: 75 mg

MAKES: 1 cup
PREP TIME: 15 minutes
COOK TIME: 25 minutes

---

2 tablespoons extra-virgin olive oil

2 shallots, diced small

¼ teaspoon red pepper flakes

1 teaspoon cumin seeds

¼ teaspoon brown mustard seeds (optional, see Cook's Notes)

2 cinnamon sticks

4 cups coarsely chopped fresh tomatoes or canned diced tomatoes with their juice

3 tablespoons maple syrup

½ teaspoon sea salt

1 teaspoon grated fresh ginger

¼ cup loosely packed chopped fresh mint leaves

Basil Lemon Drizzle

This is the little black dress of condiments—appropriate in almost any situation. What it really comes down to is mixing lemon zest, basil, and lemon juice, and—zingo!—you have a condiment that brightens and brings out the flavor in anything you put it on top of—veggies, chicken, fish, whatever. An added bonus is the blast of cancer-fighting properties, especially basil's anti-inflammatory agents and lemon's antioxidant phytochemicals.

Put all of the ingredients in a food processor and process until well blended.

GOES WITH: Italian White Bean Soup (page 52), Minestrone (page 57), Cooling Cucumber Avocado Soup (page 62), Roasted Red Roma Tomato Soup (page 69), Creamy Broccoli and Potato Soup (page 71), Basil Broccoli (page 75), Easy Eggs in a Cup (page 100), Nana's Egg Salad (page 102), Tuscan Farro and Bean Salad (page 111), Lemon Mustard Salmon Salad (page 115), Mediterranean Lentil Salad (page 144), Simple Tuscan Farro (page 147), and, as you might guess from this list, myriad other savory dishes.

VARIATION: For a richer drizzle that's more like pesto, add ¼ cup pecans or walnuts when you process the ingredients.

STORAGE: Store in an airtight container in the refrigerator for 7 to 10 days or in the freezer for 2 months.

PER SERVING: 2 tablespoons—Calories: 125; Total Fat: 14.1 g (2 g saturated, 10 g monounsaturated); Carbohydrates: 1 g; Protein: 0 g; Fiber: 0 g; Sodium: 150 mg

MAKES: ½ cup
PREP TIME: 5 minutes
COOK TIME: Not applicable

1 cup loosely packed fresh basil leaves

2 tablespoons freshly squeezed lemon juice

1 teaspoon lemon zest

¼ cup extra-virgin olive oil

1 teaspoon maple syrup (optional)

¼ teaspoon sea salt

Avocado Dressing

MAKES: 1 cup

PREP TIME: 5 minutes

COOK TIME: Not applicable

¾ cup water

2 tablespoons extra-virgin olive oil

2 tablespoons freshly squeezed lime juice

½ teaspoon sea salt

½ ripe avocado

¼ cup loosely packed chopped fresh cilantro or basil

1 clove garlic, chopped

This is my riff on green goddess dressing. I've omitted the buttermilk, but you won't miss it a bit, as the luscious avocado blends with the lime juice to create a mellow dressing. It's ideal tossed with crunchy salads—a mix of tastes and textures that gives your palate an invigorating massage.

Combine all of the ingredients in a blender or food processor and blend until smooth and creamy.

GOES WITH: All of your favorite salads, or on top of fish or chicken.

STORAGE: Store in an airtight container in the refrigerator for 1 to 2 days.

PER SERVING: 2 tablespoons—Calories: 25; Total Fat: 2.4 g (0.3 g saturated, 1.7 g monounsaturated); Carbohydrates: 1 g; Protein: 0 g; Fiber: 0 g; Sodium: 75 mg

Avocado Cream

Putting avocado and cream in the same title is almost redundant; as any guacamole lover can attest, avocados have one of the creamiest textures in the fruit kingdom. Avocado has fantastic proportions of healthy fats, vitamins, and minerals, especially potassium. In fact, avocados contain more potassium than bananas, making them ideal for combating potassium loss that can occur from dehydration. Whether on a cracker or over a dish, this creamy dollop guarantees you fantastic taste and superb nutrition.

Combine all of the ingredients in a blender or food processor and process until smooth. Do taste; you may want to add some extra lime juice or a pinch of salt.

GOES WITH: Rockin' Black Bean Soup (page 63) and Black Bean Hummus (page 132), and also makes a great sandwich spread.

COOK'S NOTE: Want a little heat? Add a pinch of cayenne. Want a bright taste? Add a few tablespoons of chopped fresh mint.

STORAGE: Store in an airtight container in the refrigerator for 3 days.

PER SERVING: 2 tablespoons—Calories: 15; Total Fat: 1.3 g (0.2 g saturated, 0.8 g monounsaturated); Carbohydrates: 1 g; Protein: 0 g; Fiber: 1 g; Sodium: 40 mg

MAKES: 1 cup
PREP TIME: 5 minutes
COOK TIME: Not applicable

1 ripe avocado, pitted and peeled

¼ cup loosely packed fresh cilantro (optional)

1 tablespoon water

1 tablespoon freshly squeezed lime juice

¼ teaspoon sea salt

Cashew Cream

MAKES: About 3½ cups
PREP TIME: 5 minutes
COOK TIME: Not applicable

---

2 cups raw cashews

2 cups water

2 teaspoons freshly squeezed lemon juice or orange juice

½ teaspoon sea salt

⅛ teaspoon freshly ground nutmeg

You know that old *Sesame Street* song that goes, "One of these things is not like the others . . ."? Put a cashew next to butter and margarine and you'll probably think, "Hey, I know which one of these doesn't belong." Think again. By using nut creams—in this case pulverized cashews—I've pleased many a client who swears by butter but wants to go dairy free. Not only is the cashew taste fulfilling and delightful, but nuts are far better for you than any store-bought buttery spread made from corn oil.

Grind the cashews in a mini food processor or nut grinder to give them a head start in the blender. (If you have a Vitamix, you can skip this step.) Put the water in a blender, then add the lemon juice, salt, nutmeg, and cashews and blend until creamy smooth. This takes several minutes, but your taste buds will reap the rewards of your patience.

GOES WITH: Emerald Greens with Orange (page 78), Warm and Toasty Cumin Carrots (page 96), Simple Tuscan Farro (page 147), and Poached Pears with Saffron Broth (page 205). Cashew Cream is also a tasty and nutritious addition to any smoothie.

VARIATIONS: Substitute other nuts, such as almonds, pecans, pistachios, or hazelnuts.

For a variation that's similar to pesto, add 1½ cups fresh basil. This is great tossed with your favorite pasta or rice.

If you want more citrus flavor without an acidic taste, add 1 teaspoon lemon or orange zest.

STORAGE: Store in an airtight container in the refrigerator for 2 weeks or in the freezer for 2 months.

PER SERVING: 1 tablespoon—Calories: 30; Total Fat: 2.2 g (0.4 g saturated, 1.2 g monounsaturated); Carbohydrates: 2 g; Protein: 1 g; Fiber: 0 g; Sodium: 20 mg

Pistachio Cream

When I was in high school, my idea of a great time was sitting on the floor with my best friend, Jill, and devouring a huge bag of pistachios while discussing the cute boys we had crushes on. By the time we were done, we were knee-deep in shells and soul-deep in feminine solidarity. Little did I know we were also improving our health. Turns out those pistachios are their own wellness center, rich in potassium (for cell fluid balance and nerve function), magnesium (for enzymes that help catalyze the body's energy), thiamine (for appetite stimulation), and vitamin B6 (for protein absorption).

Combine all of the ingredients in a blender or food processor and process until very smooth.

GOES WITH: Summer's Best Zucchini Soup (page 67) and Poached Pears with Saffron Broth (page 205).

STORAGE: Store in an airtight container in the refrigerator for 2 weeks or in the freezer for 2 months.

PER SERVING: 1 tablespoon—Calories: 30; Total Fat: 2.4 g (0.3 g saturated, 1.2 g monounsaturated); Carbohydrates: 2 g; Protein: 1 g; Fiber: 1 g; Sodium: 25 mg

MAKES: 1½ cups
PREP TIME: 5 minutes
COOK TIME: Not applicable

1 cup water

2 teaspoons freshly squeezed lemon juice

¼ teaspoon sea salt

1 cup raw pistachios

Cilantro Lime Vinaigrette

MAKES: ½ cup

PREP TIME: 5 minutes

COOK TIME: Not applicable

3½ tablespoons freshly squeezed lime juice

¼ teaspoon sea salt

¼ teaspoon ground cumin

Pinch of cayenne

1 teaspoon maple syrup

¼ cup extra-virgin olive oil

2 teaspoons finely chopped fresh cilantro

Vinaigrettes, at least the way we design them, are dual-purpose. First, they kick up greens and put their taste over the top. They also double as marinades for fish and meats. There's nothing like a meat that's marinated until it practically slides off the bone and into your mouth. In Middle Eastern cuisine, some dishes are marinated for days. Okay, so few us are that patient—and in truth it's really not necessary. Even just a little cuddle time between a dish and these vinaigrettes/marinades is enough to make any meal succulent. I like Cilantro Lime Vinaigrette as a marinade for fish and chicken recipes.

Combine all of the ingredients and whisk until thoroughly blended.

GOES WITH: Arugula with Edamame, Radish, and Avocado (page 89). In addition, this vinaigrette makes a great marinade for fish and chicken.

STORAGE: Store in an airtight container in the refrigerator for 7 days.

PER SERVING: 1 tablespoon—Calories: 65; Total Fat: 7 g (1 g saturated, 5 g monounsaturated); Carbohydrates: 1 g; Protein: 0 g; Fiber: 0 g; Sodium: 75 mg

Zesty Lemon Fennel Vinaigrette

Like Cilantro Lime Vinaigrette, this recipe works wonderfully with salads or as a quick way to dress up fish or meat. The lemon kick makes this a great partner for chicken.

Toast the fennel seeds in a small sauté pan over medium heat, shaking a few times for even toasting, until they become aromatic and start to brown slightly. Be careful that they don't burn. Let cool slightly, then pulse a couple of times in a spice grinder or clean coffee grinder, just until the fennel is broken up a bit.

Transfer to a small bowl and stir in the lemon juice, maple syrup, shallot, and salt. Slowly pour in the olive oil, whisking all the while, and continue whisking until smooth. Transfer to a small container with a fitted lid and shake well and taste. Depending on the type and taste of the lemons, you may want to add a teaspoon of olive oil or a pinch of salt.

GOES WITH: My Family's Favorite Chicken (page 110) as a marinade. It also makes a good marinade for fish and is wonderful drizzled over roasted asparagus and other vegetables.

COOK'S NOTE: Although toasting the fennel seeds may seem like a time-consuming and unnecessary step, I assure you that it isn't. Toasting unleashes the natural oils of the fennel seeds, coaxing out their tremendous flavor and healing properties.

STORAGE: Store in an airtight container in the refrigerator for 5 to 7 days.

PER SERVING: 1 tablespoon—Calories: 65; Total Fat: 7 g (1 g saturated, 5 g monounsaturated); Carbohydrates: 1 g; Protein: 0 g; Fiber: 0 g; Sodium: 75 mg

MAKES: ½ cup
PREP TIME: 5 minutes
COOK TIME: 1 minute

1 teaspoon fennel seeds

3 tablespoons freshly squeezed lemon juice

1 teaspoon maple syrup

½ teaspoon minced shallot

¼ teaspoon sea salt

¼ cup extra-virgin olive oil

Blueberry Compote

MAKES: 1¼ cups

PREP TIME: 5 minutes

COOK TIME: 10 minutes

1½ cups frozen blueberries

1 teaspoon freshly squeezed orange juice or lemon juice

1 teaspoon orange zest or lemon zest

1 teaspoon maple syrup

¼ teaspoon ground ginger

Blueberries contain lots of pectin, which helps soothe the stomach, and one of their active compounds can help prevent cancer cells from getting nourishment.

Combine all of the ingredients in a small saucepan over medium heat. Cook, stirring occasionally, for 3 to 4 minutes, until the mixture bubbles, pulls away from the sides of the pan, and becomes syrupy.

GOES WITH: Best Oatmeal Ever (page 128), Quinoa Porridge with Walnut Cream (page 142).

VARIATION: If you have fresh blueberries, all the better. Just add 2 tablespoons of water to the recipe.

STORAGE: Store in an airtight container in the refrigerator for 7 days or in the freezer for 2 months.

PER SERVING: 1 tablespoon—Calories: 30; Total Fat: 0.4 g (0 g saturated, 0 g monounsaturated); Carbohydrates: 8 g; Protein: 0 g; Fiber: 2 g; Sodium: 0 mg

Dried Fruit Compote

This is an absolute go-to dish for people taking pain medication. Such meds, especially opiates, can stop up the works, if you get my meaning. This isn't your typical fiber-laden, tasteless concoction, aka bran muffins. In addition to prunes, the traditional constipation remedy, this compote includes dried apricots and cherries. We've also brought ginger and cardamom to the party. The result is a delicious compote that smells incredible while it's cooking and goes great over oatmeal or on toast. For days when your digestion need a kick start, this blend will nudge you in the right direction. Believe me, it works. Before cooking the compote, it's best to soak the fruit for a few hours (preferably overnight), so plan ahead. This is great served warm or at room temperature.

Combine the prunes, apricots, cherries, cinnamon, cardamom, ginger, and salt in a saucepan and add water to cover. Soak overnight, if possible, or for a few hours before cooking.

Bring the mixture to a boil over high heat, then lower the heat and gently simmer for about 1 hour, until the fruit is very, very soft and the liquid is syrupy. Stir in the lemon juice and remove from the heat. Remove and discard the cinnamon sticks.

GOES WITH: Best Oatmeal Ever (page 128) and Quinoa Porridge with Walnut Cream (page 142).

COOK'S NOTES: You can use dried apples, pears, figs, or any combination of dried fruit to equal 3 cups.

The compote is a versatile condiment that crosses culinary boundaries and can be used on both sweet and savory dishes. Stir it into yogurt, spoon it alongside a sweet potato, or serve it atop oatmeal. You can even use it like jam: spread a dollop on a piece of toast with almond butter.

STORAGE: Store in an airtight container in the refrigerator for 7 days or in the freezer for 2 months.

PER SERVING: Calories: 303; Total Fat: 0 g; Carbohydrates: 70 g; Protein: 3 g; Fiber: 12 g; Sodium: 85 mg

MAKES: 4 to 5 cups
PREP TIME: 5 minutes
COOK TIME: 1 hour

---

1 cup pitted prunes

1 cup unsulfured dried apricots

1 cup dried cherries or raisins

3 cinnamon sticks

6 cardamom pods, or ¼ teaspoon ground cardamom

½ teaspoon chopped fresh ginger, or ¼ teaspoon ground ginger

Pinch of sea salt

¼ teaspoon freshly squeezed lemon juice

Seasonal Stewed Fruit

MAKES: 1¼ cups

PREP TIME: 10 minutes

COOK TIME: 15 minutes

---

4 large apricots, pitted and quartered

1 teaspoon freshly squeezed lemon juice

Pinch of sea salt

10 cherries, stemmed and pitted

1 teaspoon maple syrup

A foodie friend of mine was in the hospital for leukemia treatments when his caregiver called me. Our buddy wasn't having a great day, and it didn't help that his doctors were saying he couldn't have his favorite pick-me-up food, fruit. This is a guy who can eat a quart of strawberries at a sitting. In a sense, the docs were right; raw fruit can contain bacteria, a problem for people with low white blood cell counts that can leave them prone to infection. But I had a solution. I told his caregiver, "He can have fruit; you just have to cut it up and heat it thoroughly to kill off the germs." The docs had no objections, the caregiver came in with a beautiful medley of stewed seasonal fruit, and my friend was thrilled. So if you're concerned about raw fruits, this is the recipe for you. The heat, along with a little bit of lemon juice and a pinch of sea salt, breaks down the fruit's fiber, making it soft but not mushy. I used apricots and cherries here, but any fruit in season will do.

Combine the apricots, lemon juice, and salt in a small saucepan over low heat and cook, stirring occasionally, until the fruit begins to soften, about 10 minutes. Stir in the cherries, cover, and cook, stirring often, until all of the fruit has softened, about 5 minutes. Remove from the heat and stir in the maple syrup. Serve hot, at room temperature, or chilled.

VARIATIONS: Make a yogurt parfait. Let the fruit cool to room temperature, then spoon ¼ cup of plain organic yogurt into a glass, spoon in ¼ cup of fruit, repeat with another layer of yogurt and then fruit. Serve topped with a sprinkle of Maple-Glazed Walnuts (page 137).

Substitute 2 cups of any seasonal fruit that is available at your local farmers' market or grocery store. Some of my favorite duets are apples with pears, strawberries with rhubarb, and nectarines or peaches with blueberries. Cook firmer fruits first, and adjust the cooking time as needed.

COOK'S NOTE: This fruit is warm and comforting, the perfect topping for hot cereal, like Best Oatmeal Ever (page 128) or Quinoa Porridge with Walnut Cream (page 142).

STORAGE: Store in an airtight container in the refrigerator for 3 to 5 days.

PER SERVING: Calories: 30; Total Fat: 0.2 g (0 g saturated, 0 g mono-unsaturated); Carbohydrates: 7 g; Protein: 1 g; Fiber: 1 g; Sodium: 75 mg

Olive and Caper Relish

I think of capers as my utility condiment, capable of blending into many dishes from eggs to polenta. Capers, which are actually flower buds, are usually pickled. They may be tiny, but they pack a flavorful punch. Here, they're blended with chopped olives and lemon zest to create a mouth-popping relish.

Stir all of the ingredients together.

GOES WITH: Nana's Egg Salad (page 102), My Family's Favorite Chicken (page 110), Lemon Mustard Salmon Salad (page 115), Baked Citrus Halibut with Signora's Tomato Sauce (page 120), and Creamy Polenta (page 134). This relish is also great on a variety of fish, chicken, pasta, and rice dishes, or use it as a sandwich spread or a topping for crostini.

STORAGE: Store in an airtight container in the refrigerator for 7 days.

PER SERVING: 1 tablespoon—Calories: 20; Total Fat: 2 g (0.3 g saturated, 1.5 g monounsaturated); Carbohydrates: 1 g; Protein: 0 g; Fiber: 0 g; Sodium: 110 mg

MAKES: ½ cup
PREP TIME: 5 minutes
COOK TIME: Not applicable

⅓ cup pitted Kalamata olives, rinsed and chopped

2 teaspoons capers, rinsed and chopped

1 teaspoon extra-virgin olive oil

¼ teaspoon freshly squeezed lemon juice

⅛ teaspoon lemon zest

2 tablespoons chopped fresh basil

Moroccan Pesto

This dazzling emerald green sauce is incredibly versatile.

MAKES: 1 cup
PREP TIME: 5 minutes
COOK TIME: Not applicable

---

1 cup tightly packed fresh parsley

½ cup tightly packed fresh cilantro or basil leaves

6 fresh mint leaves

½ teaspoon ground cumin

½ teaspoon paprika

1 clove garlic, chopped

¼ cup extra-virgin olive oil

3 tablespoons freshly squeezed lemon juice

¼ teaspoon salt

2 tablespoons water (optional)

Combine all of the ingredients in a food processor and process until well blended. Do a FASS check to see whether you need to add another squeeze or two of lemon juice, and add water to achieve the desired consistency.

GOES WITH: My Family's Favorite Chicken (page 110), Middle Eastern Chickpea Burgers (page 112), poached salmon (see page 116), and Triple-Citrus Ginger Black Cod (page 119).

STORAGE: Store in airtight container in the refrigerator for 7 days or in the freezer for 2 months.

PER SERVING: 1 tablespoon—Calories: 35; Total Fat: 3.6 g (0.5 g saturated, 2.5 g monounsaturated); Carbohydrates: 1 g; Protein: 0 g; Fiber: 0 g; Sodium: 40 mg

Parsley Basil Drizzle

Drizzles and dollops are very helpful for people whose taste buds are impaired from treatment. Drizzles are a bit like Roman candles; they explode upon the palate, much to the observer's/diner's delight. They're lighter than dollops, but don't be fooled; the parsley in this drizzle is like a whiff of pure oxygen. It's that energizing.

Combine the basil, parsley, lemon juice, water, and salt in a blender or food processor and process until finely chopped. With the motor running, slowly pour in the olive oil and continue to process until very smooth. Do a quick FASS check. If the drizzle tastes too sour, add another pinch of salt.

GOES WITH: Italian White Bean Soup (page 52), Minestrone (page 57), Cooling Cucumber Avocado Soup (page 62), Roasted Red Roma Tomato Soup (page 69), Creamy Broccoli and Potato Soup (page 71), Basil Broccoli (page 75), Easy Eggs in a Cup (page 100), Nana's Egg Salad (page 102), My Family's Favorite Chicken (page 110), Tuscan Farro and Bean Salad (page 111), Lemon Mustard Salmon Salad (page 115), Mediterranean Lentil Salad (page 144), and Simple Tuscan Farro (page 147). It's also great over poached eggs (see page 103).

COOK'S NOTE: This is the base recipe for pesto. If you want a richer, thicker sauce, add ¼ cup of pine nuts or chopped walnuts along with the herbs.

STORAGE: Store in an airtight container in the refrigerator for 3 days. Shake well before serving.

PER SERVING: 1 tablespoon—Calories: 60; Total Fat: 7 g (1 g saturated, 5 g monounsaturated); Carbohydrates: 1 g; Protein: 0 g; Fiber: 0 g; Sodium: 75 mg

MAKES: ½ cup
PREP TIME: 5 minutes
COOK TIME: Not applicable

¼ cup tightly packed fresh basil leaves

½ cup tightly packed fresh flat-leaf parsley leaves

2 tablespoons freshly squeezed lemon juice

1 tablespoon water

¼ teaspoon sea salt

¼ cup extra-virgin olive oil

Herbed and Spiced Yogurt

MAKES: 2 cups

PREP TIME: 20 minutes

COOK TIME: 15 minutes to chill

⅓ cup finely chopped and loosely packed fresh flat-leaf parsley

⅓ cup finely chopped and loosely packed fresh cilantro

⅓ cup finely chopped and loosely packed fresh mint leaves

1 tablespoon extra-virgin olive oil

1 teaspoon maple syrup

1 teaspoon freshly squeezed lemon juice

¼ teaspoon sea salt

¼ teaspoon ground cumin

⅛ teaspoon ground cinnamon

2 cups organic plain yogurt

Yogurt is a wonderful international culinary staple that's been subverted by American agribusiness. Contrary to popular belief, genuine yogurt is anything but the thick, overly sweetened blend you're likely to find in the refrigerated section at your local grocery store. Designed as quickie substitutes for breakfast, too often such yogurts are laden with copious sugar for a rapid ride on the glucose express. Real yogurt—the healthier version known to the rest of the world—is generally much lighter. It's also served in a wider variety of contexts, such as Indian *raitas*, served as a condiment, and Greek *tzatziki*, a combination of cucumbers and yogurt served as a dip, condiment, or spread. Yogurt (the name is Turkish) is meant to refresh, and this version is an ideal topping on cucumbers, lamb, or Middle Eastern Chickpea Burgers. When I first proposed this blend, one of my recipe testers looked at the long list of ingredients and asked, "All this for yogurt?" And then she took a taste . . .

Stir all of the ingredients together until thoroughly combined. Taste; you may want to add a pinch of salt, a spritz of lemon juice, or a bit more sweetener.

Cover tightly and chill for 15 minutes before serving.

GOES WITH: Middle Eastern Chickpea Burgers (page 112), Poached Salmon with Moroccan Pesto (page 116), Orange Pistachio Quinoa (page 141), and Mediterranean Lentil Salad (page 144).

VARIATION: Add 1½ to 2 teaspoons of curry powder.

STORAGE: Store in a covered container in the refrigerator for 3 to 5 days.

PER SERVING: 2 tablespoons—Calories: 300; Total Fat: 12.9 g (3.6 g saturated, 4.3 g monounsaturated); Carbohydrates: 10 g; Protein: 7 g; Fiber: 4 g; Sodium: 270 mg

Signora's Tomato Sauce

I cooked for a lot of crazy signoras when I lived in Italy, and one of them whipped me into shape by insisting that the tomatoes for tomato sauce must FIRST go through a food mill. For the uninitiated, it's kind of like an old coffee mill, but with a more tightly geared hand crank. In would go the roasted tomatoes, and each crank by hand would squeeze them through holes in the side of the mill. I needed a tube of Bengay for my arms after the first batch, but the result is a far lighter sauce than any store-bought variety. If you're not up for the workout, just lightly pulse the tomatoes in a food processor.

Preheat the oven to 400°F.

Gently squeeze the tomatoes by hand to remove excess seeds, then put them in a bowl and toss with 1 tablespoon of the olive oil and ½ teaspoon of salt. Place the tomatoes, cut side down, in a single layer on sheet pans and roast for 20 to 30 minutes, until the skins are just browning and the juices are bubbly. Let cool for 5 minutes, then lift off the skins with a fork.

Meanwhile, heat the remaining 1 tablespoon olive oil in a large saucepan, then add the onion and a pinch of salt and sauté until golden, about 5 minutes. Add the carrots, garlic, and ¼ teaspoon of salt and continue to sauté until the carrots become just tender, about 5 minutes.

Lift the tomatoes off the sheet pans and transfer to a food processor, then pour in any pan juices. Add the carrot mixture and the basil and pulse until pureed but still a little chunky.

Transfer back into the saucepan and stir in ¼ teaspoon of salt. Do a FASS check. Tomatoes can sometimes be acidic, so you may want to add a pinch of sweetener and another pinch of salt.

GOES WITH: Baked halibut (see page 120), Creamy Polenta (page 134), and a wide variety of pasta dishes.

VARIATION: If fresh tomatoes aren't available, you can substitute two 28-ounce cans of plum tomatoes with their liquid.

STORAGE: Store in an airtight container in the refrigerator for 5 days or in the freezer for 2 months.

PER SERVING: Calories: 120; Total Fat: 5.4 g (0.8 g saturated, 3.5 g mono-unsaturated); Carbohydrates: 17 g; Protein: 4 g; Fiber: 5 g; Sodium: 230 mg

SERVES: 6
PREP TIME: 20 minutes
COOK TIME: 30 minutes

4 pounds Roma tomatoes, halved

2 tablespoons extra-virgin olive oil

Sea salt

1 onion, diced small

2 carrots, scrubbed and diced small

2 cloves garlic, chopped

2 cups loosely packed fresh basil leaves, chopped

Chapter 8

Sweet Bites

"Sweet dreams are made of this . . . who am I to disagree?" Okay, maybe I can't sing like Annie Lennox (more like Ethel Merman, if you ask my friends), but I agree with Annie's sentiment: I've never been a fan of making people feel deprived of their favorite tastes, no matter what their health status, and that's especially true of healthy sweets.

I realize I'm treading on somewhat controversial ground here, but here's my thinking: Biologically, sweet is the first taste we develop as babies (especially if we were breastfed), which is one of the reasons we're so drawn to that particular taste throughout life. I firmly believe that if we are cut off from a food group we love, including desserts and sweets, we'll be at risk for disconnecting from food altogether. I've seen that happen.

The challenge, of course, is coming up with desserts that aren't full of empty calories and/or contain foods we truly should avoid during treatment, such as processed flours and sugars.

I credit my baking friend extraordinaire, Wendy Remer, for helping me come up with a host of Sweet Bites that fit the bill. "Meet me at the bottom of the hill," became our inside joke, as we'd converge there constantly by car to share and sample the treats we were working on. It was even more fun than running out for the ice cream truck when I was a kid. We're talking "yum" to the max!

My team and I have really amped up the cancer-fighting herbs and spices in these sweet bites—proof positive that you can, with a little forethought, put health into nearly any dish in the culinary canon. As a further benefit for those with sensitive systems, these treats are dairy and gluten free.

So when that craving for a sweet bite hits, go for one of these delicious morsels. Satisfaction guaranteed.

Almond Muffin Mania

A little saying around my kitchen is, "If it's white, it's just not right." Many white products, especially white sugar and white flour, have been processed and stripped of both color and nutrients. These foods contain empty calories, meaning calories without meaningful amounts of vitamins, minerals, and other micronutrients. Empty calories aren't a good idea for anyone, and they're a definite no-no for people already dealing with diminished appetites. These muffins aren't the monsters so often seen in bakeries—they're smaller and healthier, but no less flavorful. The basic recipe, which is delicious on its own, is built on a foundation of nutrition-rich spelt flour and almonds. I've also provided variations for chocolate orange muffins and ginger lemon muffins. All three versions have one thing in common: They're little powerful bites of joy!

Preheat the oven to 350°F. Prepare a mini muffin tin by generously oiling each cup.

Combine the almond meal, spelt flour, baking powder, and salt in a bowl and stir with a whisk until very well combined. Separately, combine the maple syrup, mashed banana, milk, eggs, oil, almond extract, and vanilla and whisk until smooth. Add the wet mixture to the dry and mix well with a rubber spatula.

Spoon the batter into the muffin cups, filling each about three-fourths full. Bake for 13 to 15 minutes, until a muffin springs back when touched in the center. Let cool on a wire rack for 15 minutes, then gently run a knife or small offset spatula around the sides of the muffins to loosen them before turning them out.

continued

MAKES: 24 mini muffins
PREP TIME: 7 minutes
COOK TIME: 15 minutes
(plus time to cool)

1½ cups almond meal

½ cup spelt flour

1 tablespoon baking powder

⅛ teaspoon sea salt

⅓ cup maple syrup

½ cup mashed banana

¼ cup organic milk, almond milk, or rice milk

2 organic eggs

¼ cup unrefined virgin coconut oil, almond oil, or a neutral-flavored extra-virgin olive oil

1½ teaspoons almond extract

½ teaspoon vanilla extract

VARIATIONS: To make chocolate orange muffins, replace ¼ cup of the flour with ¼ cup unsweetened cocoa powder. Omit the extracts and instead add 1 tablespoon of orange zest or 1 teaspoon of orange oil (not orange extract) to the wet ingredients. Fold ⅓ cup chopped chocolate or mini chocolate chips into the batter once it's mixed.

For ginger lemon muffins, add 1 teaspoon of ground ginger to the dry ingredients. Omit the extracts, and instead add 3 tablespoons of finely chopped peeled fresh ginger, 2 to 3 tablespoons of lemon zest, and 1 tablespoon of freshly squeezed lemon juice to the wet ingredients.

For gluten-free muffins, replace spelt flour with brown rice flour or all-purpose gluten-free flour.

COOK'S NOTES: Mini muffin tins come in a variety of sizes. I prefer using tins with a wide base, around 1½ inches in diameter. Don't despair if you can find that exact size, as most anything will work.

To prevent muffins from sticking to the bottom of the pan, make sure you oil the pan really, really, really well or use paper muffin cups. Then, after baking, you must exercise patience and allow the muffins to cool completely before removing them from the tin.

STORAGE: Store in an airtight container at room temperature for 5 to 7 days or in the freezer for 2 months.

PER SERVING: Calories: 100; Total Fat: 6.4 g (2.4 g saturated, 0.4 g mono-unsaturated); Carbohydrates: 8 g; Protein: 3 g; Fiber: 1 g; Sodium: 75 mg

Baked Apples Filled with Dates and Pecans

When I told my coauthor about this baked apple dish, he said it reminded him of an old folk recipe. When he was little and had an upset tummy, his Russian grandmother would cut up an apple and leave it out on the counter for a few minutes, until it began to brown. His grandmother would then affectionately say, "Come eat, *tatellah*" ("little man" in Yiddish). Lo and behold, a few minutes later his stomach felt better. He always figured it was love at work (and, of course, it was), but years later he found out there was also some science involved: As they brown—or cook, in this case—apples release pectin that naturally soothes the belly. Baking makes the pectin and the rest of the apple easier to digest. In this recipe, the apples are complemented by tasty morsels and spices—toasted pecans, dates, orange zest, and cinnamon—and as they bake, they smell heavenly.

Preheat the oven to 350°F.

Combine the pecans, dates, orange zest and juice, cinnamon, and salt in a small bowl and stir to combine.

Core the apples, leaving half an inch at the bottom, and peel the top edges. Stuff the apples with the pecan filling, then dot the butter on top or melt the butter and brush it on the apple tops.

Put the apples in a baking pan, pour in about 1 inch of apple juice, and cover tightly with foil. Bake for 40 to 60 minutes, until the apples are tender but not mushy. Test for doneness by poking a fork into the apples; they should be tender and yield easily to pressure.

Serve warm, drizzled with the warm apple juice from the baking pan.

COOK'S NOTES: If you don't have dates or pecans, be creative! You can substitute currants or raisins and walnuts or almonds, and if nuts are a problem, you can simply omit them. You can use clarified butter if you like, or for a dairy-free version, use coconut oil.

Use a melon baller to scoop out the apple core; it's important to keep the base intact.

STORAGE: Store in an airtight container in the refrigerator for 3 days.

PER SERVING: Calories: 205; Total Fat: 5.8 g (0.5 g saturated, 3.1 g monounsaturated); Carbohydrates: 41 g; Protein: 2 g; Fiber: 7 g; Sodium: 150 mg

SERVES: 4
PREP TIME: 20 minutes
COOK TIME: 60 minutes

¼ cup finely chopped toasted pecans (see page 93)

¼ cup pitted and finely diced Medjool dates

Zest and juice of 1 orange

¼ teaspoon ground cinnamon

¼ teaspoon sea salt

4 baking apples, such as Pink Lady, Pippin, or McIntosh

1 tablespoon organic butter (optional)

Unfiltered apple juice, for baking

Chocolate Tapioca Pudding

SERVES: 8

PREP TIME: 5 minutes (after soaking the tapioca overnight)

COOK TIME: 25 minutes

½ cup small pearl tapioca

2 cups water, for soaking

3 cups organic milk, almond milk, rice milk, or soy milk

⅛ teaspoon sea salt

2 organic eggs

⅓ cup maple syrup

⅓ cup finely chopped bittersweet or semisweet chocolate

2 teaspoons vanilla extract

Comfort foods are such a big part of this book because, in times of stress, it's natural to seek out foods that have never let you down. So it is with tapioca pudding, a staple throughout the world. The cassava root, which is made into tapioca pearls, is rich in carbohydrates and is gluten free. That makes this dessert a good treat for people seeking to maintain weight without taxing the digestive system. A little chocolate sweetens the package. If you can, use very high-quality chocolate to enhance the yum factor. You can make tapioca without presoaking, but plan on an extra 10 to 20 minutes of cooking time.

Soak the tapioca in the water overnight.

Drain the tapioca and discard the liquid. Combine the milk and salt in a heavy-bottomed saucepan and bring almost to a simmer; tiny bubbles will form around the edges of the pan. Stir in the tapioca and bring to a boil, stirring constantly, then turn down the heat as low as possible and cook, stirring frequently, for 10 to 15 minutes, until the tapioca pearls have swollen and are translucent and tender. (If the tapioca is not presoaked, the extra cooking time will come in here.)

Whisk the eggs and maple syrup together in small bowl, then gradually add 1 cup of the tapioca mixture to the eggs while whisking constantly. Whisk the egg mixture back into the saucepan with the tapioca and continue to cook over very low heat, stirring constantly, until the pudding is bubbling gently. Cook for about 5 minutes, until somewhat thickened. The pudding will do most of its thickening while it cools, so don't overcook it at this point or the texture will be rubbery.

Remove from the heat and stir in the chopped chocolate. Let stand for 1 minute, then stir until the chocolate has melted and is thoroughly mixed into the pudding. Stir in the vanilla.

Transfer to a heatproof bowl or serving dish and serve warm or place a piece of parchment paper directly on the surface of the pudding, to prevent a skin from forming, and refrigerate for at least 2 hours to serve chilled.

STORAGE: Store in an airtight container in the refrigerator for 3 to 5 days.

PER SERVING: Calories: 180; Total Fat: 6.1 g (3.2 g saturated, 1.2 g mono-unsaturated); Carbohydrates: 26 g; Protein: 6 g; Fiber: 0 g; Sodium: 95 mg

Great Pumpkin Custard

When I was in college, I always loved coming home at the holidays—in part because of my mother's pumpkin pie. I still love pumpkin, as does my husband, so this recipe is for him. I was looking for something that could deliver that awesome pumpkin taste without a fat-laden crust, and the homey familiarity of custard provided a perfect vehicle.

Preheat the oven to 325°F.

Stir the pumpkin, cinnamon, salt, ginger, cloves, allspice, and nutmeg together in a large bowl. In a smaller bowl, beat the eggs lightly, then whisk in the maple syrup, molasses, vanilla, and milk. Whisk the egg mixture into the pumpkin mixture until well combined.

Pour the custard into 6 (½-cup) ramekins. Place the ramekins in a baking pan and add enough hot water to the dish to come up 2 inches high around the ramekins. Carefully transfer to the oven and bake for 45 to 55 minutes, until a knife inserted into the center comes out clean. Serve warm or chilled.

COOK'S NOTES: Make sure that the baking pan you use to hold the ramekins has sides that are at least 3 inches high. This will ensure that the hot water you pour in doesn't slosh over when you transfer the pan to and from the oven. Two teaspoons of pumpkin pie spice mixture can be substituted for the spices listed. Molasses adds a real depth of flavor; however, if you don't have it in your pantry, use an additional tablespoon of maple syrup.

STORAGE: Store in an airtight container in the refrigerator for 3 days.

PER SERVING: Calories: 110; Total Fat: 3.2 g (1.4 g saturated, 1 g mono-unsaturated); Carbohydrates: 18 g; Protein: 4 g; Fiber: 1 g; Sodium: 240 mg

SERVES: 6
PREP TIME: 10 minutes
COOK TIME: 60 minutes

1 cup canned pumpkin puree

1 teaspoon ground cinnamon

½ teaspoon sea salt

½ teaspoon ground ginger

¼ teaspoon ground cloves

¼ teaspoon ground allspice

¼ teaspoon grated nutmeg

2 organic eggs

2 tablespoons grade A dark amber maple syrup

1 tablespoon molasses

1 teaspoon vanilla extract

1 cup organic milk or coconut milk

Cardamom Maple Mini Macaroons

MAKES: 24 macaroons
PREP TIME: 20 minutes
COOK TIME: 15 minutes

2 cups unsweetened shredded coconut

1 teaspoon ground cardamom

¼ cup maple syrup

½ teaspoon vanilla extract

3 organic large egg whites

Pinch of sea salt

I knew I wanted to do a cardamom macaroon recipe for this book because my grandmother, Doris, got me hooked on them when I was knee-high. These bite-size morsels are made using maple syrup for just the right amount of sweet. Cardamom adds a warm, spicy touch, while aiding digestion and possibly slowing tumor growth.

Preheat the oven to 350°F and line a baking sheet with parchment paper.

In a medium bowl, mix together the shredded coconut and the cardamom. Add the maple syrup and vanilla and mix together until well combined.

In another bowl, whisk together the egg whites and salt until stiff peaks form. Gently fold the coconut mixture into the egg whites and refrigerate for 20 minutes or freeze for 10 minutes.

Using a teaspoon and your fingers, form the dough into 24 small mounds on the prepared pan. Bake for 12 to 15 minutes, until golden brown. Let cool completely before serving.

VARIATION: For a more decadent dessert, dip the macaroons in chocolate. Chop 4 ounces of your favorite dark chocolate, place it in a dry metal or glass bowl, and set it over a pan of gently simmering hot water (or use a double boiler if you have one). Stir the chocolate constantly until just melted, then remove it from the heat. Now for the fun part: dip the macaroons into the melted chocolate, then place them on a pan or plate lined with wax or parchment paper. Chill in the refrigerator until the chocolate hardens, then enjoy!

STORAGE: Store in an airtight container at room temperature for 5 to 7 days.

PER SERVING: Calories: 55; Total Fat: 3 g (2.7 g saturated, 0.1 g mono-unsaturated); Carbohydrates: 5 g; Protein: 1 g; Fiber: 1 g; Sodium: 20 mg

Coconut Rice Pudding

Rice pudding is a soothing must-have for many people. The challenge here was figuring out how to create a delicious, healthier version that still had all of that creamy goodness without too much dairy. After a lot of tinkering together with my dessert maven, Wendy, we found that combining coconut milk—which has great nutritional qualities—and regular milk gave us the taste and consistency we were looking for. We added a kick of flavor by including cardamom and orange zest. If you want to go completely dairy free, see the variation.

Combine the rice and water in a heavy-bottomed saucepan and bring to a boil. Lower the heat and simmer gently, uncovered, for 10 minutes.

Drain the rice, rinse the saucepan, then put the milk, coconut milk, maple syrup, cardamom, and salt in the saucepan and bring to a boil. Stir in the rice, turn down the heat to medium-low, and simmer gently, stirring occasionally, for about 30 minutes; during the last 10 minutes of cooking, stir more frequently to prevent sticking or scorching. The pudding is done when the rice is tender and starts to stick to the bottom of the pan and the pudding has the consistency of loose oatmeal. It will thicken as it cools.

Remove from the heat and stir in the orange zest, vanilla, and raisins. Transfer to a heatproof bowl or serving dish and serve warm or place a piece of parchment paper directly on the surface of the pudding, to prevent a skin from forming, and refrigerate for at least 2 hours to serve chilled. Top with compote just before serving.

VARIATIONS: To make a dairy-free version of this recipe, use 2¼ cups of almond milk or rice milk in place of the regular milk and increase the amount of coconut milk to 1 cup. The dairy-free version will take about 5 minutes less to cook.

To increase the yum factor, and for a bit of crunch, sprinkle some toasted coconut or sliced almonds on top before serving.

STORAGE: Store in an airtight container in the refrigerator for 3 to 5 days.

PER SERVING: Calories: 455; Total Fat: 9.4 g (7.2 g saturated, 1.1 g monounsaturated); Carbohydrates: 84 g; Protein: 7 g; Fiber: 12 g; Sodium: 177 mg

SERVES: 6
PREP TIME: 5 minutes
COOK TIME: 40 minutes

1¼ cups Arborio rice

2 cups water

2½ cups organic milk or rice milk

¾ cup coconut milk

2 tablespoons maple syrup

¼ teaspoon ground cardamom

Pinch of sea salt

½ teaspoon orange zest

2 teaspoons vanilla extract

¼ cup raisins or currants (optional)

Blueberry Compote (page 182), Dried Fruit Compote (page 183), or Seasonal Stewed Fruit (page 184), for serving

Chocolate Apricot Date Nut Truffles

MAKES: 20 truffles

PREP TIME: 15 minutes

COOK TIME: 2 hours in the refrigerator

¼ cup finely diced dried apricots

2 tablespoons boiling water

2 ounces dark chocolate with a 64 to 72 percent cacao content, finely chopped

⅓ cup plus 2 tablespoons almonds

1 cup pitted and halved Medjool dates

1½ teaspoons orange zest

⅛ teaspoon sea salt

½ cup unsweetened shredded coconut

For chocolate aficionados, nothing provides a better fix than a truffle. These confections are a scrumptious mélange of chocolate, dates, orange zest, and ground nuts, all rolled in coconut. I could tell you that the reason to eat these is because they're high in protein and phytochemicals, but how 'bout we just call that a nice side benefit of yum! Since you're going to indulge in a chocolate dessert, be sure to make it the best by using high-quality chocolate.

Soak the diced apricots in cold water for 5 minutes.

Stir the boiling water into the chopped chocolate and let stand for 30 seconds. Using a small whisk, stir until the chocolate is completely melted and glossy.

Coarsely grind the almonds in a food processor, then add the dates, orange zest, salt, and the chocolate mixture and process until smooth, about 1 minute. Transfer to a bowl; drain the apricots well and stir them into the chocolate mixture. Cover and chill for approximately 2 hours in the refrigerator or 15 minutes in the freezer, until the mixture is firm.

Scatter the coconut on a large plate. Scoop up approximately 1 tablespoon of the chocolate mixture and roll it into a smooth ball between your palms, then roll it in the coconut to coat. Repeat with the remaining mixture, then place the truffles in an airtight container until you're ready to serve them.

VARIATION: Substitute ½ cup of pecans or walnuts for the almonds.

COOK'S NOTES: Cacao content is the amount of pure cocoa bean used in the chocolate; the higher the percentage, the more chocolate, which also means less sugar. Plus, the higher the cacao content, the more antioxidants in the chocolate.

STORAGE: Store in an airtight container in the refrigerator for 1 week or in the freezer for 2 months.

PER SERVING: Calories: 145; Total Fat: 7.5 g (3.6 g saturated, 2.1 g mono-unsaturated); Carbohydrates: 19 g; Protein: 2 g; Fiber: 3 g; Sodium: 30 mg

Poached Pears with Saffron Broth

I call this "company food"—as in, what can I make for company that's easy but impressive? Poaching a pear sounds fancy, but all you're doing is simmering it in a fruity broth. The poaching softens up the pear, making it a breeze to chew and digest. The saffron broth turns the pears a beautiful sunset yellow color. If you're looking for extra calories, top with a generous dollop of nut cream.

Stir the pear nectar, lemon zest, ginger, maple syrup, and saffron together in a large saucepan or 3-quart sauté pan over medium-high heat. Bring to a boil.

Place the pear halves in the saucepan, flat side down. Place a piece of parchment paper over the pears and cover with a small plate to weight the pears down as they simmer. Lower the heat and simmer until the pears are tender and a knife pierces them all the way through without resistance.

Remove the pears from the saucepan. Return the liquid to the heat, bring to a lively simmer, and cook until syrupy, about 10 minutes. Taste the liquid; it may need a pinch of salt and a squeeze of lemon juice to balance the flavors.

Serve the pears drizzled with the poaching liquid and topped with a dollop of nut cream if you like.

COOK'S NOTES: To seed and stem a pear beautifully, once it's cut in half, use a melon baller to scoop out the center, making sure to remove all of the seeds. Then use a sharp paring knife to make a small angled slice on each side of the core, running out from the center of the pear to the stem. This will leave a clean and even triangle-shaped channel where the stem and the core had been.

You can garnish the pears with the solids from the broth. Lemon peel, vanilla pods, star anise pods, and cloves all make beautiful garnishes.

STORAGE: Store in an airtight container in the refrigerator for 3 to 5 days.

PER SERVING: Calories: 225; Total Fat: 0.2 g (0 g saturated, 0 g mono-unsaturated); Carbohydrates: 59 g; Protein: 1 g; Fiber: 4 g; Sodium: 15 mg

SERVES: 4
PREP TIME: 10 minutes
COOK TIME: 40 minutes

4 cups pear nectar

Zest of 1 lemon, in long pieces

4 inches peeled fresh ginger, cut into ¼-inch pieces

1 tablespoon maple syrup

Generous pinch of saffron (12 to 15 threads)

2 ripe but firm pears, preferably Bosc or Comice, peeled, cut in half, seeded, and stemmed

Salt (optional)

Lemon juice (optional)

Pistachio Cream (page 179) or Cashew Cream (page 178), for serving (optional)

Strawberries with Mango Coconut "Sabayon" Sauce

SERVES: 4

PREP TIME: 5 minutes

COOK TIME: 20 minutes

1 (14-ounce) can coconut milk

1½ cups chopped mango, fresh or frozen

Pinch of sea salt

½ teaspoon freshly squeezed lime juice

3 cups organic strawberries, hulled and halved

4 sprigs fresh mint, for garnish (optional)

This recipe is a little like karaoke: not exactly the original, but still a lot of fun, and without all the production. One of my fondest kitchen memories is making the dessert or sweet topping that the French call *sabayon* and the Italians call *zabaglione*. A combination of whisked egg yolks, marsala wine, and sugar, it's a high-wire act that has to go right from the heat to the plate. Get it right, and it's a froth of pure delight. Put it under the flame for a few seconds too long, and you're toast. This immensely more healthful version, which features mango and coconut, provides a similarly flavorful lightness, minus the need for perfectly timed kitchen pyrotechnics. It's great alone, or serve it drizzled over berries or rice pudding.

Put the coconut milk in a saucepan and stir until homogenous. Stir in the mango and salt and simmer, covered, over medium-low heat until the mango is soft, 15 to 20 minutes.

Pour the mixture into a food processor, add the lime juice, and process until smooth. Spoon over fresh organic strawberries and serve garnished with the mint.

GOES WITH: Coconut Rice Pudding (page 201), sorbets, and fresh fruit, especially raspberries.

VARIATION: For a more pudding-like texture, leave out the lime juice and cook for an additional 10 minutes. Pour into 4 small ramekins and chill for at least 2 hours before serving.

STORAGE: Store in an airtight container in the refrigerator for 5 days.

PER SERVING: Calories: 275; Total Fat: 21.7 g (18.8 g saturated, 1 g monounsaturated); Carbohydrates: 22 g; Protein: 3 g; Fiber: 5 g; Sodium: 90 mg

Triple Ginger Snap Cookies with Pecans

For people (and especially kids) who like crisply textured sweets, there's nothing like a ginger snap to scratch that itch. Many of my clients worry that they'll have to give up sweet treats like cookies during treatment. Nonsense. You just have to be smart about it, and this recipe shows you how. It uses quality ingredients (and no refined flour) and many cancer-fighting spices. There's just one caveat: make the dough at least three hours before you want to bake the cookies, and preferably an entire day ahead. Once you make the dough, it can be stored in the refrigerator for up to five days. Chilling the dough makes it easier to cut the cookies and also gives the flavors a chance to come together so the cookies taste their very best.

Line a loaf pan with plastic wrap, with several inches overhanging on each side.

Combine the coconut oil, sugar, butter, molasses, cinnamon, ginger, and cloves in a saucepan over medium heat, and cook, stirring constantly, until the mixture comes to a boil. Pour into a heatproof bowl or measuring cup and let cool to room temperature.

Combine the flour, baking soda, and salt in a large bowl and stir with a whisk. Whisk the egg into the cooled oil mixture until well combined, then pour the oil mixture into the flour mixture and mix well using a rubber spatula. Stir in the pecans, candied ginger, and grated ginger.

Transfer the dough to the prepared loaf pan, fold the flaps of plastic wrap over the dough, and press gently into an even layer. Chill for at least 3 hours, or preferably overnight.

When you're ready to bake the cookies, preheat the oven to 400°F and line two baking sheets with parchment paper. Lift the dough from the pan, unwrap it, and cut it in half lengthwise. Rewrap one piece and return it to the fridge. Slice the other piece crosswise into very thin cookies, about the thickness of a graham cracker, and place on the prepared pans, leaving 1 inch between cookies. Bake one pan at a time for 7 to 9 minutes, until the edges of the cookies begin to brown visibly. (If you have a convection oven, you can bake both pans of cookies at the same time.) Let cool on the pans for 5 minutes, then transfer to a cooling rack to cool completely.

continued

MAKES: 38 cookies

PREP TIME: 15 minutes (plus at least 3 hours to chill the dough)

COOK TIME: 9 minutes per sheet

Scant ½ cup unrefined virgin coconut oil, melted

⅔ cup evaporated cane sugar or coconut sugar

2 tablespoons organic butter or unrefined virgin coconut oil

⅓ cup unsulphured molasses

1½ teaspoons ground cinnamon

1 tablespoon ground ginger

¼ teaspoon ground cloves

2⅔ cups spelt flour

1 teaspoon baking soda

⅛ teaspoon sea salt

1 organic egg

¾ cup chopped raw pecans

3 tablespoons chopped uncrystallized candied ginger (see Cook's Notes)

1 tablespoon grated fresh ginger

Triple Ginger Snap Cookies with Pecans, *continued*

COOK'S NOTES: These cookies freeze beautifully, both in dough form and baked. If freezing the dough, wrap it tightly in plastic wrap.

If you can't find uncrystallized candied ginger, use the crystallized version; just rinse and pat dry before chopping.

STORAGE: Store in an airtight container in the refrigerator for 5 to 7 days or in the freezer for 2 months.

PER SERVING: Calories: 110; Total Fat: 5.6 g (3.1 g saturated, 1.4 g mono-unsaturated); Carbohydrates: 14 g; Protein: 2 g; Fiber: 1 g; Sodium: 50 mg

Resources

Where can you find that 16-quart stockpot or sharp chef's knife? The Internet, of course. Here's a list of websites you might find useful; they ship anywhere in the United States and offer sale items on a regular basis.

Kitchen Equipment

AMAZON: amazon.com

BED BATH & BEYOND: bedbathandbeyond.com

KITCHEN EMPORIUM: for airpots and insulated carafes, kitchenemporium.com

SUR LA TABLE: surlatable.com

VITAMIX: for the blender I use to puree everything, vitamix.com

WILLIAMS-SONOMA: williams-sonoma.com

Specialty Ingredients

ARTISANA: for organic and raw nut butters, coconut butter, and coconut oil made in a vegan facility that processes tree nuts, but not peanuts, gluten, or soy, artisanafoods.com

BIG TREE FARMS: for organic coconut palm sugar; we used the blonde variety for these recipes, but vanilla would work well in the cookie recipes, bigtreefarms.com

BIONATURE: for Italian organic fruit nectars, bionaturae.com

BOB'S RED MILL: for teff flour, almond meal, and gluten-free oats, bobsredmill.com

BLACK WING: for organic, free-range chicken, blackwing.com

CELTIC SEA SALT: for sea salt, selinanaturally.com

EDEN FOODS: for kombu, kudzu, dried tart cherries, and many other high-quality ingredients, edenfoods.com

LOTUS FOODS: for heirloom and alternative varieties of rice, including forbidden rice, lotusfoods.com

MAINE COAST SEA VEGETABLES: for kombu, seaveg.com

MAPLE VALLEY: for Grade B maple syrup from an organic maple cooperative, maplevalleysyrup.coop

SPICELY ORGANICS: a one-stop shop for a wide variety and comprehensive selection of spices and herbs in small packages, spicely.com

SPECTRUM: for healthful cooking oils, spectrumorganics.com

TRADITIONAL MEDICINALS: for certified organic herbal and medicinal teas, traditionalmedicinals.com

US WELLNESS MEATS: for grass-fed and humanely raised bison, beef, chicken, and lamb, grasslandbeef.com

VITAL CHOICE: for wild, line-caught salmon, including lox, and other high-quality seafood; organic specialty foods; and grass-fed beef, vitalchoice.com

National Grocery Chains and Online Markets

LOCAL HARVEST: immense directory to sources of locally grown organic food, plus an online catalog for items not available locally, localharvest.org

ORGANIC PROVISIONS: online organic grocery, orgfood.com

SAFEWAY: mainstream supermarket with its own line of organic food and produce, safeway.com

SPROUTS FARMERS MARKETS: chain of supermarkets in the western United States, with a focus on natural and high-quality products, sprouts.com

SUN ORGANIC FARM: online organic market, sunorganic.com

TRADER JOE'S: nationwide grocery store with organic products, traderjoes.com

WHOLE FOODS: the first certified organic supermarket in the United States, wholefoodsmarket.com

Farmers' Markets and Local Foods

EAT WELL GUIDE: directory to local, sustainable, and organic farmers' markets, restaurants, stores, bakeries, and more, eatwellguide.org

EAT WILD: state-by-state directory of local sources for grass-fed meats, poultry, and dairy products, eatwild.com

EPICURIOUS SEASONAL INGREDIENTS MAP: for info on local produce that's ripe and in season in your area at any given time, epicurious.com/articlesguides/seasonalcooking/farmtotable/seasonalingredientmap

LOCAL HARVEST: immense directory to sources of locally grown organic food, plus an online catalog for items not available locally, localharvest.org

ORGANIC KITCHEN: resource guide with listings for organic markets, restaurants, farms, vineyards, and more, organickitchen.com

REAL TIME FARMS: directory of local farmers and restaurants that use local foods, along with information on how food travels from field to plate, realtimefarms.com

US DEPARTMENT OF AGRICULTURE: nationwide farmers' market finder, search.ams.usda.gov/farmersmarkets

Environmental Resources

ENVIRONMENTAL WORKING GROUP: for a shopper's guide to pesticides in produce, ewg.org/foodnews

MONTEREY BAY AQUARIUM: for a list of sustainable seafood, seafoodwatch.org/cr/seafoodwatch.aspx

More Learning Resources from Rebecca

THE CANCER FIGHTING KITCHEN ONLINE COURSE: surviving and thriving during treatment and beyond, rebecca-katz.teachable.com

CONNECTING THE DOTS: blog at rebeccakatz.com

Bibliography

Aggarwal, B. B., and Shishodia, S. (2004). "Suppression of the nuclear factor-kappaB activation pathway by spice-derived phytochemicals: Reasoning for seasoning." *Annals of the New York Academy of Sciences* 1030:434–441. PMID: 15659827.

Alarcon de la Lastra, C., Barranco, M. D., Motilva, V., and Herrerias, J. M. (2001). "Mediterranean diet and health: Biological importance of olive oil." *Current Pharmaceutical Design* 7(10):933–950. PMID: 11472248.

American Cancer Society. (2007). "Lycopene." July 12. www.cancer.org/docroot/ETO/content/ETO_5_3X_Lycopene.asp

Balendiran, G., Dabur, R., and Fraser, D. (2004). "The role of glutathione in cancer." *Cell Biochemistry and Function* 22(6): 343–352.

Blomhoff, R., Carlsen, M. H., Andersen, L. F., and Jacobs, D. R., Jr. (2006). "Health benefits of nuts: Potential role of antioxidants." *British Journal of Nutrition* 96(Suppl 2): S52–S60. PMID: 17125534.

Boyles, S. (2003). "Eggs may lower breast cancer risk: Vegetable oils and fiber also may be protective." March 16. http://women.webmd.com/news/20030221/eggs-may-lower-breast-cancer-risk

Caldwell, E. (2008). "Turning up the heat on tomatoes boosts absorption of lycopene." August 21. http://researchnews.osu.edu/archive/lycoproc.htm.

Canene-Adams, K., Lindshield, B. L., Wang, S., Jeffery, E. H., Clinton, S. K., and Erdman, J. W., Jr. (2007). "Combinations of tomato and broccoli enhance antitumor activity in Dunning R3327-H prostate adenocarcinomas." *Cancer Research* 67(2):836–843. PMID: 17213256.

Cao, Y., and Cao, R. (1999). "Angiogenesis inhibited by drinking tea." *Nature* 398(6726):381.

Chen, C. Y., and Blumberg, J. B. (2008). "Phytochemical composition of nuts." *Asia Pacific Journal of Clinical Nutrition* 17(Suppl 1):329–332.

Chen, D., Daniel, K. G., Kuhn, D. J., et al. (2004). "Green tea and tea polyphenols in cancer prevention." *Frontiers in Bioscience* 9:2618–2631. PMID: 15358585.

Cheng, A., Has, C. H., Lin, J. K., et al. (2001). "Phase I clinical trial of curcumin, a chemopreventative agent, in patients with high-risk or pre-malignant lesions." *Anticancer Research* 21(4B):2895–2900.

Cotterchio, M., Boucher, B., Kreiger, N., et al. (2007). "Dietary phytoestrogen intake—lignans and isoflavones—and breast cancer risk." *Cancer Causes and Control* (19)3: 259–272.

Crowell, P. (1999). "Prevention and therapy of cancer by dietary monoterpenes." *Journal of Nutrition* 129:775–778.

Cumashi, A., Ushakova, N. A., Preobrazhenskaya, M. E., et al. (2007). "A comparative study of the anti-inflammatory, anticoagulant, antiangiogenic, and antiadhesive activities of nine different fucoidans from brown seaweeds." *Glycobiology* 17(5):541–552.

Dietrich, M., Traber, M. G., Jacques, P., Cross, C. E., Hu, Y., and Block, G. (2006). "Does gamma-tocopherol play a role in the primary prevention of heart disease and cancer?" *Journal of the American College of Nutrition* 25(4):292–299.

Edris, A. E., and Farrag, E. S. (2003). "Antifungal activity of peppermint and sweet basil essential oils and their major aroma constituents on some plant pathogenic fungi from the vapor phase." *Die Nahrung* 47(2):117–121.

Elgayyar, M., Draughon, F. A., Golden, D. A., and Mount, J. R. (2001). "Antimicrobial activity of essential oils from plants against selected pathogenic and saprophytic microorganisms." *Journal of Food Protection* 64(7):1019–1024. PMID: 11456186.

Erhardt, J. G., Meisner, C., Bode, J. C., and Bode, C. (2003). "Lycopene, beta-carotene, and colorectal adenomas." *American Journal of Clinical Nutrition* 78(6):1219–1224.

Fowke, J. H., Chung, F. L., Jin, F., et al. (2003). "Urinary isothiocyanate levels, brassica, and human breast cancer." *Cancer Research* 63(14):3980–3986. PMID: 12873994.

Galeone, C., Pelucchi, C., Levi, F., et al. (2006). "Onion and garlic use and human cancer." *American Journal of Clinical Nutrition* 84(5):1027–1032.

George, S. L., Polascik, T. J., Albala, M., et al. (2007). "Impact of flaxseed supplementation and dietary fat restriction on prostate cancer proliferation and other biomarkers: Results of a phase II randomized controlled trial (RCT) using a presurgical model." *Journal of Clinical Oncology, 2007 ASCO Annual Meeting Proceedings Part I,* 25(Suppl 18):1510.

George Mateljan Foundation. (2008). "The world's healthiest foods: Kale." www.whfoods .com/genpage.php?tname=foodspice&dbid=38

"Ginger 'could halt bowel cancer'" (2003). http://news.bbc.co.uk/2/hi/health/3221547.stm

Golden E., Lam P., Kardosh A., Gaffney K. (2009). "Green tea polyphenols block the anticancer effects of bortezomib and other boronic acid-based proteasome inhibitors." *Journal of the American Society of Hematology* https://www.ncbi.nlm.nih.gov/ pubmed/19190249

Honan, W. (2004). "Researchers rewrite first chapter for the history of medicine." March 2. *New York Times.* www.nytimes.com/2004/03/02/science/02MEDI.html?ex=1393563600 &en=c3177ebac2572d43&ei=5007&partner=USERLAND

Hou, D., Kai, K., Li, J., et al. (2003). "Anthocyanidins inhibit activator protein 1 activity and cell transformation: Structure-activity relationship and molecular mechanisms." September 22. *Carcinogenesis* http://carcin.oxfordjournals.org/cgi/content/abstract/ bgg184v1

Iberg, A. J., Chen, J. C., Zhao, H., Hoffman, S. C., Comstock, G. W., and Helzlsouer, K. J. (2000). "Household exposure to passive cigarette smoking and serum micronutrient concentrations." *American Journal of Clinical Nutrition* 72(6):1576–82.

Jankun, J., Selman, S. H., Swiercz, R., et al. (1997). "Why drinking green tea could prevent cancer." *Nature* 387(6633):561.

Murray CJ, Atkinson C, et al. (2013), "The State of US Health, 1990–2010," JAMA; 310(6):591–608.

Karadeniz, F., Durst, R. W., and Wrolstad, R. E. (2000). "Polyphenolic composition of raisins." *Journal of Agricultural and Food Chemistry* 48(11):5343–5350. PMID: 11087484.

Kato K., Takahashi, S., Cui, L., et al. (2000). "Suppressive effects of dietary genistin and daidzin on rat prostate carcinogenesis." *Japan Journal of Cancer* 91(8):786–791.

Kawa, J. M., Taylor, C. G., and Przybylski, R. (1996). "Buckwheat concentrate reduces serum glucose in streptozotocin-diabetic rats." *Journal of Agricultural and Food Chemistry* 51(25):7287–7291. PMID: 14640572.

Kim, Y. (2004). "Will mandatory folic acid fortification prevent or promote cancer?" *American Journal of Clinical Nutrition* 80(5):1123–1128.

Linus Pauling Institute. (2007). "Molybdenum." http://lpi.oregonstate.edu/infocenter/minerals/molybdenum

Linus Pauling Institute. (2005). "Ligans: hormone-associated cancers." http://lpi.oregonstate.edu/infocenter/phytochemicals/lignans

Li, T., Molteni, A., Latkovich, P., Castellani, W., and Baybutt, R. C. (2003). "Vitamin A depletion induced by cigarette smoke is associated with the development of emphysema in rats." *Journal of Nutrition* 133(8):2629–34. PMID: 12888649.

Lui R. (2002). "Long-cooked corn higher in antioxidant." www.psa-rising.com/eatingwell/corn/cooked-phenolics-0802.htm

Marimuthu, S., Adluri, S., and Venugopal, M. (2007). "Ferulic acid: Therapeutic Potential through its antioxidant property." *Journal of Clinical Biochemical Nutrition* 40(2):92–100. PMCID: PMC2127228.

De, M., De, M. K., Sen, P., and Banerjee, A. (2000). "Antimicrobial properties of star anise." *Phytotherapy Research* 16(1): 94–95.

Miyazawa, K., Kasuga, I., Minemura, K., et al. (2003). "Apoptosis induction of vitamin K_2 in lung carcinoma cell lines: the possibility of vitamin K_2 therapy for lung cancer." *International Journal of Oncology* 23(3):627–32. PMID: 12888897.

Mujumdar, A. M., Dhuley, J. N., Deshmukh, V. K., et al. (1990). "Anti-inflammatory activity of piperine." *Japanese Journal of Medical Science and Biology* 43(3):95–100. PMID: 2283727.

National Cancer Institute. "Glycosaminoglycan." www.cancer.gov/publications/dictionaries/cancer-terms?cdrid=44206

National Cancer Institute. "Piperine extract." www.cancer.gov/templates/drugdictionary .aspx?CdrID=440023

National Cancer Institute. "Psoralen." www.cancer.gov/publications/dictionaries/ cancer-terms?cdrid=44900

National Cancer Institute. "Salvia." www.cancer.gov/templates/drugdictionary .aspx?CdrID=574480

Nevin, K. G., and Rajamohan, T. (2004). "Beneficial effects of virgin coconut oil on lipid parameters and in vitro LDL oxidation." *Clinical Biochemistry* 37(9):830–835. PMID: 15329324.

Nimptsch, R., Rohrmann, S., and Linseisen, J. (2008). "Dietary intake of vitamin K and risk of prostate cancer in the Heidelberg cohort of the European Prospecetive Investigation into Cancer and Nutrition (EPIC-Heidelberg)." *American Journal of Clinical Nutrition* 87(4):985–992.

Nutrition Data. (2008). "Beans, kidney, all types, mature seeds, cooked, boiled, without salt." www.nutritiondata.com/facts/legumes-and-legume-products/4297/2

Nutrition Data. (2008). "Lentils, raw." www.nutritiondata.com/facts/legumes-and-legume-products/4337/2

Ogbolu, D. O., Oni, A. A., Daini, O. A., and Oloko, A. P. (2007). "In vitro antimicrobial properties of coconut oil on *Candida* species in Ibadan, Nigeria." *Journal of Medicinal Food* 10(2):384–387. PMID: 17651080.

Ouellet, V., Marois, J., Weisnagel, S. J., and Jacques, H. (2007). "Dietary cod protein improves insulin sensitivity in insulin-resistant men and women." *Diabetes Care* (11): 2816–21. PMID: 17682120.

Prakash P., Krinsky, N. I., and Russell, R. M. (2000). "Retinoids, carotenoids, and human breast cancer cell cultures: A review of differential effects." *Nutrition Reviews* 58(6):170–176.

Queensland Institute of Medical Research. (2008). "Bromelain: New cancer fighting properties uncovered." August 5. *The Daily Health* www.thehealthierlife.co.uk/ natural-health-articles/cancer/bromelain-cancer-fighting-properties-00075.html

Sartippour, M. R., Seeram, N. P., Rao, J. Y., and Moro, A. (2008). "Ellagitannin-rich pomegranate extract inhibits angiogenesis in prostate cancer in vitro and in vivo." *International Journal of Oncology* 2(2):475–80. PMID: 18202771.

Schmandke, H. (2005) "Betalains in beetroot and prickly pear fruit." http://eurekamag .com/research/004/054/004054580.php

Sengupta, A., Ghosh, S., and Bhattacharjee, S. (2005). "Dietary cardamom inhibits the formation of azoxymethane-induced aberrant crypt foci in mice and reduces COX-2 and iNOS expression in the colon." *Asian Pacific Journal of Cancer Prevention* 6(2):118–22. PMID: 16101317.

Sereiti, M. R., Abu-Amer, K. M., and Sen, P. (1999). "Pharmacology of rosemary (*Rosmarinus officinalis* Linn.) and its therapeutic potentials." *Indian Journal of Experimental Biology* 37(2):124–30. PMID: 10641130.

Stoner, G. (2001). "Black raspberries show multiple defenses in thwarting cancer." http://researchnews.osu.edu/archive/canberry.htm

Wood, R. (1988). *The Whole Foods Encyclopedia.* New York: Prentice-Hall Press.

Yuan, J. M., Stram, D. O., Arakawa, K., Lee, H. P., and Yu, M. C. (2003). "Dietary cryptoxanthin and reduced risk of lung cancer: The Singapore Chinese Health Study." *Cancer Epidemiology, Biomarkers and Prevention* 12(9):890–898.

Yuan, Y. V., and Walsh, N. A. (2006). "Antioxidant and antiproliferative activities of extracts from a variety of edible seaweeds." *Food and Chemical Toxicology* 44(7):1144–1150.

Acknowledgments

This book would never have come to pass without the following people. I'm awed by their generosity of spirit and time, as well as their heartfelt desire to make this book all that it could be.

My heartfelt thanks to Donald Abrams, MD, for your lovely foreword to this second edition. You are a true gift to all of your patients, and I'm grateful for your support and the teaching we've done together over the years. Thank you, Jeanne Wallace, PhD, for keeping me so impeccably informed in the ever-changing world of cancer nutrition, and to Fredi Kronenberg, PhD, for your insights and encouragement during my journey.

Thank you to Jeremy Katz, my agent and friend, for sitting me down and insisting that this was the book I needed to write.

A heaping amount of praise to my coauthor, Mat Edelson, a brilliant and gifted writer, for transforming copious amounts of dense information into easy digestible and delectable words, not once but twice! A big 16-quart hug to Julie Burford, my soup sister, whose valuable insights and support helped shape both editions of this book, and a special kiss on the head to both her husband, Stan, and Josie, pooch supreme, for their moral support.

Many thanks to my original team, Catherine McConkie, amazing person and recipe tester extraordinaire; Wendy Remer, dear friend and baker supreme; and Christine Kaddaras, my assistant, whose hard work, good cheer, and positive attitude are essential ingredients in this book.

Kudos to the amazingly talented team at Ten Speed Press, old and new: A special thank-you to my original editor, Melissa Moore, for her deft skills in shaping this manuscript and her keen editorial eye; the late Phil Wood, Lorena Jones, and Jo Ann Deck, who saw the possibilities of this subject matter with my first book, *One Bite at a Time,* written before there was Google! Many thanks to photographer Leo Gong and his wife, Harumi Shimizu; and the lovely food stylists Jen Straus and Alexa Hyman for the beautiful images. And on this second edition: senior vice president and publisher Aaron Wehner; editorial director Julie Bennett; my editor, Kelly Snowden; assistant editor Clara Sankey; copyeditor Kristi Hein; and proofreader Jean Blomquist, for making the new content sing; art director Kara Plikaitis, senior design manager Chloe Rawlins, creative director Emma Campion, photographer Leo Gong (again!), Leo's assistant, Agustina Perretta; prop stylist Christine Wolheim, food stylist Jeffrey Larsen, and his assistant,

Victoria Laramie, for making this book look fabulous; Hannah Rahill, Michele Crim, and Ashley Matuzak, for their sales and marketing expertise; and Erin Welke, for her PR and social media savvy.

A huge debt of thanks to Keith I. Block, MD, and Penny B. Block, PhD, of the Block Center for Integrative Cancer Treatment, for their commitment to state-of-the-art integrative cancer care and their understanding of the critical role nutrition and nourishment play in healing; Kathie Swift, MS, RD, LDN; Jim Gordon, MD; Debu Tripathy, MD; Gerry Mullin, MD; Joel Evans, MD; Linda Bartoshuk, PhD; Suzanne Dixon, MPH, MS, RD; Teressa Koetters, RN, MS; the late Annemarie Colbin, PhD; and Nancy Novack, PhD, for their time and expertise.

To my colleagues at Commonweal's Cancer Help Program, I am so honored to have been witness to your collective wisdom and incredible program participants. To Michael Lerner, the late Lenore Lefer, Waz Thomas, Claire Heart, Arlene Allsman, Oren Slozberg, Rachael Remens, MD; Kate Holcombe, Stuart Horance, Jhani Chapman, Irene Gallway, Katrina Smith, Elizabeth Evans, Jenepher Stowell, and Mimi Mindel—you've allowed me to watch magic and healing happen, and I love you all. Thanks to the folks at Smith Farm Center for Healing and the Arts, especially cofounder Shanti Norris, and executive director Laura Pole, RN, MSN.

A shout-out to Gina Gallo, Gia Passalaqua, and the charming Jean Charles Boisset. Jo Cooper, dear friend and colleague, for your gracious support of my work; Jill Leiner, for your lifelong friendship; Paul and Vicki Remer; Jen Yasis; and my mentor, Judy Witts Francini, who, many years ago, steered me toward the kitchen, where I belonged.

My gratitude to my mother, Barbara Katz, and my late father, Jay Katz, for their love and support, along with my family, Jeff, Harry and Amelia, Andy, Asako, and Branden; my canine muses, Bella, Lola, and Blossom; and my husband, Gregg Kellogg, for his belief in my work, unwavering support, and patience. And, finally, thank you to all my readers and students for all you have taught me along the way.

Mat wants to thank the following: "My parents, Clair and Charlie, for giving me the opportunities they dreamed about but never themselves had. Also, much love to Deb, my Sweet Baboo, who has the spirit of a warrior, the compassion of an angel, and the never-ending belief that everyone is capable of wondrous things. To Sweet Pea and Ollie, you guys always make me laugh (if you're a dog person, you get it; if not, go save a pound puppy and become one). Finally, to *Apollo 13* Flight Commander Gene Kranz, whose stern visage stares out at me from a picture at his console at Mission Control. *Failure is not an option* was your motto. Sometimes a writer on deadline needs to be reminded of such things."

Index

All rights reserved.
Published in the United States by Ten Speed Press, an imprint of the
Crown Publishing Group, a division of Penguin Random House LLC, New York.
www.crownpublishing.com
www.tenspeed.com

Ten Speed Press and the Ten Speed Press colophon are registered trademarks
of Penguin Random House LLC.

A previous edition published in hardcover by Ten Speed Press, Berkeley, in 2009.

Library of Congress Cataloging-in-Publication Data
Names: Katz, Rebecca, author. | Edelson, Mat, author.
Title: The cancer-fighting kitchen, second edition : nourishing, big-flavor recipes
for cancer treatment and recovery / by Rebecca Katz with Mat Edelson.
Description: Second edition. | Berkeley : Ten Speed Press, [2017] |
Includes bibliographical references and index.
Subjects: LCSH: Cancer—Diet therapy—Recipes. |
BISAC: COOKING / Health & Healing / Cancer. | COOKING / Specific Ingredients /
Natural Foods. | COOKING / Courses & Dishes / General.
Classification: LCC RC271.D52 K375 2017 | DDC 641.5/631—dc23
LC record available at https://lccn.loc.gov/2016023828

Hardcover ISBN: 9780399578717
eBook ISBN: 9780399578724

Printed in China

Design by Chloe Rawlins
Art direction by Kara Plitaikis
Food styling by Jen Strauss and Jeffrey Larsen

10 9 8

Second Edition